Studies in International Performance

Published in association with the International Federation of Theatre Research

General Editors: **Janelle Reinelt** and **Brian Singleton**

Culture and performance cross borders constantly, and not just the borders that define nations. In this new series, scholars of performance produce interactions between and among nations and cultures as well as genres, identities and imaginations.

Inter-national in the largest sense, the books collected in the *Studies in International Performance* series display a range of historical, theoretical and critical approaches to the panoply of performances that make up the global surround. The series embraces 'Culture' which is institutional as well as improvised, underground or alternate, and treats 'Performance' as either intercultural or transnational as well as intracultural within nations.

Titles include:

Khalid Amine and Marvin Carlson
THE THEATRES OF MOROCCO, ALGERIA AND TUNISIA
Performance Traditions of the Maghreb

Patrick Anderson and Jisha Menon (*editors*)
VIOLENCE PERFORMED
Local Roots and Global Routes of Conflict

Elaine Aston and Sue-Ellen Case
STAGING INTERNATIONAL FEMINISMS

Matthew Isaac Cohen
PERFORMING OTHERNESS
Java and Bali on International Stages, 1905–1952

Susan Leigh Foster (*editor*)
WORLDING DANCE

Helen Gilbert and Jacqueline Lo
PERFORMANCE AND COSMOPOLITICS
Cross-Cultural Transactions in Australasia

Helena Grehan
PERFORMANCE, ETHICS AND SPECTATORSHIP IN A GLOBAL AGE

Susan C. Haedicke
CONTEMPORARY STREET ARTS IN EUROPE
Aesthetics and Politics

James Harding and Cindy Rosenthal (*editors*)
THE RISE OF PERFORMANCE STUDIES
Rethinking Richard Schechner's Broad Spectrum

Silvija Jestrovic and Yana Meerzon (*editors*)
PERFORMANCE, EXILE AND 'AMERICA'

Silvija Jestrovic
PERFORMANCE, SPACE, UTOPIA

Ola Johansson
COMMUNITY THEATRE AND AIDS

Ketu Katrak
CONTEMPORARY INDIAN DANCE
New Creative Choreography in India and the Diaspora

Sonja Arsham Kuftinec
THEATRE, FACILITATION, AND NATION FORMATION IN THE BALKANS AND MIDDLE EAST

Daphne P. Lei
ALTERNATIVE CHINESE OPERA IN THE AGE OF GLOBALIZATION
Performing Zero

Carol Martin (*editor*)
THE DRAMATURGY OF THE REAL ON THE WORLD STAGE

Carol Martin
THEATRE OF THE REAL

Y. Meerzon
PERFORMING EXILE, PERFORMING SELF
Drama, Theatre, Film

Lara D. Nielson and Patricia Ybarra (*editors*)
NEOLIBERALISM AND GLOBAL THEATRES
Performance Permutations

Alan Read
THEATRE, INTIMACY & ENGAGEMENT
The Last Human Venue

Shannon Steen
RACIAL GEOMETRIES OF THE BLACK ATLANTIC, ASIAN PACIFIC AND AMERICAN THEATRE

Marcus. Tan
ACOUSTIC INTERCULTURALISM
Listening to Performance

Maurya Wickstrom
PERFORMANCE IN THE BLOCKADES OF NEOLIBERALISM
Thinking the Political Anew

S. E. Wilmer
NATIONAL THEATRES IN A CHANGING EUROPE

Evan Darwin Winet
INDONESIAN POSTCOLONIAL THEATRE
Spectral Genealogies and Absent Faces

Forthcoming titles:

Adrian Kear
THEATRE AND EVENT

Studies in International Performance
Series Standing Order ISBN 978–1–403–94456–6 (hardback)
978–1–403–94457–3 (paperback)
(*outside North America only*)

You can receive future titles in this series as they are published by placing a standing order. Please contact your bookseller or, in case of difficulty, write to us at the address below with your name and address, the title of the series and the ISBN quoted above.

Customer Services Department, Macmillan Distribution Ltd, Houndmills, Basingstoke, Hampshire RG21 6XS, England

Contemporary Street Arts in Europe

Aesthetics and Politics

Susan C. Haedicke

© Susan C. Haedicke 2013

Softcover reprint of the hardcover 1st edition 2013 978-0-230-22026-3

All rights reserved. No reproduction, copy or transmission of this publication may be made without written permission.

No portion of this publication may be reproduced, copied or transmitted save with written permission or in accordance with the provisions of the Copyright, Designs and Patents Act 1988, or under the terms of any licence permitting limited copying issued by the Copyright Licensing Agency, Saffron House, 6–10 Kirby Street, London EC1N 8TS.

Any person who does any unauthorized act in relation to this publication may be liable to criminal prosecution and civil claims for damages.

The author has asserted her right to be identified as the author of this work in accordance with the Copyright, Designs and Patents Act 1988.

First published 2013 by
PALGRAVE MACMILLAN

Palgrave Macmillan in the UK is an imprint of Macmillan Publishers Limited, registered in England, company number 785998, of Houndmills, Basingstoke, Hampshire RG21 6XS.

Palgrave Macmillan in the US is a division of St Martin's Press LLC, 175 Fifth Avenue, New York, NY 10010.

Palgrave Macmillan is the global academic imprint of the above companies and has companies and representatives throughout the world.

Palgrave® and Macmillan® are registered trademarks in the United States, the United Kingdom, Europe and other countries.

ISBN 978-1-349-30585-8   ISBN 978-1-137-29183-7 (eBook)
DOI 10.1057/9781137291837

This book is printed on paper suitable for recycling and made from fully managed and sustained forest sources. Logging, pulping and manufacturing processes are expected to conform to the environmental regulations of the country of origin.

A catalogue record for this book is available from the British Library.

Library of Congress Cataloging-in-Publication Data
Contemporary street arts in Europe: aesthetics and politics/by Susan C. Haedicke.
   p. cm.
Includes bibliographical references and index.

1. Street theater—Europe.   2. Street theater—Political aspects—Europe.
I. Title.
PN3220.H34 2013
792.094′09051—dc23   2012034813

10 9 8 7 6 5 4 3 2 1
22 21 20 19 18 17 16 15 14 13

Contents

List of Illustrations	vi
Series Preface	ix
Preface: Into the Street	x
Acknowledgements	xiii
Introduction: Aesthetics and Politics of Street Arts Interventions	1
1 Looking Back: A Socio-Historical and Intellectual Context for Contemporary Street Arts in Europe	22
2 Democratic Performatives and an Aesthetics of Public Space	44
3 Performing Democracy on a Grand Scale	71
4 Trespassing in Urban Places	91
5 Subversive Imaginaries: Performing the Other	125
6 Community Performance: Community Performatives	149
Postscript: Beyond the Street	176
Notes	184
Bibliography	199
Index	220

List of Illustrations

Colour plate section

1. Street arts collage. Designed by Monica Lira
2. Générik Vapeur, *Bivouac* (Villeurbanne, France, June 2008)
3. Tony Clifton Circus, *La Morte di Babbo Natale: Eutanasia di un mito sovrappeso* (Morlaix, France, August 2010). Photograph by Abdoul Aziz Soumaïla. Courtesy of Tony Clifton Circus
4. Ilotopie, *Les Gens de Couleur* (Sotteville-lès-Rouen, France, June 2009)
5. Royal de Luxe, *The Sultan's Elephant* (London, England, May 2006)
6. Compagnie Willi Dorner, *Bodies in Urban Spaces* (London, England, October 2009)
7. Compagnie Willi Dorner, *Bodies in Urban Spaces* (London, England, October 2009)
8. Jeanne Simone, *Mademoiselle* (Paris, France, September 2010)
9. Opéra Pagaï, *Safari Intime* (small town near Aurillac, France, August 2008)
10. Compagnie Kumulus, *Les Squames* (Paris, France, 2007)
11. Pascal Laurent, *Melgut* (Paris, France, June 2002)
12. Compagnie Osmosis, *Transit* (Marseille, France, February 2005). Photograph by Vincent Lucas. Courtesy of Compagnie Osmosis
13. Friches Théâtre Urbain, *Witness/N14* (France, 2008–10)

Monochrome figures in text

1. Opéra Pagaï, *Les Sans Balcons* (St Flour, France, August 2008) — 15
2. Stephen Bain, *Baby, Where Are the Fine Things You Promised Me?* (Rennes, France, July 2009) — 18

List of Illustrations

3 Compagny Teatro Gestual de Chile, *Su-Seso Taladro* (Béthune, France, June 2011) — 48

4 Opéra Pagaï, *Mobil-Home Container* (Port Saint Louis, France, April 2006) (Courtesy of Opéra Pagaï) — 62

5 Desperate Men, *Darwin and the Dodo* (Chew Valley Lake near Bristol, England, June 2011) — 67

6 Royal de Luxe, *The Sultan's Elephant* (London, England, May 2006) — 82

7 Royal de Luxe, *The Sultan's Elephant* (London, England, May 2006) — 87

8 Compagnie Willi Dorner, *Bodies in Urban Spaces* (London, England, October 2009) — 100

9 Compagnie Willi Dorner, *Bodies in Urban Spaces* (London, England, October 2009) — 101

10 Lili Jenks, *La Mecanista* (Ghent, Belgium, July 2010) — 106

11 Jeanne Simone, *Mademoiselle* (Béthune, France, June 2011) — 112

12 Jeanne Simone, *Mademoiselle* (Béthune, France, June 2011) — 113

13 Opéra Pagaï, *Safari Intime* (Sotteville-lès-Rouen, France, June 2007) — 119

14 Opéra Pagaï, *Safari Intime* (Rennes, France, July 2009) — 122

15 Compagnie Kumulus, *Les Squames* (Paris, France, June 2007) — 130

16 Pascal Laurent, *VitupErrance* (Paris, France, September 2011) Photograph by Juliette Dieudonné (Courtesy of Friches Théâtre Urbain) — 135

17 Compagnie Osmosis, *Alhambra Container* (Aurillac, France, August 2008) — 138

18 Back to Back Theatre, *Small Metal Objects* (Sydney, Australia, January 2007) — 142

19 Compagnie Kumulus, *Les Rencontres Internationales de Boîtes* (banlieue near Paris, June 2007) — 144

20 Compagnie Kumulus, *Les Rencontres Internationales de Boîtes* (banlieue near Paris, France, June 2007) — 147

21	Friches Théâtre Urbain, *Witness/N14, Parcours 1: D'Ici-Là!* (Paris, France, April 2008)	157
22	Friches Théâtre Urbain, *Witness/N14, Parcours 2: Au-delà du périph* (October 2009)	165
23	Friches Théâtre Urbain, *Witness/N14, Parcours 2: Au-delà du périph* (October 2009)	167
24	Friches Théâtre Urbain, *Witness/N14, Parcours 5: Un pas de côté* (May 2010)	169
25	Friches Théâtre Urbain, *Witness/N14, Parcours 5: Un pas de côté* (May 2010)	170

Series Preface

The 'Studies in International Performance' series was initiated in 2004 on behalf of the International Federation for Theatre Research, by Janelle Reinelt and Brian Singleton, successive Presidents of the Federation. Their aim was, and still is, to call on performance scholars to expand their disciplinary horizons to include the comparative study of performances across national, cultural, social, and political borders. This is necessary not only in order to avoid the homogenizing tendency of national paradigms in performance scholarship, but also in order to engage in creating new performance scholarship that takes account of and embraces the complexities of transnational cultural production, the new media, and the economic and social consequences of increasingly international forms of artistic expression. Comparative studies (especially when conceived across more than two terms) can value both the specifically local and the broadly conceived global forms of performance practices, histories, and social formations. Comparative aesthetics can challenge the limitations of national orthodoxies of art criticism and current artistic knowledges. In formalizing the work of the Federation's members through rigorous and innovative scholarship this Series aims to make a significant contribution to an ever-changing project of knowledge creation.

Janelle Reinelt and Brian Singleton

International Federation for Theatre Research
Fédération Internationale pour la Recherche Théâtrale

Preface: Into the Street

Pedestrians filled the street. I glanced to my left and saw a woman in a beret being pulled along by her dog on a leash, except there was no dog. She gave a coquettish smile as she hurried by. An eight-foot tall figure all in white with tiny wings budding out of his shoulders bent over to whisper in people's ears as they ambled by. I could hear percussion music coming from a side street and laughter and applause in the square in front of the cathedral. In the park, I saw musicians performing while suspended from the branches of a tree. In the town centre, I watched very large blue chickens wander down the street in a line and enjoyed the four seasons represented by dancing stilt walkers. I followed a musical ensemble of pilgrim monks in brown robes and wooden shoes until tiny finger puppets caught my attention. Performers, some on stilts and others on aerial equipment, enacted a loose adaptation of the Cassiopeia story. Without realizing it, I stepped into the middle of a performance as a woman standing at a window with a balcony full of flower pots called down to ask what she should make for supper – only the window and balcony were atop a tall pole and she was standing on a ladder. She gossiped with passers-by about her neighbours at other tiny balconies: the man smoking cigarette after cigarette, another listening to the radio, or the woman hanging out her oversized lingerie to dry. Suddenly, I heard what sounded like a power lawn mower and saw a man in a red-and-white checked suit transformed into a robot attached to a motor on wheels guided by a lively woman dressed the same. His jerking, angular movements and mask-like expression that never changed were somewhat disconcerting, especially when he seemed to look me in the eyes as he passed. I arrived at the square in front of the cathedral in time to see the end of a show with an old bearded man and a golden angel, both on stilts. It was lyrical, melancholy and beautiful. As I photographed a group of performers playing with and mocking uncomfortable members of the public, I was suddenly picked up by one of them. He ran with me down the street as spectators snapped photographs of the astonishment and embarrassment that must have filled my face. After dark, as I walked down one of the main streets, I glimpsed gargoyle performers lurking in the darkened doorframes, but even though I knew they were there, when one jumped in front of me, my heart started to race and a startled cry escaped my lips.

Going to my first street theatre festival changed my attitude toward participatory performance and my understanding of its potential for lasting impact. I thought I knew what to expect – jugglers, magicians, musicians, living statues, clowns. I had seen street performance in New Orleans, New York City, on university campuses, or in front of the Centre Pompidou in Paris, but the range of shows and the complexity and professionalism of much of the work at the festival was astounding. Since that first summer experience, I have attended many street theatre festivals as well as single street arts events of all sizes in cities and towns in the UK and continental Europe, and I have worked on several professional street theatre productions. I have often taken students from the United States or England and have frequently been accompanied by colleagues, all attending their first street theatre festival or large outdoor performance. Their astonished reactions are always the same – breathless thrill that they are experiencing a very different kind of theatrical event and startled realization that the way they experience performance in the future will never be the same.[1]

One of the goals of this book is to begin to understand, articulate, and analyse the visceral responses to European street arts that my students, my colleagues, and I have all experienced. The term *street arts*[2] covers an enormous range of performance practices: stilt-walking, puppetry, aerial acrobatics, inflatable floating sculptures, musical ensembles, urban dance, living statues, walkabout characters, theatre of fire, theatre of sound, theatre of objects, performance installations, storytelling, multimedia, promenade performances, walking performance, flash mobs, large-scale spectacles, and more. (See Colour Plate 1 that offers a visual collage of the overabundance of varied performances. The photographs were taken at several different festivals throughout Europe since 2001.) More than 1,000 professional street theatre companies are listed in *Le Goliath 2008–2010*, the guide to circus and street arts published by HorsLesMurs, the national archive for street theatre and circus in Paris.[3]

While some street arts events are performed outside the festival circuit, many more are performed in festivals around the world. Every summer, over three hundred street theatre festivals take place in Europe alone. Hat Fair in Winchester has been an annual event since 1974, and others (for example, those occurring in Tàrrega in Spain, Stockton-on-Tees in the UK, and Aurillac, Chalon-sur-Saône, and Sotteville-lès-Rouen in France) began in the 1980s. The festivals vary in size (from under twenty to over one hundred shows), in length (a few days to several weeks), and in offerings (from street theatre to circus, music, installations, and site-specific events). Most festivals invite a limited number of companies to perform, but several also have an 'off' (or fringe) programme for companies to present shows at their own expense. Both the 'in' (invited) and 'off' shows are listed in the programme, but sometimes artists just show up and perform, so it is not at all unusual to see performances and not know the name of the show or the company. Some festivals, like MiramirO in Ghent, Belgium, are part of a larger arts festival; others are stand-alone events, like Terschelling Oerol where performances happen all over a small island off the coast of the Netherlands. In Europe, the majority of street theatre and circus festivals take place in France, but theatre festivals that include street theatre or even focus exclusively on it occur throughout the world, usually annually, but sometimes on a one-time basis, like the New Island Festival on Governors Island in New York in 2009.

This book focuses on street arts interventions in public spaces occurring in cities and towns all over Europe.[4] These interventions offer a range of street arts practices that intervene, often unexpectedly, in daily activities. They disrupt expectations, unsettle routines, and transform ordinary places of commerce or relaxation into places of art. From amusing to annoying, diverting to challenging, the interventions interrupt and interact with everyday life. Not all performance interventions are exciting or even memorable, but the best ones touch the audience in a variety of ways: entertaining certainly, but also visceral, emotional, thought-provoking or disturbing.

Acknowledgements

Many people helped me to complete this book from audiences at several conferences at which I presented my ideas to spectators at street theatre events who enthusiastically expressed their reactions to me and my students who share my enthusiasm for street arts. I am grateful to all the festival programmers, curators, educators and researchers who helped me along the way, especially the staff at HorsLesMurs and FAI AR. I want to thank Anne Gonon, researcher at HorsLesMurs, who challenged my ideas, shared her own scholarship at various stages of completion and helped with translations and Floriane Gaber, who has written extensively on street arts, for her advice, insights and willingness to introduce me to several artists. I am grateful to all the artists who inspired me with their exciting performances and who took time after a show to talk to me, even if briefly. I am especially grateful to those artists who generously shared anecdotes and unpublished documentation of their work and willingly answered all my questions: Sarah Harper, Pascal Laurent, Laure Terrier, Cyril Jaubert, Ali Salmi, Françoise Léger, Lili Jenks, Jon Beedell, Richard Headon, Nicola Danesi de Luca, Iacopo Fulgi, Eric Blouet and Willi Dorner. All of my colleagues at University of Warwick have been very supportive and deserve a special thanks for their patience as I struggled to finish the book, especially Robert Batterbee who helped me with the images. I would like to thank my friend and colleague Baz Kershaw for our numerous conversations that challenged and inspired me. I would also like to thank Janelle Reinelt and Brian Singleton, the editors of the series in which this book appears, who offered excellent editorial advice and suggestions along the way.

Finally, I would like to acknowledge the incredible love and encouragement from my family without whom this book would not have been possible: my sons and their partners, Michael and Kathleen who discussed ideas and read drafts, Stephen and Kris who attended many street theatre events with me, and Daniel and Monica, artists themselves who helped me understand the work with new eyes. I want to thank my sister Sally Chandler who has always offered support when I needed it. And a special thank you goes to David who has been by my side for many years and whose patience and encouragement sustained me. Last but not least, an exuberant thank you to the newest member of my family, Torunn Elizabeth, whose birth coincided with a completed draft of the book.

Introduction: Aesthetics and Politics of Street Arts Interventions

Art, activism, affect

Street arts interventions invade a public space, shake it up and disappear, but the memory of the disruption haunts the place for audiences who experience it. The artists seek to interrupt daily life, startle onlookers with an inversion of a familiar place and quotidian activities, and test the limits of what they can do in public and what they can encourage the public to do. The artists do not try to hide or erase the everyday world that encases their performance interventions. Instead, their participatory practices establish a dynamic experiential rapport with the audience in actual public spaces: an amalgamation of production, reception, and place. Here *fiction* does not work in opposition to *reality*; rather the *imaginary* re-frames, re-interprets, confuses, subverts or challenges notions of the *real*. This palimpsest of the world of imagination and the world of the everyday created by a street arts intervention works like a collage juxtaposing incongruous images, ideas or logics to construct new interpretations, and it uses the city as its medium and passers-by as its found objects. Street theatre does more than offer outdoor entertainment; it *frames* the public space and the everyday with art. As the boundaries between participation in a performance and participation in daily activities, between art and non-art, become porous, the public can experience a disorientation that often initiates reflection and a critical reassessment of the surrounding situation. This book questions whether street arts acquire a practical and social significance as they offer the public the opportunity to view everyday life and familiar locations through a lens of art and thus potentially to re-evaluate the meaning and function of quotidian activities and urban spaces. It asks whether the dynamic interrelationship between performance, participant and place creates a unique politicized aesthetic of public space that, in turn, enables the public to *rehearse* democratic practices.

Artists and writers have often asserted that European street theatre is political, seeking justification in its roots in the turmoil of the 1960s and its opposition to the status quo. Pioneering radical theatre companies responded artistically to the social unrest by trying to democratize culture through accessible and populist forms that would attract an audience indifferent to more elite art and to develop alternative and counter-cultural practices in the non-hierarchical organizational structures of their theatre companies and in the communal life styles of the artists. Those working outside[1] hovered at the edge of legality when they created social disturbances to make political statements opposing the state or socio-cultural institutions and challenged social norms with characters whose appearance or behaviour identified them as Other, thus exposing metaphorically who was welcome in public spaces and who was not. These provocative performance tactics certainly dominated the outdoor work of theatre companies in the 1960s and 1970s. Many artists and critics lament that street theatre in the early twenty-first century lacks the anti-establishment stance of its predecessors. They argue that its popular success has led to its co-option by municipal governments or corporations that recognize its utility and versatility and so use it to support official narratives of cultural tourism and to participate in the production of social interpretations, identities and inhabitations according to the ideology of growth, redevelopment and rejuvenation so much a part of the model of late capitalism and liberal democracy.[2] Shannon Jackson questions, however, whether oppositional or resistant 'social practice' is the only way to define political engagement: 'When a political art discourse too often celebrates social disruption at the expense of social coordination, we lose a more complex sense of how art practices contribute to inter-dependent social imagining. Whether cast in aesthetic or social terms, freedom and expression are not opposed to obligation and care, but in fact depend upon each other' (2011: 14).[3]

The connection between art in public spaces and political engagement is complicated in the first decades of the twenty-first century. Public space is contested both as a concept and an actuality, and that ambivalence makes it appealing to street artists who often seek to expose the normative behavioural codes, social constructions and ideological operations at work there. The aims of these artists can be resistance to socio-political and cultural institutions certainly, but they can also be collaboration with these institutions on initiatives focusing

Introduction: Aesthetics and Politics of Street Arts 3

on individual empowerment, community development, urban renewal and, significantly, the creation of safe public spaces that encourage gathering and dialogue. What is key in terms of political engagement, whether these street performances are resistant or not, is that many artists create events where the public, consciously or unconsciously, can question or *re-view* the workings of the city and can initiate a debate (in words or actions) about the city's priorities, processes and agendas.

Sometimes opposition and support, disruption and co-operation, coexist simultaneously in the arts event regardless of artistic intention as many of the case studies in subsequent chapters demonstrate. While artistic and political ambitions have become more ambiguous and contradictory, they are no less significant. This book investigates the symbiotic relationship between aesthetics and politics in a range of contemporary street interventions as it interrogates what interventionist performance *does* rather than what it *is*. The ideas of Jacques Rancière suggest a conceptual framework within which one can think about the inseparability of the aesthetic and political dimensions of street arts interventions, and Gilles Deleuze's interpretations of 'percepts' and 'affects', as well as the work of scholars who have adapted his ideas, help explain what street arts can do or, in other words, the reception and the potential for efficacy of the art form.

Rancière identifies three artistic regimes in the history of western art. The 'ethical regime of images' focuses on the authenticity (or 'truth content') of the images and how they are to be used (their purpose). The 'representative regime' identifies what is appropriate for artistic representation and how it should be represented (mimesis). The 'aesthetic regime' breaks from these strictures. 'The word aesthetics,' he clarifies, 'does not refer to a theory of sensibility, taste, and pleasure for art amateurs. It strictly refers to the specific mode of being of whatever falls within the domain of art, to the mode of being of the objects of art' (2004: 22). The aesthetic regime disengages the arts from rigid rules of subject matter and form, and it establishes a connection between the art work and the social world that influences and shapes it:

> The aesthetic regime of the arts did not begin with decisions to initiate an artistic rupture. It began with decisions to reinterpret what makes art or what art makes....The aesthetic regime of the arts is first of all a new regime for relating to the past. It actually sets up as the very principle of artisticity the expressive relationship inherent in a time and a state of civilization, a relationship that was previously considered to be the 'non-artistic' part of works of art...it devotes

itself to the invention of new forms of life on the basis of an idea of what art *was*, and idea of what art *would have been*. (2004: 25)

The aesthetic regime breaks down 'the mimetic barrier that distinguished ways of doing and making affiliated with art from other ways of doing and making' (2004: 23). And, Rancière links aesthetics and politics through their 'ways of doing and making', through their participation in determining and often reconfiguring what is seen, heard, and understood about the contemporary world. They are not linked through forms of representation, but instead both art and politics are activities, he claims, that propose innovative perceptions and conceptions of the current situation and that map the visible, the sayable and the thinkable. They challenge notions of free speech by expressing what is unspoken or taboo, and they propel people out of their societally assigned identities and locations:

> Art is not political owing to the messages and feelings that it carries on the state of social and political issues. It is not political owing to the way it represents social structures, conflicts or identities. It is political by virtue of the distance it takes with regard to those functions. It is political as it frames a specific space-time sensorium, as it redefines on this stage the power of speech or the coordinates of perception, [and] shifts the places of the actor and the spectator. (2006a: n.p.)

Art and politics, for Rancière, are acts of intervention that contest the status quo by challenging a *natural* hierarchical order of individuals or ideas and giving voice to those not usually heard. Thus, artistic and political acts legitimate new partners in aesthetic-socio-political debate. As a consequence, they are necessarily democratic practices that *stage* equality and resistance. Politics, Rancière argues, is synonymous with democracy since it is characterized by ' "liberty" of the people' and resistance to domination. Democracy is not one of several political systems but 'the very institution of politics itself – of its subject and the form of its relationship' (2010: 32). Democratic political activity occurs when individuals challenge the political order, and the task of that political action must be to disrupt the accepted connection between perception and meaning. 'Politics, before all else, is an intervention in the visible and the sayable' (2010: 37). Aesthetic practices, like political actions, seek to disrupt the social experience and to alter perception and understanding. Thus, both artistic and political activities are forms of what Rancière calls 'dissensus' since both rely on innovative ways to interrupt rules governing social experience and to present images and ideas that cut across normative beliefs. Dissensus 'is not a conflict of interests, opinions or values; it is a division inserted in "common sense": a dispute over what is given and about the frame within which we see something as given' (2010: 69). It is a political process that has a 'way of dissensually inventing scenes and characters' (2006: 83) in order to challenge the status quo by demanding the right to speak and be heard, but it is equally an aesthetic process that disrupts the norm and insists on 'configurations of experience that create new modes of sense perception and induce novel forms of political subjectivity' (2004: 9). For Rancière, a democratic community is one 'whose lived experience does not rend itself into separate spheres of activity....Where art and life, art and politics, life and politics are not severed from each other' (2006a: n.p.).

Rancière argues that societies are identifiable by what the members share in common, but also by who and what cannot participate in that community. He refers to Aristotle's assertion that a citizen is one 'who *has a part* in the act of governing and being governed' and to Plato's rejection of artisans from that 'community of citizens' since 'they do *not* have the time to devote themselves to anything other than their work. They cannot be *somewhere else* because *work will not wait*' (2004:12. Italics in original). It is what Rancière calls the 'distribution of the sensible' (*partage du sensible*) that reveals this coexistence of inclusive and exclusive parts, of participation and separation. Rancière defines the distribution of the sensible as 'a system of self-evident facts of sense perception that simultaneously discloses the existence of something in common and the delimitations that define the respective parts and positions within it.... The distribution of the sensible reveals who can have a share in what is common to the community based on what they do and on the time and space in which this activity is performed' (2004: 12). The translation of *partage du sensible* into *distribution of the sensible* complicates the notion for an English-speaking reader. The word *partager* in French means both a *sharing* (establishing conditions for a collectivity) and a *splitting or dividing* (creating divisions and disruptions), so *partage du sensible* not only refers to shared views (what is seen, heard and understood in common), but also to what and who is excluded from that 'common habitat' (2004: 42). And *sensible* as used by Rancière refers to a 'space/time sensorium' (2006a: n.p.) or sense experience, but it also resonates with *sensibilisation* that refers to an increase in public awareness. Aesthetics and politics, for Rancière, are practices or actions that reconfigure the status quo by troubling the commonality with alternate voices inventing new ways of seeing, hearing, and thinking and suggesting innovative strategies to alter what can be said or done about those perceptions and experiences. They disrupt a complacent stability and certainty by overturning a sense of a common social order and affecting a shift in the understanding of social space: 'Politics and art, like forms of knowledge, construct "fictions," that is to say *material* rearrangements of signs and images, relationships between what is seen and what is said, between what is done and what can be done' (2004: 63).

Rancière does add a word of caution, however, about a simple equation between aesthetics and politics. If the boundaries between them become too porous, he warns, they are in danger of cancelling each other out. While aesthetics and politics share dynamic characteristics and practices of rupture, instability and transformation, they do not function in the same way: 'If there is such a thing as an "aesthetics of politics", it lies in the re-configuration of the distribution of the common through political processes of subjectivation. Correspondingly, if there is a politics of aesthetics, it lies in the practices and modes of visibility of art that re-configure the fabric of the sensory experience' (2010: 140). Political rupture and transformation assume equality among individuals and test that assumption in public spaces. Aesthetic rupture introduces the notion of equality into the art form itself.

Rancière's ideas provide a theoretical basis from which to interrogate a politicized dramaturgy of contemporary street arts interventions that does not necessarily depend on political content, but rather on practices that displace the boundaries of artistic and political activities and reconfigure social space. Here artists may choose not to offer a political message or represent political issues in the content or in the visual images of the artwork, and instead to intervene in the visible, sayable and thinkable through '*material* rearrangements of signs and images' (2004: 63. Italics in original) in public spaces so that spectators must reassess what they see and understand. The artists do not necessarily make political art in terms of ideas, characters or narratives, but they 'make art politically', to use the words of contemporary artist, Thomas Hirschhorn.[4] What that actually means in street arts interventions is twofold. First, it refers to a reconfiguration of the aesthetic experience through a superimposition of an unfamiliar world of imaginative possibility on the familiar world of everyday life. The spectator participates imaginatively and physically in activities that take place both in an actual public space and in a fictional theatrical space. Rancière's concept of collage offers a way to understand this experiential palimpsest. He explains:

> Collage in the most general sense of the term is the principle of a 'third' aesthetic politics. Prior to mixing paintings, newspapers, oilcloth or clock parts, it mixes the strangeness of the aesthetic experience with the becoming-life of art and the becoming-art of ordinary life. Collage can be carried out as a pure encounter of heterogeneities, testifying wholesale to the incompatibility of two worlds. It's the surrealist encounter of the umbrella and the sewing machine, showing the absolute power of desire and dreams against the reality of the everyday world, but using its objects. Conversely, collage can be seen as evidence of the hidden link between two apparently opposed worlds. (2006b: 84)

For Rancière, collage is necessarily political (or *democratic*) because its reassembling of ordinary objects and sites into new and often startling creations and spaces hovers at the spatio-temporal point of tension where a comfortable comprehension of a logical reality coexists with an unsettling disorientation caused by a nonsensical possibility. Thus collage often 'takes the form of a shock, which reveals one world hidden beneath another' (2006b: 87). This shock causes a disruption in 'the relationship between the visible, the sayable, and the thinkable', a rupture that overturns expectations and 'resists signification' (2004: 63).[5] The experiential shock of this disorienting contradiction elicits an initial somatic response that then stimulates a desire to understand critically what had seemed natural moments before and is now unfamiliar. Grant Kester, explains that 'we meet the epistemological challenge posed by aesthetic shock not by abandoning ourselves to the pleasures of ontic dislocation but by renewing, and expanding, our efforts to grasp the complexity of our surrounding world' (2004: 84).[6] Given the nature of collage, it is possible, therefore, to claim that a spectator achieves an enhanced understanding of the socio-political world from street arts *collages* of fictional and everyday worlds, of art and non-art.

Secondly, making art politically refers to a shift away from representational art-making where the art work reflects or *re-presents* (and so is *about*) external events, situations or issues. Street artists often eschew what they see as the stasis of *about-ness* and instead pursue *event-ness* since *event* implies that something is happening. Their artworks demand more than an interactive exchange between actor and spectator. They thrive on the interplay of the occasion of performance, the social participation of a public, and the overturning of a familiar place: an aesthetics of public space that embodies *event* by heightening the rhythms, sounds and textures of a public space, often so familiar that they are invisible. As a consequence, traditional dramaturgical elements, particularly narrative plot or dramatic character, tend to be simplistic or even non-existent. Interventions insert the art in the socio-political world itself by occupying places not usually associated with art and questioning distinctions between art and non-art. While socio-political issues may be represented in the text or imagery, the political impact of street theatre depends on a form of encounter, sometimes confrontational, sometimes consensual, between a public (individuals that become a theatrical audience through the act of witnessing or participating in the performance event[7]) and an artwork in a public space. The artists go beyond the telling of a story (or reject storytelling altogether) and try to make something happen, to initiate a visceral and active reaction in the audiences. Rancière asserts that the 'dream of a suitable political work of art is in fact the dream of disrupting the relationship between the visible, the sayable and the thinkable without having to use the terms of a message as a vehicle. It is the dream of an art that would transmit meanings in the form of a rupture with the very logic of meaningful situations' (2004: 63). He insists that 'meaning' alone cannot change understanding and behaviour. To make a difference, meaning and message must work in tandem with shock, a conviction that grew out of Rancière's experience of the May 1968 uprising in France that I will explore in more detail in Chapter 1.

Street arts interventions thus sometimes function as a form of activism changing, even temporarily, how the onlookers see public spaces *and* what they do there. These performances in public spaces overturn the notion that spectators may be objective or 'disinterested' observers by catapulting them from an ordinary space into one transformed into an aesthetic space and by inserting the art into daily life. These performances, hovering between art and non-art, elicit a strong kinaesthetic reaction, often well before an intellectual response; they are felt before they are understood and so elude analysis through traditional aesthetic theories. Understanding the art is inextricably linked to experiencing it.

It is, thus, important to establish a critical framework that enables both thoughtful interpretation of the performance in a public space and analysis of the audience's somatic reception of this art form. Rancière provides a way to understand the link between aesthetics and politics in these works and foregrounds the crucial role that a visceral response plays. Scholars associated with what is variously called the 'affective

Introduction: Aesthetics and Politics of Street Arts 9

turn', the 'performative turn' or the 'corporeal turn' in critical theory add useful concepts and methodologies to understand and evaluate the significance of a visceral response and the symbiosis between body and mind, emotion and thought. Michael Hardt insists that:

> the challenge of the perspective of affects [is]...the synthesis it requires. This is, in the first place, because affects refer equally to the body and the mind, and, in the second, because they involve both reason and the passions....The perspective of affects requires us constantly to pose as a problem the relation between actions and passions, between reason and the emotions. (2007: ix–x)

Affect, he argues, refers to our ability both to be affected by an event or situation *and* to affect its direction or nature. This paradox of a co-existence of seemingly contradictory states – passivity as one is *affected* and activity as one can *affect* – is precisely where individual agency and thus a potential for efficacy thrive. In street arts interventions, the spectator experiences these liberatory 'affective' insights in large part through participation in the event by his or her acting body and thinking mind, whether that participation is following artists down the middle of the street, contributing to the art-making process or any number of other participatory practices. Thus these interventions have the potential to shift the paradigm of individual and community agency from the social to the aesthetic realm.

The interdependence of the acting body and the thinking mind goes back to ideas articulated by Baruch Spinoza. In *Looking for Spinoza*, neurologist Antonio Damasio credits Spinoza with pioneering analysis on links between feelings and the mind and on how 'affects' (emotions, feelings, motivations) were key to being human. In spite of Spinoza's relevance to the 'affective turn', it is to Gilles Deleuze that many contemporary scholars turn, particularly his emphasis on the critical relevance of a mind/body synthesis in affects as the way to understand the power of art. Although his writings on theatrical production are primarily in one article, entitled 'One Less Manifesto', his ideas on the nature of art in many other works are relevant to performance analysis.[8] For Deleuze, art represents a power of 'becoming', not through a transformation of one thing into something already in existence, but by a creation of something new, different, and potentially life-transformative. Thus art, by very its nature, is revolutionary as it constantly replaces the old with the new. Deleuze, often in works co-authored with Félix Guattari, insisted that art is not about representation, but rather a mode of thinking that is affective, not cognitive, and so relies on sensations to imagine and create new worlds. Art struggles with chaos to compose a *vision* that results in sensation: 'Art is not chaos but a composition of chaos that yields the vision or sensation' (1994: 204) and 'sensation is pure contemplation...contemplating is creating, the mystery of passive creation, sensation' (1994: 212). For Deleuze, 'composition is the sole definition of art, and what is not composed is not a work of art. However, technical composition... is not to be confused with aesthetic composition, which is the work of sensation. Only the latter fully deserves the name *composition*, and a work of art is never produced by or for the sake of technique' (1994: 191–2). Thus, art, as Deleuze and Guattori define it, does not express opinions that remain firmly entrenched in lived experience. Art seeks to 'pass through the finite in order to discover, to restore the infinite' (1994: 197). It does not mirror or reproduce the world, but rather offers a way of seeing and thinking that provokes, shocks or disrupts as it discovers possibilities, creates new experiences and celebrates concepts of difference.

Deleuze argues that art *is* what it *does*, and what it does is to provide a way to transcend representation and encourage an encounter with difference. Representation implies stasis; encounter, becoming and affect. While affect offers a way to understand the impact of a performance on a spectator, for Deleuze who writes in the realm of abstract theory, affect is not reducible to a personal emotion or sensation; it is a disruption of individual experiences that challenges understanding. As Claire Colebrook explains, 'art may well have meanings or messages but what makes it *art* is not its content but its *affect*, the sensible force or style through which it produces content' (2002: 24–5). *Affect* and *percept* (the other key aspect in relation to art) are difficult to define. Deleuze explains:

> Percepts aren't perceptions, they're packets of sensations and relations that live independently of whoever experiences them. Affects aren't feelings, they're becomings that spill over beyond whoever lives through them (thereby becoming someone else)....Affects, percepts, and concepts are three inseparable forces, running from art into philosophy and from philosophy into art. (1995: 136–7)

Percepts and affects go beyond the individual experiencing them, and Deleuze insists that 'the aim of art is to wrest the percept from perceptions of objects and the states of the perceiving subject, to wrest the affect from affections as the transition from one state to another: to extract a bloc of sensations, a pure being of sensations' (1994: 167). Thus, affect is not an individual emotional response; it is a 'nonhuman becoming....Becoming is neither an imitation nor an experienced sympathy, not even an imaginary identification' (1994: 173). Becoming is not a transformation of one thing into another, but a dynamic instability, a condition of chaos, difference and change, a way of asking and establishing new connections, new beginnings. It is either a coupling of disparate sensations to create a hybrid or a 'third' sensation or it is a juxtaposition of the contradictory sensations with both visible and tangible simultaneously. And 'sensory becoming is the action by which something or someone is ceaselessly becoming-other (while continuing to be what they are)...sensory becoming is otherness caught in a matter of expression' (1994: 177).

While Deleuze views art as pure sensation apart from the spectator who experiences it, in one provocative passage in *What is Philosophy?*, he and Guattari hint at the possible impact of an artwork on the audience:

> creative affects [in the work of art] can link up or diverge, within compounds of sensations that transform themselves, vibrate, couple, or split apart: it is these beings of sensation that account for the artist's relationship with a public....It should be said of all art that, in relation to the percepts or visions they give us, artists are presenters of affects, the inventors and creators of affects. They not only create them in their work, they give them to us and make us become with them, they draw us into the compound. (1994: 175)

The spectators are able not only to experience the affects of the artwork, but can participate in art's 'becoming'; they can be moved and they can be inspired to act. Art can place the spectators in a liminal state of emergence that not only causes a somatic response but also leads to a somatic understanding of the social world that rattles rational interpretations. Early in his career, Deleuze had acknowledged the power of an affective response: 'The truths which intelligence grasps directly in the open light of day have something less profound, less *necessary* about them than those which life has communicated to us *in spite of ourselves* in an impression, a material impression because it has reached us through our senses' (1964: 161. Italics in original.). He thus opens the door to the possibility of a shift from pure affect to *applied* affect, to reception and efficacy, and scholars inspired by the power of affect did not miss the opportunity to enter. As Brian Massumi writes, 'There seems to be a growing feeling within media, literary and art theory that affect is central to an understanding of our information- and image-based late capitalist culture, in which so-called master narratives are perceived to have foundered' (2002a: 27).

Deleuze's foregrounding of affect has been adapted by scholars in many disciplines.[9] In theatre and performance studies, Deleuzian affect is reshaped primarily by shifting the emphasis toward an affective response in the audience. The affective response is evident, for example, in Eve Kosofsky Sedgwick's analysis of texture and affect in embodied experience in *Touching Feeling* and in Jill Dolan's 'utopian performatives' in *Utopia in Performance: Finding Hope at the Theater*, discussed later in the book. And Erika Fischer-Lichte's belief in the 'transformative power of performance' compels her to question the relationship between affect and meaning. Describing Marina Abramovic's *Lips of Thomas*, she claims that the:

> reality [of the performance] was not merely interpreted by the audiences but first and foremost experienced. It provoked an array of sensations in the spectator...which stirred them to actions that equally constituted reality. It can be assumed that the affects that were triggered...by far transcended the possibility and the effort to reflect, to constitute meaning, and to interpret the events. The central concern of the performance was not to understand but to experience it and to cope with those experiences, which could not be supplanted there and then by reflection. (2008: 16–17)

She argues that such performances constitute 'events' in which lines between production and reception, artist and spectator, are erased.

In contrast, cultural theorist, Nigel Thrift, in *Non-Representational Theory: Space, Politics, Affect*, is not particularly interested in affect in relation to individuals, but rather asks '"How do political formations generate affect?" and "To what extent is affect a political form in itself?"' (2008: 222). He seeks to use affect to understand social and political mechanisms that propel people into action. Thus, he expands the notion of affect beyond individual emotional responses in order to highlight their potential for affecting social change. Affect 'refers to complex, self-referential states of being, rather than to their cultural interpretation as emotions or their identification as instinctual drives' (2008: 221). Thrift refuses to discount the biological aspects of affect and insists that they are something that 'cannot be either wished away, shoved into a box marked "naturalism," or made secondary to the social' (2008: 226). Affect, he argues, is felt or experienced, but not necessarily rationally understood, but it 'brings together a mix of hormonal flux, body language, shared rhythms, and other forms of entrainment... to produce an encounter between the body (understood in a broad sense) and the particular event' (2008: 236). Again, not remaining in the area of individual affect, Thrift argues that this idea of encounter reveals that another key element of affect is 'space, understood as a series of conditioning environments that both prime and "cook" affect' (2008: 236). He uses the concept of affect and its power to change behaviour as a way to re-think social and political processes. Approaches like these offer a critical language to analyse the politicized dramaturgy of a street arts event and the public's visceral–critical responses to it. A focus on affects legitimates a foregrounding of what these performance interventions *do* with/to/for a public and what a public does in response. It does not replace meaning with visceral response, or mind with body, but expands and enriches meaning and critical analysis of the events and connects them to the *social* through actions undertaken within the frame of the performance event, but that resonate beyond the theatrical moment to 'cook up an affective storm', as Thrift says (2008: 243).

But how can a street performance even begin to have that kind of impact? In performances that use public space as an element in the aesthetic experience, the boundaries between art and non-art become porous. And as these lines of demarcation become blurred, the public is startled into seeing recognizable cultural signs and familiar sites through a lens of artistic imagination and thus is compelled to experience a *re-vision* of what seemed normative, established or permanent. The art represents 'becoming', not a transformation into something else that already exists, but a hovering at the moment of potentiality. The spectator's response to this tension of *almost-but-not-quite* is a *personal* embodied interaction with the experience, but it is also a *social* (or communal) participation in the performance event in public spaces saturated with a blend of affects. The audience, viewing a familiar place through the lens of art, can see and experience possibilities in real-life places that may have seemed unimaginable just moments before and can be *affected* by those insights, but, as already discussed, the affective response also includes the power to *affect* a situation. To *affect* sociopolitical change requires a shift in how people view the surrounding world and an ability to imagine an alternative world but it also needs a crucial additional step: people need to believe that they have the power and the tools to transform their world. Street arts interventions can offer the public an opportunity to work with those tools since the actions undertaken by the spectator within the frame of the intervention have a *reality* and significance not only in the performance space, but also in the actual public space and thus merge art and non-art both spatially and somatically. Participation in the performance is thus politically charged because the public can imagine and *rehearse* alternative models of society within the theatrical event. These events can rely on tactics of opposition or on those foregrounding collaboration as they offer an experience of a new social world. Here, in these events, the artists immerse the public in the work to dislodge expectations, long-held assumptions, and even habitual behaviour and thus to change how their audiences understand and interact with daily life and urban spaces. Here, the artists 'make us become with them, they draw us into the compound' (Deleuze and Guattari, 1994: 175) as the public has the opportunity to try out alternative worlds and engage in democratic practices of questioning the status quo and intervening 'in the visible and the sayable' (Rancière, 2010: 37).

As the book proceeds, I seek to develop a critical language to interrogate the 'rehearsal'[10] of citizen activism and democratic action, whether resistant or not and whether recognized as a form of activism by the spectator or not. I will explore how these performance interventions initiate a corporeal and critical encounter between a public, the aesthetic experience and the surrounding real-life environment, and I will look at how participation in the event constitutes a rehearsal of civic acts that can reinvigorate and re-form public spaces. These experiential moments of active democratic participation create what I call *democratic performatives*. Obviously, the source of the term 'performative' is J.L. Austin's *How To Do Things With Words* where he establishes a correspondence between words and actions 'in which to *say* something is to *do* something; or in which *by* saying or *in* saying something we are doing something' (1962: 12). In spite of Austin's anti-theatrical bias, many theatre and performance scholars have adapted the idea of performatives to a range of theatrical and cultural performances. Building on that work, I posit that the democratic performative creates a correspondence between audience actions within the frame of the performance and in an actual public space. The performance interventions provide the public with the chance to perform small, but significant, democratic activities in an actual space even when undertaken in the safety of a fictional event, and those activities implant democratic 'doings' into the bodies of the spectators. The audience thus both *imaginatively* experiences and *bodily* participates in alternative social practices and democratic acts. In Chapter 2, I develop the concept of democratic performatives in depth.

Introduction: Aesthetics and Politics of Street Arts

I do not claim that street arts can solve contemporary social and political ills, ensure urban regeneration, or make assessable improvements in people's lives although to see, hear, and experience the familiar in a new light is unmistakably transformative. And, I do not endeavour to prove that street arts alone mobilize their audiences or instigate social movements. I do, however, interrogate their potential for efficacy.

Theatrical intervention

I walk through the streets of a French town and as I round a corner, I am confronted with a startling sight. A woman has turned the roof of her car into a home gymnasium as she pedals vigorously on her exercise bicycle, stopping briefly for gulps of water. In the parking spot next to her, her three neighbours have transformed their car roof into a back garden patio. They sit around a small picnic table under a large umbrella chatting and sipping wine. Around them are potted plants and flowers.

Every now and then, the neighbours comment on each other activities and argue about issues of health. They defend their choices to

Figure 1 Opéra Pagaï, *Les Sans Balcons* (St Flour, France, August 2008)

passers-by who join the debate on relaxation versus exercise, as can be seen in the photograph. Further on, two women sunbathe on a car; another tends her potted plants. One family has taken over both their van and car that they park side-by-side connected by a playground slide. The parents barbecue, listen to the radio and sip wine on the roof of the van while their daughter tries to read a book in her deck chair on the car, but becomes bored and restless and so moves back and forth between the van and the car annoying her parents. A little domestic spat is placed on display. Others turn their car roofs into additional rooms. A furniture maker uses the top of his van as a carpenter's workroom with a table saw and other wood-working tools. Planks of wood lean against the sides of the van. A musician has transformed the roof of his car into his recording studio complete with a computer and musical instruments. Although he is watched often for quite a while by passers-by as he busily mixes tapes, he acts as though he is surrounded by walls and makes no contact with those who stop and stare. Other automobile roof-top dwellers chat quite happily with interested onlookers explaining that the tiny flats in which they live allow only the basics and lack a garden, a terrace, or even a small balcony. They cannot afford to move to a larger place, so they have decided to claim the roofs of their cars as a piece of their own private space even though it lacks any privacy. They point out that it is a space that is just wasted when the car sits idle and encourage the curious bystanders to use their own cars as free additions to their homes too.

The performance installations in Opéra Pagaï's *Les Sans Balcons*[11] are visually amusing and engaging, but they are also subtle provocations and playful social protests. Cyril Jaubert, director of Opéra Pagaï, says that the use of the roof of one's car parked on the street as a private space blurs boundaries between domestic space and public space. But it also imaginatively raises issues of urban overcrowding due to migration to the city and the resulting high cost of living, obstacles to sustainable gardening in urban environments, and challenges to health. Often the faux neighbourhood residents explain to the curious onlookers that they used to live in a village where they had a big garden, but they could not find work there so they had to move to the city where housing is so expensive. Or they claim that they cannot afford a vacation, so they have converted the car roof into a tiny beach or meadow. The idea behind *Les Sans Balcons* is to suggest a far-fetched, and yet vaguely plausible, way to increase one's living space and simultaneously to highlight the porous boundaries between public and private space in city life.

The intervention takes place in a residential urban area where most inhabitants live in small apartments. Scattered throughout the neighbourhood are the parked cars and vans whose roofs have been transformed into open-air rooms or small patches of garden. The incongruity of an occupied intimate space in the heart of a public space is disquieting, but the simplicity of the solution to a very real problem of lack of space in tiny homes is astonishing and encourages comment. For actual city inhabitants who live in small spaces, especially those in cities and towns that do not have many public parks, the installation offers a whimsical way to complain about urban population explosion and the resulting pressures it causes in a public forum and to play with seemingly extremist measures to which some must go. They can *share* their annoyances of urban life with their temporary pretend neighbours, and together they can intervene in urban spatial codes and challenge what had seemed a normative organization of social life with a playful credible solution to overcrowding.

New Zealand artist Stephen Bain has performed *Baby, Where are the Fine Things You Promised Me?* in cities all over Europe, Australia and New Zealand. Like Opéra Pagaï, Bain plays with issues of housing through a performance installation that intervenes in a public space by presenting an incongruous image and compelling the public to act in ways that contradict normal urban activities. Centred on a small square of astro-turf is a tiny white house with a red roof and a letter-box in front. The doll-size house is a 1:8 scale model of working class houses built in neat rows all over New Zealand at the turn of the twentieth century. They catered to families eager to participate in the dream of home ownership. Bain grew up in houses like these, he tells us. As curious passers-by approach the miniature replica of a recognizable home and bend down to peek in the windows, they discover an adult man inside surrounded by a radio, a tiny stove on which he makes tea for his *guests*, and a doll-size piano that he plays from time to time.

The interior walls are papered with the notes and drawings posted in his letterbox. The oversized inhabitant, looking a bit like Alice after she nibbled the cake that made her grow too large for the space she was in, invites conversation, and the spectators, both children and adults, some tourists but many business people on a lunch break, lie down on the astro-turf to have a chat. In spite of the whimsical incongruity of a cramped house in a public space inhabited by a full-size adult sharing a cup of tea or offering a bit of music, the performance installation raises serious social questions about who can achieve home ownership and at what cost. Bain proudly brags that he owns his tiny home, but admits

18 *Contemporary Street Arts in Europe*

Figure 2 Stephen Bain, *Baby, Where Are the Fine Things You Promised Me?* (Rennes, France, July 2009)

that it is probably the only one he will ever be able to buy. His simple intervention encourages people to lie down on the pavement and to confide their hopes for a home and family or their fears about loneliness or homelessness. Spectators must *shrink* in order to see in the house and thus experience a sensation of becoming too big for our shrinking world. Bain's *text* is all improvised in response to comments and questions by the spectators. Like *Les Sans Balcons*, the aesthetics and politics of *Baby, Where are the Fine Things You Promised Me?* are inseparable as the images and context reconfigure the visible, the sayable and the thinkable and thus hint at previously unimagined futures. The piece engages the public viscerally and critically as they participate in the event with unexpected actions that affect body and mind.

And another intervention

This book critically (and metaphorically) intervenes into the realm of street arts as it interrogates and analyses a wide range of interventionist performance practices. It looks at the shared aesthetico-political democratic practices of dissensus that can lead to moments of rupture and initiate an affective response in the public to many street arts interventions. Whether the art relies on oppositional tactics that equate political art with resistance to the state and its institutions (so evident in the pioneering street theatre work in the mid-twentieth century) or on relational or dialogic tactics that seek to forge interpersonal or inter-agency connections (as in the work of an increasing number of artists in the twenty-first century), Grant Kester claims that:

> The goal, in either case, is the transformation of a human consciousness in a way that enhances our capacity for the compassionate recognition of difference, both within ourselves and in others. In one case the ability of a certain form of disruption or dislocation to produce this transformation is taken as axiomatic, while in the other this transformation is achieved, or not, through a form of practical or experiential production, the outcome of which is not predetermined". (2011: 185)

The connection of both these forms of intervention to democratic practices is through 'becoming', affect and event-ness rather than content. Political ideas surface through actions, not only of the actors, but also of the spectators, 'actions that equally constitute reality', Fischer-Lichter claims (2008: 17). These participatory activities (acts of encounter) have a potential for efficacy through what the spectator *does* within the frame of the theatrical experience, but enacted in an actual public space: these activities enact a performance of everyday life in a state of becoming.

My choice of performances discussed in the book is based on what I have seen with just a few exceptions. I believe that actually *being there* is key to understanding and appreciating the work since the intervention in a public space needs to be moved through. Physical and emotive characteristics of a particular site, size and composition of a particular audience, and the ratio of passers-by and intentional spectators all have an impact on reception. The *script* is the interaction of place, performance and public, not the narrative content that is often quite problematic, silly, politically incorrect, retrogressive, or even offensive. To help the reader *be there*, I have included as much description and as many images as possible. There are online videos of many of the productions that I discuss posted on YouTube, Daily Motion, or on the HorsLesMurs website (directly accessible at www.rueetcirque.fr).[12] And one can see the shows live at over three hundred festivals in Europe every year.

Chapter 1, 'Looking Back: A Socio-Historical and Intellectual Context for Contemporary Street Arts in Europe', places the performance strategies and democratic performatives of contemporary street arts interventions within the socio-historical context of the 1960s in which it began to flourish. Although adapting centuries-old techniques, the current form of street arts developed in the 1960s and 1970s in response to the same anti-establishment impulses and seeds of rebellion that initiated social unrest and led to the vivid, and often violent, demonstrations and riots around the world in 1968.

Chapter 2, 'Democratic Performatives and an Aesthetics of Public Space', explores how the experience of these performance interventions in an actual place has a latent dissentient implication whether or not it leads to actual active engagement in political activities. I explore how the three general forms of activities of the democratic performatives begin to develop a critical language that can be used to identify that engagement, to interrogate tensions between aesthetic form and socio-political activist concerns and to evaluate the potential for efficacy in street theatre productions.

Chapter 3, 'Performing Democracy on a Grand Scale', further develops the concept of an aesthetics of public space through a detailed analysis of the London production of Royal de Luxe's *The Sultan's Elephant* in 2006. This chapter contrasts the 'feel-good' utopian performatives of a participatory democracy in the primary narrative surrounding the event with an edgier set of radical democratic performatives in the counter-narrative.

Chapter 4, 'Trespassing in Urban Places', looks at the democratic performatives of several contrasting performance interventions that aim to change how audiences experience the urban landscape; that alter, albeit temporarily, the function of these urban sites; and that overturn social expectations about the daily activities of the city inhabitants. The chapter explores how these street artists 'trespass' into other people's spaces and bring the public with them so that together they take over urban territory and, even momentarily, change its function.

Chapter 5, 'Subversive Imaginaries: Performing the Other', explores the various strategies used by several street theatre companies not only to perform 'otherness', but also to place the audience participants into an experience of otherness. These performance interventions engage specifically with socio-political issues and meanings of insider/outsider status, social citizenship and immigration.

Chapter 6, 'Community Performance: Community Performatives', looks at a complex, durational performance/community event. Friches

Théâtre Urbain's *Witness/N14* is a multi-stage project that develops ties with particular communities along the ancient route connecting Paris and Rouen and enables the communities to showcase (or not) performances, installations, or guided tours of their neighbourhoods.

The Postscript, 'Beyond the Street', looks at artists who seek to expand the notion of the *street* or public space beyond that of a geographic location as a way to establish an interactive connection between art and democracy and to problematize that connection.

The overall aim of the book is to question and consider the potential for efficacy at the intersection of aesthetics and politics in forms of contemporary street arts that inject art into public spaces. It seeks to offer an analytic *intervention* into the *event-ness* of street arts, and it strives to understand the thrill that these practices can arouse and to interlace entertainment with critical reflection.

1
Looking Back: A Socio-Historical and Intellectual Context for Contemporary Street Arts in Europe

Legacy of 1968

Performances have taken over the streets and squares of European cities for centuries: ancient mimes, jugglers, acrobats, and bards; the medieval cycles, miracles and morality plays; royal entries of the Renaissance; itinerant commedia dell'arte troupes; *tableaux vivants*; showmen exhibiting anything out of the ordinary from religious relics to freaks of nature throughout the centuries; and the popular entertainments of the great fairs, like Bartholomew Fair and Southwark Fair in London and Foire Saint-Germain, Foire Saint-Laurent, and Foire Saint-Ovide in Paris (some of which lasted into the 19th century).[1] All these street performances and many others used *art* to shift the focus of their audiences from ordinary day-to-day activities to special events of religious celebration, entertainment, or displays of power and transformed the function of the public space in which they took place. The long and vivid history of outdoor performance clearly contributed to what is called street arts today, but contemporary street theatre in Europe is not simply a continuation, an elaboration, or a modernization of the traditions of the past. Although adapting centuries-old outdoor performance techniques, the current form of street arts was deeply influenced by and developed as an artistic response to the same anti-establishment impulses and seeds of rebellion that initiated social unrest in the 1960s and led to the vivid, and often violent, demonstrations and riots around the world in 1968.

The earliest radical theatre companies[2] in this tumultuous period, in many ways anticipating the events of 1968, devised militant performances to challenge dominant discourses and traditional values through performance practices linking theatre to social issues, political struggles, and democratic initiatives. They sought to politicize the public by encouraging them to make cultural choices and to restore the participatory role of active citizenship. The elite art establishment often dismissed their communally devised pieces as amateurish, misguided, and even a degeneration of culture into a form of socio-political activism. These condemnations did not stop the young artists, and their experiments often motivated them to abandon traditional theatrical venues, texts, rehearsal procedures, and company structures. International tours and newly established festivals in Europe in the 1960s and 1970s enabled the activist artists (notably Living Theatre and Bread and Puppet Theatre) to share their innovative and oppositional theatrical languages, practices and techniques. The radical artists also shared a utopian confidence in the power of art to affect social change.

In the early 1980s, Michel Crespin (a pioneer in street arts as co-founder of an early street theatre company, Théâtracide; co-founder and director of Lieux Publics;[3] and founder of one of the earliest street theatre festivals in Aurillac, France) completed a study that cited the goals of street arts as both preserving old traditions of outdoor entertainment, carnivals, and other festivities and encouraging experimentation with new forms and practices.[4] This dual goal was echoed in 'Dossier Spécial 01', the report of a Street Arts Working Group, established by HorsLesMurs in 1998 and charged with identifying key aspects and practices of contemporary street theatre. Michel Simonot, writer and director who led the Street Arts Working Group, acknowledged the importance and influence of the ancient outdoor art forms, but at the same time he insisted that current street theatre artistic practices originated in ideological values and political goals unique to the 1960s and 1970s (1999: 5).[5] In the 2007 study entitled *Street Artists in Europe*, commissioned by the European Parliament's Committee on Culture and Education, Yohann Floch (consultant on international relations, education and cultural arts and coordinator of Circostrada Network at HorsLesMurs) claims that looking for these links to the past arises from an imagined need for historical legitimacy. He argues that outdoor performers from earlier centuries performed outside out of necessity and sought to create the conditions of an indoor theatre with its physical distance between actor and audience as evidenced by the use of make-shift stages. Artists who in the 1960s and 1970s *chose* to go outdoors, did so to oppose traditional cultural institutions, to re-appropriate public space, to mingle with a new audience, and to establish porosity between art and non-art. 'The object of the street theatre is the street' noted French sociologist Sylvia Ostrowetsky, one of the first scholars to look at street theatre as an art form worthy of critical analysis (1997: 141; my translation). Crossing the theatre building's threshold represented a metaphoric border crossing that required finding a new home, learning new languages and codes, putting down new roots, and establishing new relationships with the *native* populations (the public that avoided art institutions). This notion of border crossings formed the foundation of street arts' aesthetics and politics. Thus their practices, while seemingly similar to earlier outdoor performance, were developed consciously in response to the vibrant socio-political moment. To understand this shift to theatre 'outside the walls' (*hors les murs*), it is important to have a sense of the unique context in which it began to flourish.

For political scientist Sheldon Wolin, the 1960s began as a 'quest to expand the meaning and practice of freedom. It was a time for seeing the world and themselves with fresh eyes, for believing that it was possible to begin things anew' (1997: 132). It came to represent a decade in which populations became politicized: 'The sixties converted democracy from a rhetorical to a working proposition, not just about equal rights but about new models of action and access to power in workplaces, schools, neighbourhoods, and local communities' (1997: 144). And it was a time when 'acts of civil disobedience, communal experiments, aesthetic innovations...did not spring from a desire to 'participate,' but from a newly discovered passion for significant action' (1997: 143). In western democracies, the conflicts of the 1960s were flamed by the sons and daughters of the middle class, the students at universities, who were disillusioned by the world around them and believed that they were on the brink of revolutionary changes. Paul Potter, president of the radical group Students for a Democratic Society in the United States, claimed that the young people 'had everything their society could give them, found that gift hollow and rejected it' (quoted in Cavallo, 1999: 2). They were motivated by a distrust of those in authority and a moral outrage against the injustices and inequalities in their supposedly democratic societies.

The summative year of 1968 was, in the words of one popular history writer, 'the year that rocked the world' (Kurlansky, 2005). The events of 1968, however, were the explosion of ideas that had been in the air certainly throughout the 1960s and most likely since the end of World War II, ideas that crossed national borders to create global unrest and citizen activism.[6] Carole Fink, Philipp Gassert, and Detlef Junker, in the 'Introduction' to their interdisciplinary and international anthology on the 1960s, write: 'The events of 1968 happened within national contexts yet took place across the globe—from Berkeley to Berlin, Bangkok to Buenos Aires, Cairo to Cape Town, Paris to Tokyo' (1998: 1). Local groups, emboldened by the mass media coverage of protests elsewhere, felt a part of a larger and more powerful socio-political movement that could possibly find an alternative to both communism and capitalism: a 'third way' beyond state or party politics. Paul Berman calls this period a time of 'utopian exhilaration' when many believed that a 'superior new society was already coming into existence' (1996: 9). Images and reports of demonstrations and the often aggressive response of the police or the brutal suppression of democratic initiatives appeared daily on television, on radio, and in newspapers around the world. In countries without a free press, underground broadcasts, posters and leaflets, and even word-of-mouth kept the population informed of successful and unsuccessful protests and provided a network of information on issues and strategies (Fink *et al.*, 1998: 1–27). While the social revolt in each country was in response to national issues, the global unrest represented a world-wide discontent with the cultural, economic and political status quo; a rejection of authority, Western imperialism, dictatorships, and rampant consumerism; and a longing for 'freedom, justice, and self-determination' (ibid., 1998: 21) on personal levels in some countries and on a state level in others as citizens fought against totalitarian governments.

While demonstrations, marches, and unrest occurred in cities around the world, the events of May 1968 in France were arguably the most dramatic and transmissible. Fink *et al.* write:

> The 'export' of the Paris May, which proved to be particularly contagious, is perhaps the most striking example of the global nature of 1968....The gains made in Paris convinced protesters in other countries that it was possible to make similar demands elsewhere, leading to the exchange of ideas and methods of revolution across national borders....Paris provided both the model for dissent and a cautionary lesson for the authorities. (1998: 18)

Daniel Singer, Paris-based correspondent for *The Nation* during these years who wrote about the events soon after they happened, concurs: 'The lessons of the May crisis are not only true for France, but extend well beyond French frontiers' (2000: x).

It was only in France that the student protesters were joined by workers nationwide who went on strike with similar, although sometimes more practical, sometimes more ambiguous, demands. In Italy, workers also responded to student protests, but not until a year later and not on a national level. And in Germany and the United States, student and worker movements sometimes intersected, but not to the extent of the coordination in France. The uprising caused the largest strike in French history that put the power of the ruling party into question and paralyzed the economy. Georges Pompidou, prime minister at the time, worried that 'the only historical precedent [of the May events] is the fifteenth century when the structures of the Middle Ages were collapsing and when students were revolting at the Sorbonne. Right now, it is not the government which is being attacked, not the institutions, nor even France. It is our own civilization' (quoted in Seidman, 2004: 1–2). While the words may seem hyperbolic, there is no question that the protests of May 1968 challenged the societal and intellectual status quo in French society profoundly.

In spite of this apparent upheaval, the 'third way' of the May 1968 protesters failed to achieve radical political change. Historian Peter Starr, in his analysis of what he calls the 'failed revolution', argues that the 'third way' rejected 'direct political action', organizing and coordination and instead relied on iconic gestures, proclamations and street interventions, often inspired by artistic practices, to spread the idea of revolution (1995: 8). But, while that approach did not result in actual revolution, it did achieve a radical socio-cultural shift that located the site of opposition and subversion in art. Social historian, Michael Seidman writes that:

> The events [of May '68] are still viewed as a rupture with the past and the beginning not of a proletarian revolution (as many radicals thought at the time), but rather of a cultural rebellion that led to a more emancipated society. Almost all agree that the crisis of the spring of 1968 changed France profoundly. (2004: 1)

And, Ingrid Gilcher-Holtey, who describes this revolt as a 'new social movement' (or a mobilization of a group of people over a sustained period of time who seek to affect social change through protests and demonstrations), argues that this movement opposed the 'total structure of society' and was guided by ideas of the New Left, one of which insisted 'that changes in the cultural sphere must precede social and political transformation' (1998: 257).

In October following May 1968, Michel de Certeau wrote *The Capture of Speech*, in which he tried to make sense of the events of a few months earlier and assess their impact in the cultural sphere. He calls the crisis a:

> symbolic revolution... because it *signifies* more than it effectuates, or because of the fact that it contests given social and historical *relations*

in order to create authentic ones. After all, the 'symbol' is the indication that affects the entire movement, in practice as well as in theory. From the beginning to the end, speech is what played the decisive role. (1998: 5–6)

He explains quite passionately:

> Last May, speech was taken the way, in 1789, the Bastille was taken. The stronghold that was assailed is a knowledge held by the dispensers of culture, a knowledge meant to integrate or enclose student workers and wage earners in a system of assigned duties. From the taking of the Bastille to the taking of the Sorbonne, between these two symbols, an essential difference characterizes the event of May 13, 1968: today it is imprisoned speech that was freed. (1998: 11)

For de Certeau, the protests succeeded in hijacking cultural knowledge and social language by inverting the meaning of their signs and thus stating or depicting the seemingly impossible, representing the unrepresentable. It is this creation of 'symbolic sites' with their contradictory signs that constituted the 'exemplary action' of the revolt. The exemplary action:

> 'opens a breach,' not because of its own efficacity [sic.], but because it displaces a law that was the more powerful in that it had not been brought to mind; it unveils what was latent and makes it contestable....The exemplary action changes nothing; it creates *possibilities* relative to *impossibilities* that had until then been admitted but not clarified. (1998: 8)

These symbolic sites and exemplary actions are forms of shock, discussed earlier, and they acquired an aesthetic form in the oppositional street interventions of the 1970s and 1980s.[7]

Henri Lefebvre, also writing in 1968, gave the revolt more than the symbolic success claimed by de Certeau, insisting that it was:

> profoundly political from the outset....The extraordinary fact is that, following a relatively minor confrontation, a substantial number of the superstructures and institutions of a great country should have been severely shaken and in certain cases even made to collapse. For such were the results of the movement as it spread. (1969: 112–13)

The protests shifted from student demands for reforms in housing and classrooms to societal issues of hierarchy, freedom, personal agency and 'autogestion' or self-management. As Lefebvre warned, 'the crisis of authority is but the outward appearance of a much deeper crisis which extends, beyond everyday existence, to the institutions and the state which holds them together' (1969: 107). Celebration and struggle characterized this cultural revolution for Lefebvre as the students, in particular, reclaimed the streets and re-appropriated public spaces in their quest to refashion society. And like de Certeau, Lefebvre applauded 'the explosion of unfettered speech....Speech manifested itself as a primary freedom, now reconquered and re-appropriated' (1969: 119). And Jean-Jacques Lebel, artist and activist who played a significant role in the student street activities, passionately claimed that the 'May Revolution dynamited the limits of 'art' and 'culture' as it did all other social or political limits. The old avant-gardist dream of turning 'life' into 'art,' into a collective creative experience, finally came true' (1998: 180).

It is difficult to deny the significant impact of the vivid events of 1968 on a generation of French thinkers whose work has crossed national and disciplinary borders: de Certeau and Lefebvre certainly, but also Deleuze, Guattari, Derrida, Foucault, Debord, Lefort, and Rancière to mention just a few. For them, May 1968 represented an irreversible rupture in the socio-political and intellectual foundations of French society that required a 'third way' of oppositional thought retaining the revolutionary impulses but avoiding inevitable consequences and compromises that would result from actual revolutionary action. 'The solution', explains Grant Kester in his analysis of art theory and history of this period:

> was a tactical withdrawal into the protected field of the text. The novel, the poem, the film, the work of art, and theory itself would become the site for a process of 'subtle' or 'discrete' subversion. The revolutionary would decamp to the institutional margins of political life—the university, the gallery, and the publishing house—to create a heterotopic space of experimentation. (2011: 45–6)

Thus, for these French thinkers, the arts had a crucial role to play in the new society.[8] The enormous impact of their ideas on both intellectual thought and art practices is impossible to measure since, as Kester argues, 'What would have been identified twenty years ago as a distinct 'post-structural' strand within the larger field of critical theory has been so successfully assimilated that it's now largely synonymous with critical theory *per se*' (2011: 54).

It is easy to see the impact of these ideas and the conviction that societal transformation could only be achieved indirectly through cultural interventions on the burgeoning street theatre movement, particularly in France, in the 1970s. Sadie Plant claims that the 'events of 1968 are remembered for the irruption of play, festivity, spontaneity, and the imagination into the political realm' (1992: 70), and clearly the mass demonstrations relied on performance practices of burning effigies, beating objects to create drum-like rhythms, or participating in processions. The highly visible role of the Living Theatre in the events of 1968 reinforced the belief in the centrality of the arts, and performance in particular, in initiating a shift toward a more just and democratic society, and students, activists, scholars and theatre practitioners began to understand and use the close link between performance and political act. Lebel and his fellow activists turned to agit-prop skits on the street as a way to 'provoke discussions and awaken the people to the fact that imperialism is present in their daily life...as a means of breaking down the Berlin Wall in people's heads and helping them out of their state of passive acceptance' (1998: 182). The early French street theatre companies, like Théâtre de l'Unité, Oposito, Royal de Luxe, Ilotopie, Transe Express, and Générik Vapeur, took these ideas further as they abandoned traditional theatre buildings for the freedom and populist appeal of the street, offered their shows to the public for free, and insisted on a revolutionary aesthetic of innovation, provocation, and overthrow of norms. Their performance practices did not seek to present alternative social structures and behaviours for static spectators, but to compel participation as they tore down conventional barriers between actor and audience and between the fiction of art and the reality of daily life. The artists sought to politicize the public by blurring the boundaries between participatory acts in the art event and democratic practices of resistance. Thus, through their art, they 'converted democracy from a rhetorical to a working proposition', as Wolin claimed (1997: 144).

One of Générik Vapeur's shows, *Bivouac*, created in 1988, seems to draw on the street demonstrations of the late 1960s for inspiration.[9] The actors, dressed in suits and ties but with thick bright blue make-up on their faces and hair, take back the streets as they advance like a protest march through the center of town furiously and ominously banging their large blue oil drums on the pavement. (See Colour Plate 2.) They are accompanied by fireworks, flares, and a flatbed truck carrying a loud rock music band. One actor pulls an oil drum with pipes sticking out to make it look like a mechanical dog on a leash. He stops every now and then to cast lighted flares into the animal's body so that it glows and he then spins around with the lighted animal creating a large and dangerous circle. The procession resembles a fantastical anarchistic demonstration with theatricalized moments: a police car is *assassinated* in a giant mousetrap, several actors with their oil drums rappel off the roof of a tall building, and the actors' *picnic* in the street as they stuff heads of lettuce and raw eggs into their mouths and often spew them onto spectators. At one point during the show, they construct a wall of oil drums, echoing Christo's 1962 'Iron Curtain', an oil barrow wall signifying the Berlin Wall blocking a narrow Paris street. The actors in *Bivouac* violently knock down their wall soon after its completion. Dramatic imagery of inverted signs, loud noise, danger, and performative anarchy replace a clear narrative as the promenade performance powerfully evokes the street protests of the 1960s.

While early street theatre companies throughout Europe experimented with a range of outdoor forms from busking to large-scale and site-specific productions, street arts developed and diversified more in France than elsewhere in the three decades after 1968. Floriane Gaber, who has documented street theatre for over two decades, claims that one of the reasons that an ever increasing number of French theatre companies chose to work in the streets in the 1970s, 1980s and 1990s when pioneering militant companies elsewhere in Europe and in the United States folded or moved indoors (with a few notable exceptions) was the existence of favourable cultural policies in France (2009b: 15–49).[10] Key policies that created a nurturing climate for French street theatre companies were the decentralization of the arts and the encouragement of 'people's theatre'. Both policies, that offered financial support in addition to words, sought to engage new audiences—what was called the 'non-public' (Gaber, 2009b: 7). Although the idea of a people's theatre was first introduced by Roman Rolland in 1903, it was Firmin Gémier who established the first TNP or Théâtre National Populaire (National Popular Theatre) in Paris in 1920. The TNP flourished under the leadership of Jean Vilar (founder of the theatre festival in Avignon in 1947) in the 1950s, and it was an important stepping stone in the democratization of culture or taking the arts to the people who rarely entered cultural institutions. However, by the 1960s, the TNP model of classics for the common man no longer seemed the 'best remedy for a "sluggish and depoliticized public, hooked on television and gadgets by consumer society"' according to Philippe Madral in *Le Théâtre hors les murs* (quoted in Gaber, 2009b: 19). Instead, the new generation of activist artists inevitably left the cultural institutions for the public spaces where the non-public lived and worked. They strove to engage these people, accidental audiences involved in their daily activities, by superimposing art on life, and they idealistically sought 'to make the populations understand the necessity of theatre as a tool for social transformation' (ibid., 2009b: 19).

The early radical street artists certainly refashioned old theatrical forms, practices and organized structures. In launching artistic interventions into the actual life of the city, the artists challenged the demarcation between the *fiction* of the theatre and *reality* of the street. The early street productions, creating what de Certeau had called 'symbolic sites', turned aesthetic expectations and socio-political assumptions upside down when theatrical moments unexpectedly appeared on the streets. The artists, in a much more extreme gesture than the state policy of democratization of culture, took the art to the people in order to change their perceptions, not only of art, but of the social world in which they lived. They decided to *go public* by choosing to perform outside cultural institutions (even the 'people's theatres' that sought to dispel the aura of elitism) and by linking their performances to actual everyday sites. In so doing, they often created public memories of familiar urban places transformed by the interventions, and thus they offered an alternative social and artistic experience based in imagination. Photographer and chronicler of street theatre, Christophe Renaud de Lage, asserted:

> To break the established rapport between stage and auditorium, to leave the beaten path created by institutions, to transform the rapport with the public, to rediscover a taste for risk and innovation, to invent new modes of production, to refuse the tyranny of money and its submission to mass appeal, to imagine other ways of living, to look for new connections with objects, things, and people, to replace the focus on 'me' with one on the collective, all that, yes, is really revolutionary, it is true that in order to change life, we must begin by transforming, each at his own pace, our rapport with the world. (2000: 16, my translation)

Underlying this passionate utopian claim are the democratic ideas and goals of those involved in the 1968 riots: a rejection of the status quo with its hierarchies, capitalism, and consumerism and a quest for justice, equality, free speech, and 'autogestion' or citizen control over one's own world.

'Situations' and 'moments'

The writings of the Situationists,[11] a group of thinkers and activists whose most famous name is Guy Debord, gave voice to many of the anti-establishment leanings and had a strong impact on the May events. Founded in July 1957, Situationist International was made up of writers and artists who were profoundly engaged in understanding and acting upon the intersections of politics and art through individual freedom, imagination, and socio-political engagement. Beginning in the realm of art, they sought to develop an avant-garde that would initiate a socio-cultural revolution overthrowing the mainstream ideas and practices relating to art, history, politics, urbanism, and everyday life. Key among their concerns was the growing alienation in all aspects of contemporary life since in capitalist society, they argued, it was impossible to participate in the lived world except through images ('spectacle'). They railed against the elite and state-sponsored cultural institutions that played a major role in the success of the capitalist state and against the commodification of all aspects of socio-cultural life from recognizable art forms (mass-produced as posters) to walking (seen as window shopping), and they sought to interrupt this rapid transformation of culture into commodity. While it is questionable how many of their ideas the Situationists actually put into practice, it would be difficult to deny that key concepts they articulated, like psychogeography, *détournement* (diversion, turn-about, or derailment), *dérive* (drift, stroll), situations, and *urbanisme unitaire* (unitary urbanism), inspired and have been adapted by street artists up to the present day as analyses later in the book will show.

Debord did not just want to create another art movement with these practices, but rather sought to transcend art (or actually to wedge it into everyday life) in order to develop a 'unified vision of art and politics' in which one is not subordinate to the other, but rather they work together to overthrow the 'society of alienation, totalitarian control, and passive spectacular consumption' (Knabb, 2006: 402–3). Central to Debord's ideas (as well as to the missions of many early street artists although not as clearly articulated) is a condemnation of what he labelled the 'society of spectacle'. Debord, like many other thinkers of his generation, notably Lefebvre, deplored the alienation and loss of agency of individuals in modern society. In *The Society of Spectacle*, he claimed that 'spectacle is not a collection of images; rather it is a social relationship between people that is mediated by images' (1994, thesis 4: 12). What that means is that a passive observation and contemplation of images of life have replaced direct, lived experience; images have become the new reality, and reality is reduced to images. People have become alienated from actual life, from each other, and even from themselves. 'All that was once directly lived has become mere representation' (1994, thesis 1: 12), and this contemplation of images privileges the sense of sight over all other senses and thus reduces 'the special place once occupied by touch' (1994, thesis 18: 17).[12] These ideas had a wide-reaching influence, like the emphasis on affect. And Sadie Plant points out that 'the situationist spectacle prefigures contemporary notions of hyperreality, and the world of uncertainty and superficiality described and celebrated by postmodernists is precisely that which the situationists first subjected to passionate criticism' (1992: 5).

But even more importantly, the passive spectatorship described by the Situationists has a significant impact on individual agency. Debord wrote:

> The more he contemplates, the less he lives; the more readily he recognizes his own needs in the images of need proposed by the dominant system, the less he understands his own existence and his own desires. The spectacle's externality with respect to the acting subject is demonstrated by the fact that the individual's own gestures are no longer his own, but rather those of someone else who represents them to him. The spectator feels at home nowhere, for spectacle is everywhere. (1994, thesis 30: 23)

Agency or individual freedom has been distorted to signify free market consumerism in which *consumers* supposedly have the freedom of choice to buy whatever they want, but from a pre-selected group of items in the shops. The choices are manipulated by the images presenting a very specific view of society determined by the ruling hegemonic order. That false freedom, warned Debord, should not be confused with the freedom of *citizens* to participate in dialogue and debate about governance in a democracy.

In the 1950s and 1960s, the Situationists, anxious to encourage active participation in daily life as a solution for the alienation and passivity of contemporary society, suggested an approach that blurred distinctions between art and life in order to stimulate an abrupt awareness of *lived experience*. Early opposition to socio-political aspects, later identified as key characteristics of Debord's society of spectacle, were first tackled within the cultural world with calls for art to 'enlarge life, not merely to express or explain it' (Knabb, 2006: 36). To do that Debord suggested the construction of 'situations' that heightened and intensified everyday experience. This quasi-art work was not meant to endure or become an exchangeable commodity, but rather to be an intense, ephemeral experience that resulted in a 'sudden expansion of knowledge' (Debord, 1994, thesis 182: 131). In 'Theses on Cultural Revolution', he explains that:

> The goal of the situationists is immediate participation in a passionate abundance of life by means of deliberately arranged variations of ephemeral moments. The success of these moments can reside in nothing other than their fleeting effect. The situationists consider cultural activity in its totality as an experimental method for constructing everyday life. (Knabb, 2006: 53)

But their ultimate goal was not simply increased awareness, it was a social transformation as Debord claimed in 1957: 'First of all, we think the world must be changed' (Knabb, 2006: 25). Art in everyday life and radical politics were considered inseparable.[13]

Like Debord, Henri Lefebvre sought to counteract what he saw as a passive spectatorship and consumption of life experiences. In *Everyday Life in the Modern World*, he insisted that contemporary life could only have meaning and coherence if it went beyond consumption, if life was seen, felt and experienced, and if individuals acquired some personal agency. Through his introduction of the concept of 'moments', he hoped to reawaken the senses, and in so doing perhaps to inspire the imagination to conceive of revolutionary or utopian possibilities. He insisted that the only 'answer is everyday life, to rediscover everyday life—no longer neglect and disown it, elude and evade it—but actively to rediscover it while contributing to its transfiguration' (2007: 202). And art can begin to point the way since creative activity is a form of freedom and a source of potentiality. David Harvey's Afterword to Lefebvre's *The Production of Space*, clarifies the concept of 'moment' as:

> fleeting but decisive sensations (of delight, surrender, disgust, surprise, horror, or outrage) which were somehow revelatory of the totality of possibilities contained in daily existence. Such movements were ephemeral and would pass instantly into oblivion, but during their passage all manner of possibilities—often decisive and revolutionary—stood to be uncovered and achieved. 'Moments' were conceived of as points of rupture, of radical recognition of possibilities and intense euphoria. (Lefebvre, 1991: 429)

The notions of 'moment' and 'constructed situation' as suggestions for ways of living that linked politics and aesthetics to lived experience led to conceptions of art forms that superseded institutional art. Simon Sadler in *The Situationist City* explains that 'the constructed situation would clearly be some sort of performance, one that would treat all space as performance space and all people as performers' (1999: 105). The clear boundary between art and non-art was breached, and while these revolutionary utopian ideas were clearly a product of their historical moment, they continue to have an impact on contemporary street performances.

Theatrical intervention

As I began working on this chapter, I saw *Est-ce que le monde sait qu'il me parle?* (Does the world know it speaks to me?), devised by the French theatre group, Ktha Compagnie.[14] To my surprise, the production seemed to dramatize Situationist ideas about passivity and loss of agency in a society of spectacle. As we wait in the lobby of Confluences (Maison des Arts Urbains) in the twentieth arrondissement in Paris for the start of the show, the audience can wander through an exhibition of hundreds of photographs of signs one sees in a range of public spaces as well as spaces that seem public but actually are privatized, like shopping malls, airports and other places that strangers can gather. These signs display words and images that announce what is permitted and forbidden to do: pictures of large bottles of liquid toiletries, cigarettes, bicycles, or drinks surrounded by red circles with red lines drawn diagonally across them, 'No Parking', 'Left Turn Only', 'Do Not Walk on the Grass', 'Please wait here' and 'Danger: Construction Zone' from countries all over Europe fill the walls.

Soon, the spectators are summoned, and we dutifully follow our guide out the door onto the street and into the large international shipping container in which the show takes place. The door is shut behind us. Inside are two actors identically dressed in workers' jumpsuits who passively watch as we enter and choose a spot to sit on the benches. Once the spectators are settled, the actors play one round of 'rock, paper, scissors'. Chance determines the winner who stands in front, very close to the audience; the other stands a few steps behind and off to the side. They just look at the audience for several minutes, quite disinterested, but their constant watching, like embodied surveillance cameras, makes me more aware of my own actions as I realize that my mundane movements are not escaping notice as the actors *copy* an unconscious movement that I or the other spectators make. It seemed as though they were training the audience to behave as a *proper* audience should as they made us aware of our fidgeting and whispering. As several spectators giggle uncomfortably, the actors just stare into the audience, and their spectatorial passivity is contagious as everyone gradually becomes silent and motionless. Suddenly, the container shakes and rattles as someone runs back and forth on the roof. The spectators look up with alarm, amusement, or even irritation and begin to comment, laugh, and gesture, but again the actors take very little notice and just look at us. Seemingly following the actors' lead, the audience becomes quiet and sits passively waiting, aware of the activity above but not responding. Finally, the trap door in the roof opens and a white faceless rag doll falls to the floor just between the actor and the audience. And yet again, the actors give it just a fleeting look, and the audience as well responds just by looking. The disinterested glance of the actors, imitated by the audience, removes a sense of humanity as we all appear like desensitized robots in reactions to actual events.

Finally, the actor in front begins to speak. All she says are familiar phrases from advertisements in newspapers, magazines, radio and television; *orders* from the Paris metro, airport security, or GPS systems; phrases from tele-marketing calls and administrative letters; commercial and governmental telephone recordings of instructions; and *common knowledge* phrases throughout the rest of the show. Everything one actor says is repeated by the other, sometimes with exactly the same intonation, sometimes quite differently. Sometimes, the second actor waits for a pause in the first actor's list; sometimes, their words overlap. Conversation is replaced by slogans and advertisements; dialogue itself is commodified. Recognizable phrases are recycled and offered as *original* insights. As the actors repeat the words of a recognizable phrase, it is easy to hear the connotative meanings change with each repetition. Many phrases, particularly those related to issues of security, repeated over and over with increasing urgency, clearly demonstrate their power to create fear of the Other. And phrases that encourage everyone to look or smell alike, when intoned repeatedly, highlight not only a desire to fit seamlessly into a group, but also the opposite of that quest for belonging in the need to identify or target difference. At one point in the show, the actors whistle familiar advertising tunes. Several spectators smile with pleasure as they recognize a tune and verify the product it is advertising with a person seated nearby, but the use of these tunes comments on how quickly and easily an individual can become absorbed or drawn in by what the world 'says to us'. The narrative text of familiar phrases and tunes often heard, but rarely noticed, suddenly becomes a keyhole through which recurrent social problems of rampant consumption, commodification, fear of the other, and need for a sense of belonging can be glimpsed.

Est-ce que le monde sait qu'il me parle? dramatizes the Situationist assertion that we experience reality second-hand through spectacle as actual involvement and content of life is replaced by its commodity form. It reveals that freedom in today's capitalist societies is, as Debord pointed out, freedom of choice to buy products that become *necessary* through compelling ads. For me, this clever adaptation of verbatim drama not only encouraged me to *actually hear* what usually becomes background noise obeyed without thought, but it also highlighted the constant cacophony in today's world. And I was left feeling disturbed and helpless as I began to realize how easy it is to allow advertising and public announcements like these to deaden a critical response and to turn the population into automatons that just do what they are told. The mesmerizing power of the repetitions of these familiar advertisements and commands of this verbatim *text* highlighted the ease with which I assumed the role of passive consumer. Once in a while, the actors asked the audience members a direct question. The responses were often giggles or grunts rather than actual answers. I think that the discomfort in answering was not about reluctance to participate, but rather it was a sudden, unexpected and acute awareness of our zombie-like enjoyment of the repetitions.

Every few minutes during the show, another white rag doll (one hundred by the end) was dropped through the hole, some as large as the actors, others the size of infants and young children: a nameless, faceless, indistinguishable and mass-produced population. They gradually fill the space. One of the actors, every now and then, casually picks up a doll, looks at it disinterestedly, and drops it again – no emotion, no concern. The other actor stacks the doll bodies in the back of the container, blocking the door. The actors change places, and the doll wall is dismantled as the bodies are tossed around the container, again with no interest in the doll's human form as the advertisements and orders drone on. The dolls clearly represent a population, any population, of the Other whose members all look alike unless one takes the time to get to know individuals (just as each doll is unique in spite of all being white faceless rag dolls). And the way they are treated is a powerful commentary on the treatment of the Other in contemporary society. Finally, the doors at the end of the container are opened to frame the actual world of the street. The night I saw the show, a young man on a bicycle stopped and stared in at us sitting in the container. For me, our passive staring out into the street became embarrassing.

Part of the power of the piece created by Ktha Compagnie came from the theatrical adaptation of the ideas of passive consumption and lack of personal agency, explored in *The Society of Spectacle*. The monotonous and yet appealingly addictive spoken text with its repetitive images, the role of passive spectatorship in which the audience quite happily let itself be cast, and the enclosed container played with the verbatim form to present a 'society of spectacle' *reality*. The company used the leitmotifs from advertising and public announcements, barely noticeable because they are so familiar, and made them strange and somewhat unsettling through humour, repetition, juxtaposition, and collage. This strangeness created experiential shocks: a gradual realization of the modern consumer's docile acceptance of what the 'world' says to do and not to do and what to feel and want, so that one no longer needs to think. That awareness, in turn, had the potential to develop a more critical response to advertising or even a more active engagement to counteract passive consumption of both products and knowledge.

In addition, many of the visual images and kinaesthetic audience experiences resonated with images of actual events and social problems in the contemporary world: the dolls (like refugees) locked in the container after the spectators left at the show's end, the actors' costumes echoing the jumpsuits of the prisoners in Guantanamo Bay prison camp, and the audience becoming like human cargo in a large international shipping container. The interpretive possibilities of the short, deceptively simple, performance expanded from the power of advertising to a troubling apathy in spite of the vivid world events. Do you see how easy it is to create a passive and obedient population, the piece seems to ask. And what are you going to do about it?

Bill Talen began his career as Reverend Billy as a one-man performance artist/street preacher, carrying his own wooden pulpit over his shoulder, on the sidewalks of Times Square in New York City in 1996. Echoing the words of the Situationists, he railed against unbridled consumption warning the public that the United States was a nation of consumers, not producers. He spoke of the violence in the consumer cycle as corporations abuse the earth and cause increased levels of pollution. The power of his campaign against consumerism caught on, and today his Church of Life After Shopping includes not only the Reverend, but also a choir of thirty-five gospel singers and seven musicians. His politico-performative interventions into large chains like Walmart or Starbucks challenge ideas of public space and free speech, and they often lead to his arrest, but they also increase the impact of his grassroots activism though performance. Echoing the ideas of the Situationists on consumerism, Reverend Billy's message focuses on the loss of individual freedom and agency in a consumer society, the privatization of many public spaces in the shift from a High Street of family-owned shops to malls of chain stores, and the Disneyfication of contemporary life with its simulacra and nostalgia. Rampant consumerism will wipe out imagination and commodify the individual, he claims. And he rants against the notion of identity being circumscribed by consumption. His persona of a hyperbolic stereotype of an evangelical preacher appropriates a religious trope of the charismatic minister and uses familiar preaching techniques to draw attention to what he insists is the dominant religion of capitalist societies: the religion of consumerism.[15] Unquestioned belief in free-market economy has replaced a spiritual religious commitment, and the goal of Reverend Billy's Church of Life After Shopping is to disrupt the dramaturgy of commercialism by highlighting how advertising *stages* the need for a product to lure the consumer into buying items that promise happiness, perfection, and beauty. The arrival of Reverend Billy and his Choir creates disorder in the choreography of shopping.

In 2009, Reverend Billy and his Life After Shopping Gospel Choir brought their anti-consumerism message to the UK on a two-week 'Shopocalypse Tour' that included performances at the Battersea Arts Centre and actual street interventions and exorcisms, one that occurred at London's Westfield Shopping Centre. Reverend Billy, in his signature white suit, preacher's collar, and puffy bleached blond hair, arrived at the mall and began preaching through his large white megaphone that 'we've got to stop shopping. There is life after shopping. Slow down your consuming. It is bad for the economy. It is time to stop our shopping. Let's go home!' He was followed by his choir in billowing green robes singing 'stop...stop shopping'. Shoppers followed them, clapping to the music. Within a few minutes of their flamboyant arrival, the mall's security guards asked them to leave and when the preacher and his choir continued, they surrounded him, roughly grabbed his megaphone, tried to hold him down and silence him, aggressively sought to separate him from the choir who stayed very close, and dispersed the gathering crowds dismissing Reverend Billy as a problem they were dealing with. The security guards approached the videographer telling him 'we don't want you recording this' and demanding repeatedly that he turn off his camera and recorder, even threatening to take them away. The videographer insisted that the camera was off when it was not, as the video posted in the Campaigns section of Reverend Billy's website attests.[16] When Reverend Billy and his choir left the mall, they were told never to return.

Shoppers responded in a range of ways to Reverend Billy's message and to the heavy-handed response of the security guards. Some angrily said he had no right to tell them not to shop; some expressed surprise that the mall was private property and not a public space; many were baffled by the event and sought clarification of the message. How could we stop all shopping was a frequent question, but with the commotion of the event that question was left unanswered. Reverend Billy does not seek to close down all shops, but rather to encourage people to abandon the mega-corporations like Starbucks, Walmart, or Tesco in favour of more ethical retail practices and to support local shops and farmers' markets. Spending money at the large corporations enriches the corporate leaders, not the community, he insists.

One of Reverend Billy's interventions is the exorcism of the cash tills at Starbucks. He puts his hands on the cash till and prays loudly as the choir sings, what he calls 'power prayers'. His success at raising consumer awareness and intimidating the corporation is evident in the court order in California banning him from entering the premises and requiring him to remain at least two hundred and fifty yards away from the door. When Reverend Billy went to the Whitechapel Road Starbucks in London to exorcize the cash tills, he was surrounded by fifteen policemen, several police vans waited outside, and a helicopter hovered overhead. To get him to leave, Starbucks closed.

The performance of Reverend Billy and his choir in Battersea Arts Centre clearly displayed the theatrical and musical talent of the company and the humour and parody in the preaching and the exorcism of the spectators' credit cards, but the *church* service became just an entertaining show. In the *religious* intervention in the mall or in Starbucks, however, the impact of the ideas of shopping as the new religion, and the interruptions of the social rituals of shopping acquired a totally different power as attention was drawn to the consumer activity and the shoppers must respond. Some stopped shopping and some shrugged and went on with their shopping; others challenged or verbally attacked the Reverend and the choir. In these privatized public spaces, the disruption is real, and shoppers become participants in or opponents of the protest against consumer society. Although his preaching began as a performance act, Talen actually became a pastor in response to people's real need for guidance and comfort after the terrorist attacks in New York on 11 September 2001. He thus uses his performing body to trouble distinctions between art and non-art.

Art work or social work

The questions and challenges raised by Ktha Compagnie and Reverend Billy about the role of art in counteracting passivity and encouraging active citizenship were also of paramount importance to artists in the 1960s and 1970s as the role of art began to shift toward an art that sought to engage with social reality. This paradigm shift from autonomy to heteronomy has been variously called the 'social turn', the 'relational turn' or the 'performative turn',[17] and it marks a rejection of modernism's notions of art divorced from sociality articulated in Clement Greenberg's famous 1940 essay, 'Towards a Newer Laocoön', and in Michael Fried's condemnation of 'objecthood' in minimal art.[18] In a prescient essay written in 1958,[19] Allan Kaprow expressed his regret that Jackson Pollock failed to take his artistic innovations to their logical conclusion, to go beyond the edge of the canvas and make the leap into the real world.[20] Kaprow's own artistic innovations, especially in happenings, sought to do just that, to include the everyday world of the audience in the artwork by assigning specific tasks to each spectator, and thus giving the audience some agency in the scripting of the event. He did not want to create an object for solitary viewing, but rather an ephemeral performance event in which the spectator became co-creator. Such artistic interventions that spilled out into daily life (Situationist constructed situations, Lefebvre's moments, and Kaprow's happenings[21]) had a great appeal for the pioneering street artists who strove to wedge ephemeral performative instants into the social life of the city to affect social change.[22] As the early artists abandoned the enclosed theatre spaces for open public spaces (both urban and rural) in which the actual sites, activities, and inhabitants necessarily became a part of the performance, they radically altered how audiences reacted to the interventions. They pushed their publics to experience a somatic and semantic engagement with the artwork that led to some form of participation in democratic activities, conscious or unconscious, great or small.[23]

The use of art to achieve revolutionary ends seemed quite possible in the ebullient years after 1968 as artists made utopian claims that aesthetic endeavours could transform the world. But what seemed so clear and attainable in the 1970s, appears in the twenty-first century as naïve or even counter-productive as it becomes increasingly evident that an artistic engagement with the social world is complex and contradictory. Writing toward the end of the twentieth century about the role and responsibility of public art to its context and its public, Rosalyn Deutsche lauded the oppositional (or interventionist) practices of early radical public art (permanent or temporary) that revealed that public spaces are not neutral. The art '*intervened* in its spatial environment by making social organization and ideological operations of that space visible' (1996: 68). She disparaged what she saw as the integrationist practices of *new* public art 'to create, rather than question the coherence of the site, to conceal its constitutive social conflicts' (1996: 68) and dismissed these works as tools for redevelopment and gentrification, cultural tourism and consensual democracy. As discussed earlier, many artists and writers agree with that assessment and accuse contemporary street arts of lacking a political core, of becoming entertainment without social critique, or of selling out to commercialism. Under the guise of community collaboration, they argue, artists avoid pointing out contradictions and injustices in the social order and thus depoliticize art in public space and public space itself.[24]

The ongoing debate about forms, practices and responsibilities of this socially engaged or dialogic art is becoming more nuanced. Claire Bishop, in 'The Social Turn: Collaboration and its Discontents', cautions against two assumptions about this work: that it forges a collaboration between artists and non-artists that is democratic and politically responsible and that socio-political engagement is synonymous with good art. She insists that dialogic art be critically analysed in aesthetic terms, not ethical ones. For her:

> the success of their work is not dependent upon authorial suppression, but upon the careful deployment of collaboration to produce a multilayered event that resonates across many registers. As such, they think the aesthetic and political *together*, rather than subordinating both within the exemplary ethical gesture. (2009: 250)[25]

Shannon Jackson, while not dismissing artistic value, looks at questions of autonomy and heteronomy from the perspective of ways to define the social context to include systems of support:

> to sustain the Life side of the supposed Art/Life binary....By emphasizing—rather than being embarrassed by—the infrastructural operations of performance, we might find different ways to join aesthetic engagement to the social sphere....To emphasize the

infrastructural politics of performance, however, is to join performance's routinized discourse of disruption and de-materialization to one that also emphasizes sustenance, coordination, and rematerialization. (2011: 29)

The street interventions discussed in this book draw on both oppositional and relational or dialogic tactics of socially engaged art often simultaneously, and that dynamic interrelationship can privilege both resistant art and the collaborative or participatory art-making. But key to these works is that the performance/audience exchange takes place in a public space and significantly uses that public space to provide intentional and accidental audiences with the opportunity to rehearse democratic activities.

2
Democratic Performatives and an Aesthetics of Public Space

Doing democracy

Street arts interventions in public spaces interrupt the everyday activities taking place there and challenge unwritten rules governing those activities. But, in addition, the artists, through their provocations, seem to grant permission to the passers-by to do what they would not normally do in a public space, to act differently. As the artists create events that blur the boundaries between actions that the spectators do in the fictional world of the performance and those that they do in the actual world of the public space – actions that challenge the status quo however minutely – the artists and their audiences shift democracy from an idea to a practice. In fact, these alternative ways of inhabiting public spaces are a key source of the performance's potential for efficacy since the spectator learns and creates new ways of thinking about urban space and civil society. 'Civil society', Kester explains, 'is a complex term that describes the capacity of individual subjects to engage in substantive debate over political issues, as well as the agency whereby this debate, in the form of consensus or "general will", could be transformed into an instrument of political decision making' (2011: 175). As the artists contrast the ordinariness of daily life with Debord 'situations' and Lefebvre 'moments' in the interventions, they also entice the spectators to break their routines, to transgress accepted behavioural norms obeyed out of habit rather than examined consideration, and thus to enter public debate about socio-political issues with their bodies. The performance events offer the audience opportunities to experience previously unimagined possibilities whether it is walking down the middle of a major London street and enjoying the city as a harmonious community as in *The Sultan's Elephant*, peeking into the private lives of neighbours as in *Safari Intime*, sharing an intimate moment with a stranger as in *Mademoiselle*, gawking at the Other as in *Les Squames*, or making art as in *Witness/N14*. What is crucial here is that these out-of-the-ordinary experiences taking place in an ordinary public space acquire a *reality* from daily life that permeates the art and cause the spectator to experience an affective response that establishes strong links connecting the performance, the rhythms of the body, the surrounding environment, and the mind making sense of the surprises and ruptures.

This complex and dynamic interrelationship, what I call an aesthetics of public space, thrives on the dynamic experiential and politicized interplay of performance, public and everyday place. Here the spectator can engage in creative actions that are entertaining and engaging certainly, but they can also provide alternative experiences of the city and civil society. These activities can potentially contribute to the construction of new knowledge as they overturn expectations and present unexpected alternatives. Thus through the actions undertaken within the frame of art but realized in an actual public space, the passer-by transformed into audience member is like Rancière's 'emancipated spectator' who does not just receive the performance as a gift, but rather tests its premises and solutions through bodily actions. The artwork, Rancière argues, remains separate from the spectator and the artist but links the two: what he calls 'a third thing' (2009:14). It is through this 'third thing' offered by one and *translated* by the other, but belonging to neither that intellectual emancipation is achieved. A spectator does not become emancipated through participation in the performance, but through what Rancière calls 'a redistribution of places' (2009: 15). A spectator achieves emancipation or critical awareness by translating the 'third thing' into his or her own experience, by linking it to what he or she already knows and, through that association, creating new knowledge. 'It is in this power of associating and disassociating that the emancipation of the spectator consists... Being a spectator is not some passive condition that we should transform into activity. It is our normal situation' (2009: 17). For Rancière, an individual learns and acts by linking new ideas and experiences to what is already known, and that process only stops if he or she accepts 'boundaries between territories' (2009: 17) While the notion of 'emancipated spectator' offers a way to understand the potential for efficacy of art, Rancière limits its usefulness by defining *art* as a completed artifact rather than an ongoing dialogue in words or actions so evident in street arts interventions.

In street theatre, the 'emancipated spectator', under the *protection* of participation in an artistic event, engages in small, but nevertheless quite *real*, acts of democratic participation, resistance or social activism in actual public spaces: what I call *democratic performatives*. These democratic performatives signify practices that are 'doings' and what they *do* is actually engage the audiences in democratic activities. The spectators' personal interventions, guided by an aesthetic sensibility manipulated by the artists but taking place in actual places, are not acts of *civil* disobedience that actually break the law, but rather acts of *social* disobedience that disrupt the status quo and draw attention to normative social codes. As such, they represent democratic acts of resistance, freedom, equality and self-determination: Rancière's acts of dissensus. The doing of these small, but surprisingly influential, acts that are repeated, shared, imitated and passed around the crowd, create *affects* that contribute to an embodied critical awareness of active citizenship. The power of these affects is that they are communal and so create what Nigel Thrift calls 'affective contagion, for affect spreads, sometimes like wildfire' (2008: 235). At one performance of Jeanne Simone's *Le Goudron n'est pas meuble* (Villeurbanne, 2009),[1] for example, the affective contagion was palpable. This piece begins invisibly as the actors blend into the crowd, all performing everyday activities (reading a newspaper, smoking, leaning against a tree) in a public space, like a train station, a bus stop, or an intersection of two busy streets. One of the actors gradually exaggerates normal behaviour until it becomes odd enough to attract attention, but the unsuspecting audience usually looks away in embarrassment until the exaggeration is bizarre or disruptive enough to signal 'performance'. There is no narrative story line although there is a clear arc to the performance, and the performers never develop 'characters' in spite of each one's distinct personality and activities. Each performance is improvised within these parameters and in response to the reactions and participation of the public. At one particular performance, an actor helped an older man with a cane across a busy intersection during rush hour. The actor took his arm and carried his bag of groceries as they walked slowly taking longer to cross the street than the time of the red light. Just before they reached the other side, one of the drivers honked to hurry them up, but instead of stepping onto the curb, the pair smiled mischievously and turned around and slowly walked back across the street. When the annoyed drivers began to increase their honking, the spectating public spontaneously rebelled against that aggressive impatience by joining in the slow crossing of the street thus taking over the intersection. Once in a while, they would let a car or two through, but the traffic was snarled for several minutes.

Augusto Boal has demonstrated with his 'poetics of the oppressed' that this type of participation can transform the:

> 'spectators,' passive beings in the theatrical phenomenon—into subjects, into actors, transformers of the dramatic action....[This audience member] assumes the protagonic role, changes the dramatic action, tries out solutions, discusses plans for change—in short, trains himself for real action. In this case, perhaps the theatre is not revolutionary in itself, but it is surely a rehearsal for the revolution. The liberated spectator, as a whole person, launches into action. No matter that the action is fictional; what matters is that it is action! (1979: 122)

Like Boal's spect-actor, the public at a street arts event does activities that can act as a 'rehearsal' for future actions, but here the actions are in actual urban spaces and have real consequences on the daily life of city inhabitants who are not members of the audience. Thus the impact of these actions spreads beyond the fictional world of the performance into the actual city streets and so blurs distinctions between art and non-art. These democratic performatives are quite varied, but they fit roughly, and a bit uncomfortably, into three broad categories of activity: the reclaiming of public spaces, the development of a critical awareness of social constructions in the everyday world, and the participation in art-making that intervenes in official socio-political discourses. These forms of activity clearly overlap and merge in practice, but they each bring about an increased sense of agency on an individual and a community level and contribute to active citizenship through participation, even within the frame of art, in democratic practices of making one's voice heard by taking the time and space to speak through actions,[2] resisting the status quo to ensure freedom and equality, and often acting for the common good.

Democratic performative: reclaiming public spaces

Street interventions challenge the co-option of public spaces by taking back the streets or *trespassing* in a variety of ways.[3] Artists initiate the trespass, the take-over, but it is the audiences who accomplish it. This voluntary reclaiming of public spaces by the people, as opposed to state-sponsored shows of power in government-organized protests or displays of grief or outrage, is an assertion of democratic civil rights. Rebecca Solnit, in *Wanderlust: A History of Walking*, explores intersections of

48 *Contemporary Street Arts in Europe*

public spaces, democracy and walking. She looks at citizenship as practices, from protests and demonstrations to religious processions or street arts events, that relate to walking and reclaiming public spaces and argues that:

> When public spaces are eliminated, so ultimately is the public; the individual has ceased to be a citizen capable of experiencing and acting in common with fellow citizens. Citizenship is predicated on the sense of having something in common with strangers, just as democracy is built on trust in strangers. (2000: 216, 218)

Compagny Teatro Gestual de Chile reclaims the streets quite literally and aggressively in *Su-Seso Taladro*, an intervention that offers a brief, but quite visceral, experience of a society in which trust is shaken. The two white face clowns take over busy intersections, stop traffic, lie down in the street, climb on and into cars, play with drivers and encourage the spectators to help them.[4] Dressed in red, black, yellow and white jumpsuits, wearing clown noses and using a language of squeaks, the

Figure 3 Compagny Teatro Gestual de Chile, *Su-Seso Taladro* (Béthune, France, June 2011)

clowns transform a commercial street into a playground for acts of social disobedience. They provoke an anarchic overthrow of rules and social norms that verge, if not cross the line, into unacceptable behaviour as they get into people's cars, take personal items from the back seats of stopped cars and exhibit them on the street, let themselves be dragged by moving cars for a few meters, ask passengers to get out of cars to dance, and even *steal* cars.

In the moments right after the photograph was taken (Figure 3), the clown on the passenger side of the car opened the door and enticed the woman to dance with him for a few moments. Sometimes, the clowns enact mini-scenes that could happen on the street: one clown pretends to be hit by a car or bus and throws himself on the ground in front of the vehicle as it quickly stops just inches away or a clown decides to leave with the people whose car has been blocked and so the two clowns have an emotional farewell scene that, of course, holds up traffic. Sometimes, the clowns provocatively stage a car-jacking using their hands as guns to stop a car and force the driver to get out. One clown then drives off in the car while the other consoles himself by crying on the shoulder of the man whose car has been *stolen*. The clowns often stop the city buses by standing or lying in the street in front of them, and they encourage the gathered crowds to board the bus and ride for free. As they force the driver to acknowledge them, they offer a particular challenge to authority as official policies in many major European cities discourage drivers from having any interaction with the public beyond collecting tickets. And as the public applauds the bus driver when he reluctantly says hello, they engage in small acts of protest against this official policy of impersonality and dehumanization.

But the clowns freely change affiliations as they shift from being allies of the public to being allies of authority figures. When they stop a car and discover alcohol in the back seat, for example, they chastise the driver and tattle to the police. This seeming betrayal of one side and then the other makes it impossible for onlookers to take comfort in being on the *right* side and puts the focus on acceptable and unacceptable behaviour in the space. But an even more provocative tactic of this edgy and extremely uncomfortable intervention is to compel the people going about their daily business to understand quite viscerally what it means to be the object of amusement or ridicule as the clowns strive to embarrass the individuals they stop during the performance. Those targeted by the clowns just happen to cross that particular intersection; they were not there to see a show. When the trapped member of the public plays along, the spectators applaud his good humour as he is finally released, but if the passer-by resists, the crowd often boos. That anti-social behaviour, however, can make the clowns turn on the offending spectators and put one or more of them into the hot seat by pulling them into the center of the intersection and emptying a handbag or stopping a car, forcing the spectator inside, and sending the driver on his way. No one is safe from embarrassment, but this extreme display of ridicule and humiliation compels the public ask themselves whether they want to live in a society that enjoys such mockery (so evident in much reality television and political discourse).

In a performance in Ghent, Belgium in 2010, the clowns blocked the way of a couple on a two-seater bicycle and displayed their shopping that included fancy lingerie to the delight of the crowd. In Béthune, France in 2011, the clowns began to empty a van and even gave some items to spectators as the annoyed, but good-humoured, driver ran around collecting his things until one clown drove the van down the street. When the driver gave up and sat on the pavement, the spectators took over, standing in front of the van forcing the clown to stop, collecting the items, repacking the van and chastising the clown for driving off. The intervention develops in response to the actions of the drivers who usually play along but sometimes get annoyed and try to drive around the clowns who keep jumping in front of the car. No car is stopped for longer than a wait at a red light, but for unsuspecting drivers embarrassed at being the focus of attention, bicyclists whose personal bags are emptied on the street to the delight of the crowds or bus drivers trying to keep to a schedule, those few minutes must seem quite long indeed.

The performance intervention relies on danger for its appeal – physical danger that comes from playing in traffic, but also from unexpected reactions of the passers-by who become objects of amusement, even ridicule, within the performance. The provocative piece transforms the location quite dramatically for one-half hour and pushes the boundaries of acceptable behaviour. It encourages the large crowds not only to support and reward the clowns' acts of social disobedience, but also to join in those acts. By testing and surpassing social limits as they challenge the patience, tolerance and good humour of a passer-by or embarrass a spectator who suddenly finds himself or herself a participant in a show, they draw attention to the social norms in public space that we take for granted. They seize the public space and rewrite what is acceptable behaviour there, thus in provocative ways they interrogate democratic concepts of freedom, individual rights and agency.

Many political scientists agree that public space is essential to democracy. Claude Lefort, in 'The Question of Democracy', claims that with the 'democratic revolution', democracy's site of power was transferred from an external and identifiable source (the monarch) to 'the people', a vague and unstable location that meant that power did not belong to any one individual, but to the 'public'. For Lefort, democracy did not constitute a new form of government control that was now in the hands of the people. Instead, democracy represented a changed form of society built on uncertainty over the identity and role of 'the people'. The 'people' did not represent a fixed entity, but rather a potential constantly on the cusp of transformation. The notion of an uncertain democratic power determined by an enigmatic *public* shook the stability of monarchical rule. And that uncertainty, in turn, caused debate about the source of democratic power: what Lefort calls the 'question of democracy'. This question identifies the dilemma at the heart of democracy: power is located in the people, but 'the locus of power is an empty place.... This phenomenon implies an institutionalization of conflict' (1988: 17). The shift in the location and nature of power means, according to art historian Rosalyn Deutsche, that:

> democratic power cannot appeal for its authority to a meaning immanent in the social. Instead, the democratic invention invents something else: the public space. The public space, in Lefort's account, is the social space where, in the absence of a foundation, the meaning and unity of the social is negotiated—at once constituted and put at risk. (1996: 273)

Thus public space becomes the core of democracy since it is in public space that debate and conflict are legitimized.[5] This legitimization of conflict in a public space is at the heart of Compagny Teatro Gestual de Chile's intervention. By usurping the public space for a random display of ridicule and ostracism, not of any particular identity or social position but through a constant reversing of loyalties, the clowns challenge the comfort of a consensual democracy and easy assumptions that reclaiming the public space is an action that necessarily leads to equality and harmony for a free and democratic population. Instead, they highlight that with democracy can come disagreement and discord, and that conflict is aired in the public space.

When Deutsche asks, 'What does it mean for a space to be "public"?', she does not limit the meaning of 'public' to places with open access, but rather asserts 'How we define public space is intimately connected with ideas about what it means to be human, the nature of society, and the kind of political community we want' (1996: 269). Public space, she claims, is 'a realm of discursive interaction about public issues' (1996: 287).[6] The notion of a public space as a discursive space for debate is invaluable for an interrogation of how art in public spaces (whether monuments and statues, park furniture and pathways, or street theatre) can contribute to active citizenship.[7] For Deutsche, the idea of a democratic public space:

> replaces definitions of public art as work that occupies or designs physical spaces and addresses pre-existing audiences with a conception of public art as a practice that constitutes a public, by engaging people in political discussion or by entering a political struggle.... Art that is 'public' participates in, or creates, a political space and is itself a space where we assume political identities. (1996: 288–9)

Through or with the art, the public, not just the artist, expresses these political debates and practices in languages using words, images and actions and thus acquires the agency needed to have a say, even temporarily, in the construction and identity of their communities. With these actions, they take a small step toward active citizenship.[8]

Deutsche does caution, however, that the equation of public space and democratic activity can be counter-productive if we forget that 'the political public sphere is not only a site of discourse; it is also a discursively constructed site' (1996: 289). Drawing on ideas of radical democracy, she argues that for democratic activities to take place in public spaces, that construction needs to be a part of the discourse of dissensus, not consensus.[9] Thus, the question must be asked how public art (and street arts interventions in particular) participates in democratic practices of resistance, agency and equality. The clowns in *Su-Seso Taladro* offer one possibility as they remind us of the instability of democratic processes by intensifying disagreement and debate as they behave outside an expected norm of social behaviour and constantly change sides or loyalties. They present an uncomfortable and disturbing view of the discourse of democratic dissensus in their provocative acts and exaggerate the idea of public space as a site of debate. Rebecca Solnit goes one step further: '"to the streets" is the classic cry of urban revolution, for the street are where people become public and where their power resides' (2001: 176). Reclaiming the street, even within an artistic frame, allows people to become public and to walk in the shoes of a active citizen.

Democratic performative: developing a critical awareness of social constructions

That question about how public art participates in or becomes a site of debate is answered in part by looking at how street interventions activate a critical awareness of seemingly *natural* social and spatial identities and functions, invisible because of their ubiquity. By creating an alternative perception, experience and understanding of familiar ideas, sites and activities, public art can expose the *constructedness* of normative behaviour or apparently neutral public spaces. And the transitory nature of street arts interventions makes them particularly effective since they do not lose their 'shock' value by becoming a permanent installation.[10] Street arts interventions place the spectator in a familiar place but in an unexpected and often bewildering situation, and that unfamiliarity requires critical reflection and possible adjustments.

The radical pedagogy of Paulo Freire, claiming 'education as the practice of freedom' (1989: 69),[11] provides a key to understanding the political significance of this form of democratic performative that develops a critical awareness of seemingly normative or natural aspects of social life, sometimes gradually and gently (as in artistic collaborative projects) and sometimes abruptly like a catapult (as in interventions that rely on shock) and in so doing elicits an affective response. Freire sought to thwart the increasing dehumanization in modern society and to liberate the oppressed, primarily in Brazil and Peru, by helping them develop a critical awareness of socio-political forces and constructions that circumscribed their lives.[12] Liberation, he argued, was not just an abstract concept, but 'a praxis: the action and reflection...upon the world in order to transform it' (1989: 66). Freire insisted that humans are unique among animals because they can construct history and culture as well as being shaped by them. Freire's claim thus parallels that of Michael Hardt (discussed earlier) as he explores 'what affects are for'. Hardt explains that:

> affects require us, as the term suggests, to enter the realm of causality, but they offer a complex view of causality because the affects belong simultaneously to both sides of the causal relationship. They illuminate, in other words, both our power to affect the world around us and our power to be affected by it, along with the relationship between these two powers. (2007: ix)

For Freire and Hardt, it is the experiential response to the situation *and* the understanding of one's agency to change the situation that can counteract dehumanization and lead to freedom. Freire argues that an individual is not trapped in a fatalistically determined social environment, but rather has the opportunity to comprehend the world as it is *and* to intervene and alter its construction and its future. These interventions, in turn, empower both individuals and communities by revealing external and internal constraints that maintain the status quo and by suggesting ways to transform it. Freire focused on literacy campaigns because he felt that reading was a political act that was not just about reading words, but about critically *re-reading* the way things are and how they got that way – the socio-political context as well as one's place or identity within that context. His radical pedagogy sought to empower people to change their lives by developing:

> their language: not the authoritarian, sectarian gobbledygook of 'educators,' but their own language—which, emerging from and returning to their reality, sketches out the conjectures, the designs, the anticipations of their new world...language as a route to the invention of citizenship. (1994: 39)

Similarly, street artists seek to help the public develop a language of democratic practices through visceral performances in public spaces.

Compelling audiences to undertake a critical re-reading of the way things are can be accomplished in a variety of ways in street arts. Although seemingly simple in concept and execution, *La Morte di Babbo Natale: Eutanasia di un mito sovrappeso* (The Death of Santa Claus, Euthanasia of an Overweight Myth) by the Italian company, Tony Clifton Circus, overturns expectations of a family entertainment that features Santa Claus.[13] Instead, the actors create a dramatic narrative that blatantly illustrates rampant consumerism by debunking cherished myths of Christmas and childhood. The two Italian clowns, Nicola Danesi de Luca and Iacopo Fulgi who founded Tony Clifton Circus in 2001, do not seek to entertain their public comfortably, but rather to shock their audiences into a critical awareness of what they see as the inevitable end results of capitalism. While they make their audiences laugh, they also shake their beliefs so that they no longer feel so secure. The performance depicts Santa Claus alternatively as an embodied advertisement, the epitome of shopping, a crooked superhero, a depressed failure and a terrorist whose big black leather belt is that of a suicide bomber, and children are revealed as greedy and impossible to satisfy. Danesi de Luca hopes that *La Morte di Babbo Natale* acts as a 'virus that remains inside the audience to instil doubts' (personal email correspondence, 3 September 2011).

La Morte di Babbo Natale uses Santa Claus as a mouthpiece to speak about contemporary malaise. For de Luca, the basis of consumerism is to convince people that whatever they have is not enough so 'unhappiness and dissatisfaction of the people are indispensable prerequisites of consumerism' (personal email correspondence, 3 September 2011). Santa Claus is the icon of that rampant consumerism as well as its victim. While he strives to make people happy by showering them with gifts, his employer (consumer society) requires that he never satisfies them or he will no longer be needed. Santa can never give enough, so his 'customers' can never be happy. He is doomed to failure. *La Morte di Babbo Natale* accuses its audiences of supporting and celebrating a commercial and rather vicious Christmas, and it exposes this repulsive side of Christmas with an offensive Santa Claus, his outrageous reindeer-helper called Adolf and their mob-like bodyguard. There is nothing reassuring about this image of Christmas used as a way to explore a materialistic consumer society and the inevitable alienation, selfishness and hatred it causes. But, Tony Clifton Circus also plays with Santa's conundrum as the clowns explore the character's desperate side as he can no longer lie to his beloved children, but the truth will make them unhappy. And, at the same time, these children who always want more infuriate him, and he longs to punish them.

The show opens as Santa arrives amid a fanfare of flashing lights, honking of car horns and loud music. His first act is to throw small gifts into the standing crowd so that spectators immediately push and grab to get as much as possible. He then mocks the greed that has just been displayed so vividly. While he repeats over and over that he is nice, the impression he leaves is of a paedophile not to be trusted with a child or with people's dreams. When he gets agitated repeating how nice he is, his bodyguard gets him to sing 'Jingle Bell Rock' but his dance that accompanies the song is sexually explicit. Early in the show, he invites a child from the audience to join him with the promise of a small balloon. As he hands the child an almost completely deflated balloon, he challenges him or her to show disappointment and then says, '"You have finished getting presents this year', as he sends the child back into the audience. He offers the children other gifts – a bottle of whiskey or cigarettes that he throws one-by-one into the crowd, and he teases them with a laptop computer that he keeps for himself. He repeats that he knows their desires and that he keeps their letters. He reads these letters aloud as he smokes a cigarette. Sometimes he assures the writer that he or she will get the item 'someday...someday' with as much credibility as a sleazy used car salesman. He cruelly mocks a child who has asked for solutions to social problems. As he reads from the letters, his reindeer assistant fondles a large doll with voluptuous bare breasts, a seemingly startled open mouth and a somewhat caved-in face. (See Colour Plate 3.) Innocence and depravity co-exist in this scene.

Later, Santa Claus promises children they will have what they want because they live in a 'world of abundance' and everything they can imagine is just behind the store window. The fact that the items are so near means that the children have the right to take them. 'All the things are for you', he explains. The child just needs to break the store window and grab the toy. At one point, he tells the children that they should get whatever they want because their parents should buy it. He admits that some 'naughty' parents might not have enough money, but 'they do have credit cards, don't they?' Of course, he points out, the use of credit cards results in personal debt and thus creates a new form of slavery to the banks. At one point, he disparages parents who say they are too poor to load their children with gifts by mocking those who lost their jobs because of the economic crisis with demeaning comparisons to racial stereotypes. He reminds the children that they live in the land of plenty and that there must be work because if unemployment is rampant, 'why do all the immigrants come here'. While that tirade made spectators around me open their mouths in disbelief, it was just a teaser of what was to come as Santa is shot by a Muslim terrorist and replaced by a needy and powerless Spiderman who tries out several superhero roles, each one more pathetic than the last, until he finally strips naked except for his mask and runs through the crowd. The newscaster relating the events as they are happening breaks taboo after taboo, and Santa's bodyguard hits the bottle, smokes marijuana, and pulls out a chain saw. Finally Santa reappears on the balcony of a nearby restaurant to let us know what he thinks about his 'job', his depression, his quest for a normal life and what he does in his time off, and then he dies and is carried through the audience in a glass coffin. Gasps from the spectators accompany his progression through the crowd. The show ends as a huge inflatable Santa towers over the crowd: Santa as spectacle. Clearly much of the appeal of this biting satiric comedy is in the number of taboos broken and offensive statements made. The crowd when I saw it seemed to love being shocked and insulted, but one woman next to me kept repeating, 'I can't believe it.' Many I spoke to after this piece recognized its embodied message and commented on how even adults struggled to catch the gifts, gleefully using their height to reach what a child could not. They admitted the titillation they felt as this depraved Santa aroused personality traits they usually strive to keep hidden.

La Morte di Babbo Natale intervenes in the nostalgic myth of Christmas as a time of happiness, generosity and community by highlighting unhappiness, greed and the inevitable social injustice associated with uneven wealth distribution. And it implicates the audience in this perversion of the spirit of Christmas by appealing to our base desires that we try to keep in check. As we catch and pocket a thrown trinket meant for a child, as we laugh at the discomfort of a spectator being mocked, or as we nod in agreement with a comment specific to a theatrical moment but that reinforces racial stereotypes, the face under our social mask is exposed. We may be shocked by the tirades and images, but also by our own reactions from exposing our greed and meanness to mourning the loss of the myth of Christmas. It is one thing to say Christmas is commercialized, but quite another to follow that accusation to its logical conclusion. Purposely controversial, if not inflammatory, this Santa provokes the crowd with accusations of their prejudices, materialist greed and perversions and asks what they will do about it. Santa has completely sold out to a consumer society, and he points out that the public has gleefully followed.

Fallen Fruit, an art collective based in Los Angeles, California, offers a contrasting example of how this type of democratic performative can aid the public in developing a critical awareness. Their participatory events, that really push the limits of *performance*, seek to change the way people understand equal and democratic use of public space by showing that what is in a public space belongs to the public. Founded in 2004, Fallen Fruit began as an art project for the *Journal of Aesthetics and Protest* by Matias Viegener, David Burns and Austin Young. They created maps of fruit trees growing in public spaces in their neighbourhood in Los Angeles and shared those maps with the public encouraging them to harvest the fruit so that the food that usually rotted on the ground could be enjoyed by the city residents. They argued that the law allows people to pick fruit from trees that grow on or have branches that hang over public space, so why not *advertise* this free food and in so doing draw attention to how we currently understand public space. By giving *permission* to take the fruit, they encourage us to re-consider the meaning of public space.

Since that initial project, the artists and their collaborators from the general public have created maps of many neighbourhoods in cities across the United States as well as in Malmo, Sweden; Copenhagen, Denmark; Madrid, Spain; Linz, Austria and Cali, Columbia. On their website, the artists ask individuals to map their neighbourhoods and send the maps to the cooperative so that they can be posted online.

In addition to the maps, they have created many other fruit-picking in public spaces events such as *Nocturnal Fruit Forages* (night-time fruit-picking tours), *Public Fruit Jams* (communal jam-making from fruit gathered on an urban forage, with the jam often given to homeless shelters), or *Public Fruit Tree Adoptions* (where the general public plants fruit trees on the margins of private space). All these events have an existence on the street as communal activities and protests, but online as well in photographic series, interviews and videos. Fallen Fruit's projects seek to convince the public to engage in democratic practices around issues of equality, ownership, social justice and the common good. They encourage communal participation in food security by showing how food can be available, affordable and accessible, and they foster community development through the sharing of food, increased use of public space, and dialogue. Although many of their tactics seem a bit like pranks, their goals echo Freire's ideas as the projects work to reconfigure awareness of and attitudes toward public and private property, class interactions, and active citizenship. In their video entitled *Double Standard*, posted on their website, for example, they document a *Neighbourhood Fruit Forage* in two videos side-by-side but overlaid with a block text of racist and homophobic comments by some observers of the event. These comments not only challenge a master narrative of community and good will, but also expose anti-social attitudes and fears about a shared communal form of land use. The video is meant as a provocation to protest such attitudes through increased urban foraging.

The significance that Freire places on developing a critical awareness of one's world is particularly relevant to an understanding of the possibilities of street arts' democratic performatives to provide a way to recognize unexamined beliefs and the unspoken rules governing normative behaviour, the social constructions of public spaces and the oppressive aspects of consensual democracy. That critical awareness relies on a dialectical perspective that constantly interrogates the relationship between subjectivity and objectivity, between individual agency to construct history and the world's material *given-ness* or inevitability. Freire argues that 'the dialectical view is incompatible with the notion that *tomorrow* is the pure repetition of today, or that *tomorrow* is something "predated," or as I have called it, a *given dictum*, a "given given"' (1994: 101). As the spectators experience the city anew or see familiar icons and myths overturned, they can begin to imagine alternate futures.

Democratic performative: participating in art-making as a social practice

An altered critical and experiential awareness of socio-political constructions of public spaces and urban identities and an embodied understanding of the power dynamics of the lived world are first steps toward a sense of individual and community empowerment. The next step is, as Freire cautions, that:

> we have to make it, produce it, else it will not come in the form that we would more or less wish it to. True, of course, we have to make it not arbitrarialy [sic.], but with the materials, with the concrete reality, of which we dispose, and more as a project, a *dream*, for which we struggle. (1994: 101)

Understanding the hegemonic order alone will not lead to political action. Like Freire, Rancière (2006b) argues that it is not lack of understanding that leads to apathy or inaction, but lack of confidence in one's ability to alter the status quo. Reclaiming public spaces contributes to a sense of individual and communal agency as the public changes, even temporarily, the function of the public space from that determined by the hegemonic order. Developing a critical awareness that questions the seemingly apparent neutrality of public space and that resists the dominant narratives begins to build a confidence that the social order can be changed. But the participatory nature of street arts goes one step further as spectatorship shifts from passive consumption of art to an active physical engagement in the art-making process whether that is discussing housing issues with faux neighbours, sharing a map that locates free neighbourhood fruit or contributing to the process of making the art work. The spectator becomes a participant in and co-creator of the artistic event in an actual public space. Guided by the artists and within the frame of the performance, the spectators participate in debate, through both words and actions, on a range of aesthetic, but also social, issues.

Participation in the theatrical event here does not mean getting up on stage to become part of the fictional action. It refers instead to encountering, questioning and responding to the larger social order through art. It means imagining *and* practicing challenges to and interrogations of popular and official discourses on significant social issues within an imaginative frame but in real public space. It means finding a voice and using that voice to engage in collective art-making that may contrast with an official narrative relating to the site of performance. It means using art-making to contribute to a community's understanding of itself and to identify and debate social issues and urban renewal projects. It means interrogating new technologies and products supposedly introduced to improve quality of life through the lens of art as opposed to corporate advertising or official statements. It is art as social practice. These acts of resistance or dissensus, in the liminal space of imagination-actuality (fiction of theatre and reality of street), sometimes occur through language, but more often through physical statements made by the body blurring the distinctions between speech and action as physical acts become a form of free speech. The spectator thus intervenes in public discourses and official narratives, sometimes unconsciously, through bodily statements that are then remembered by the body: affects. Philosopher Mark Johnson, in *The Meaning of the Body*, explores affect by looking at how physical acts made by the body make meaning. Meaning is embodied because it arises from corporeal experiences of our surroundings, he argues; it does not exist only in words and thoughts about the world around us and our place in it. We learn about our world through movement through it – our own bodily movement that alerts us to what we can do, how we can manipulate our environment, and how we experience space and time. Movement is thus intimately tied to identity construction. For Johnson, embodied knowledge is performative – 'thinking is doing, and ... cognition is action....Thinking is not something humans "bring" to their experience from the outside; rather it is *in* and *of* experience' (2007: 92). Abstract thought is based in our ability to organize our physical and perceptual experiences, and art provides an intensified pattern of organization.

How these claims work in a street arts intervention is evident in a durational performance piece specifically created to engage the community in the art-making process through debate about social issues important to them and to place those issues in a larger social context. Between 2004 and 2011, Opéra Pagaï, a street theatre company based in Bordeaux, France, developed a series of six unique site-specific performative interventions, or 'unexpected theatrical intrusions into the public space', entitled *L'Entreprise de Détournement*.[14] The six 'utopias of proximity', created for six cities in various regions in France, acted like 'a grain of sand in the cogs of daily life to jostle certainties and habits', says Cyril Jaubert, Opéra Pagaï's Artistic Director. Each intervention is tailored to the specific city and its residents for which it is created, and the durational performance lasting several days takes place only once.

Each one acts something like a protest poster (although embodied and dynamic) as it strives to encourage the public to raise questions about unexamined beliefs and positions. Its goals are to create an event close enough to the reality of the city's inhabitants that it hovers between something a bit strange but still possible and a fantastical exaggeration and then to present it as a real occurrence.[15]

The third intervention, *Mobil-Home Container*, took place 3–8 April 2006 in Port Saint Louis in southern France. The unsuspecting audiences experienced the unadvertised theatrical intervention for just one week in which the performers posed as ordinary people *actually* living an extraordinary event. Several months earlier, however, many of the city residents unknowingly participated in the art-making when company members permeated the city as curious tourists or faux-journalists asking questions about life there. A few residents – local historians, city planners, elected officials and journalists – were informed of the project and consciously participated in the art-making by sharing facts and anecdotes unique to Port Saint Louis. On their initial visit, the artists were struck by three seemingly unrelated observations. First, visible from the highway entering the city were thousands of international shipping containers. Secondly, the artists learned that Port Saint Louis, throughout its history, had a large transient population, and many long-term residents with whom they spoke originally came from outside of France. And finally, the artists discovered that many city residents had *cabanons*, small beach huts on the coast a few miles away where they escaped for a break from the stresses of the city. These huts were closely tied to the city's history as a port since many were originally the flimsy shelters of migrant dockworkers. The box-like huts, on publicly owned land, were at the centre of an urban development debate over occupation rights and increased land taxes. Although the local residents did not own the huts, they had right of occupation, based on French law, and they paid land taxes. They were passionate about their 'squatting' rights and considered the huts part of their unique heritage and identity, but the local government sought to increase the land taxes sevenfold to get the 'holiday' residents to abandon the huts. It was this issue that many residents of Port Saint Louis were willing to protest. And it was this issue that Opéra Pagaï sought to locate in a larger context of migration and international shipping. From these somewhat contradictory starting points, Opéra Pagaï developed a durational performance installation that intervened in the discourse of the city on these issues by developing an event that created a fictional intersection of transient populations, shipping containers and *cabanons* and that challenged residents' assumptions by inverting their reality and establishing a site of debate.

Early Monday morning, city residents discovered a large container with no identifying markings on the sidewalk in the centre of the city. Later that morning, two couples arrived with suitcases and a large cage with two parrots. The couples explained that they were emigrating to Canada to start a new life, but when they got to Marseille they discovered that their container with all their possessions had been dropped in Port Saint Louis, so they had come to reclaim it. They soon found out that it could not be picked up until the following Saturday. In addition, the container had to be opened to make sure it did not contain contraband. On Tuesday morning, the couples unpacked the container and soon the grass in front was covered with tables, chairs, a refrigerator, a barbeque, plates – everything for a picnic that they then organized for the city residents who happened to stop. The two couples asked the locals about hotels and quickly decided that rather than paying for a hotel and repacking the container, they would *squat* in the container until Saturday. That afternoon, a workman arrived to cut holes in the container for a door and a window, and the couples *moved in*. Over the next few days, they made their container like home as they painted

Figure 4 Opéra Pagaï, *Mobil-Home Container* (Port Saint Louis, France, April 2006) (Courtesy of Opéra Pagaï)

the exterior, connected it to an electric line, added an outdoor shower and even received a post box. They transformed the container into a *cabanon*. The transient container residents chatted with their new neighbours who simultaneously wanted to believe the story of the container and enjoyed the imaginative fiction inserted into their city. City residents quickly recognized the container as a cabanon and appreciated the joke of a *getaway* in the city centre as the couples relaxed in beach chairs. But many also began to question or at least be amused by their obsession with their cabanons.[16] The photograph shows one of the stranded shipping container residents explaining their predicament to passers-by and telling them they were transforming their container into an urban *cabanon*.

In *Mobil-Home Container*, the actors *performed the city* through the composite characters inspired by the urban residents themselves alongside the actual residents who also *performed the city* in their responses. The quirky *newcomers* to the city told the stories of the inhabitants themselves, collected as found text months before on the research foray or developed on-site, and then re-contextualized into a peculiar, and yet at the same time, credible situation. And the curious and sceptical residents entered a story space, both physically and symbolically, as they engaged with the actors. Together they transformed the actual public space into an alternative one with new rules that they ostensibly accepted.

Whether such a performance intervention is anything more than an amusing, if somewhat informative, interlude is difficult to evaluate. Rancière tackles the issue of efficacy by developing three models that correspond to his concept of the three regimes of art: the ethical regime, the representative regime, and the aesthetic regime. The *ethical immediacy* model and the *representational mediation* model are lumped under what Rancière calls the 'pedagogical model of the efficacy of art' (2010: 136). But Rancière rejects the cause-and-effect link between artistic engagement and political activism implied by these two models of efficacy and instead argues for an:

> aesthetic rupture [that] arranges a paradoxical form of efficacy, one that relates to a disconnection between the production of artistic *savoir-faire* and social destination, between sensory forms, the significations that can be read on them and their possible effects. Let us call it the efficacy of *dissensus*, which is not a designation of conflict as such, but is a specific type thereof, a conflict between *sense* and *sense*. Dissensus is a conflict between a sensory presentation and

a way of making sense of it, or between several sensory regimes and/ or 'bodies'. (2010: 139)

It is this kind of "conflict" that urban residents experienced in *Mobil-Home Container* in the overlap of fiction and reality, in the imaginative situation in dialogue with an actual one. For Rancière, this efficacy of dissensus initiates a reconfiguration of the expected logic of social life, and in so doing affects social change, even if very small.[17] Baz Kershaw explains that efficacy is 'the potential that theatre may have to make the immediate effects of the performance influence, however minutely, the general historical evolution of wider social and political realities' (1992: 1). As the residents of Port Saint Louis engaged with the container residents, they explored the city's history and their own connection to that history through the cabanons and thus *practised* arguments opposing an increased land tax: they engaged in democratic practices.

Theatrical intervention

Walkabout characters are a familiar form of street arts intervention that rely on all three categories of democratic performatives in varying degrees for their impact as illogical or even offensive Others infiltrate or invade an ordinary public space and actively engage with the onlookers in the construction of the performance text that in some way challenges the public with new ideas. While the most recognizable walkabouts are human caricatures or human-like fantastical creatures, some look quite ordinary, but their behaviour or attitudes are exaggerated. Their physical appearance or unusual actions make it clear that they to do not fit into the everyday world, and they use that difference to draw attention to socially constructed norms, unexamined assumptions, social exclusions or public policy. Walkabouts can amuse or disturb the passer-by, highlight a social issue, provide information, or even advertise a product, but the varied performance strategies all rely on interaction with the public through words or actions that become the *text* of the intervention. That text can range from improvised encounters with passers-by to a more tightly scripted or choreographed scenario, but most often, it is a pretext for an extended interaction with the audience. Usually, the interactions are quite intimate – an actor and just a few spectators, perhaps only one, so the exchange is less about performing than about establishing a dialogue in words and actions. The range of walkabout characters is enormous, and variations appear in several of the case studies in subsequent chapters.

Desperate Men, now based in Bristol, United Kingdom, have created many walkabout characters since the company was founded in 1980 by Jon Beedell and Ritchie Smith. While following an entertainment-oriented tradition of street performers, their walkabout characters often focus on social ideas and issues not only by providing information about historical events or social movements, but also by getting the passers-by to contribute to the narration through their actions. Their walkabout characters first announce their presence through anomaly. In *The Rubbish Heads*, for example, they draw attention to littering through both visual appearance and choreographed actions. Four people appear unexpectedly in a public space dressed in suits, but with their heads covered with rubbish that one sees on city streets. Their performing bodies thus become satiric figures that are both ludicrous and disturbing, symbolic images that intervene in and comment on the everyday. The Rubbish Heads carry buckets filled with cans, plastic bottles, empty bags of potato chips or candy, papers and other familiar bits of litter. As they wander through the city, they throw their rubbish on the street, sometimes one piece at a time over a relatively large area, sometimes the whole lot as the debris flies out of the bucket and cascades around them. They move quite realistically much of the time, but sometimes they *dance* in a quasi-balletic style or lurch quite robotically. They play with the litter as they arrange it, bury each other, and try to entice the crowd with it. Not only do they drop their rubbish on the street; they also pick it up, placing it gently in the bucket or throwing it in quite roughly. While the routine is comic, it raises public awareness about a significant public nuisance and inconsiderate social behaviour as well as the larger environmental problem that rubbish creates. It also makes a comment perhaps on our throwaway society and on the garbage we carry around in our heads. Desperate Men insist that their street performances are 'political and social acts' that that erase borders 'between expression and subversion' (*In Situ*: 76). It is on the street, they say, where actors and audience share the same space, where spectators play a key role in the performance and where unexpected interruptions can change the direction of the show that true radical theatre can take place.

In a piece entitled *Darwin and the Dodo*, created for the 150th anniversary of the publication of *On the Origin of Species*, Desperate Men again tackled environmental issues, but this time through an interactive comic routine that draws on the contradictions of evolution in what one character calls 'Darwin's street maxim – "Adapt or die"' (*In Situ*: 78). Like *Rubbish Heads*, this show relies on both improvised sections that depend on audience responses for their length and development and on more choreographed and set bits of dialogue, action, and often song, but the actions of the characters and their interactions with the public are the key motor behind the plot. The two characters, Darwin and Mrs Dodo, wander through the city, chatting with people having a picnic, serenading shoppers, and exploring what the public knows about evolution through questions, activities and prompting so that the spectators can contribute to the mini-science lesson about evolution and Darwin. This collaborative text is the core of the performance. Combining science and comedy, Darwin discusses how evolution can lead to higher life forms, but it also means that other forms die out. The poor dodo is one of those extinct forms, and Darwin pushes her in a wheel chair (and gets spectators to push her) on a journey through the city on her 'last day'. Even though she carries a huge egg in the hole in the seat of her wheel chair, visible when she gets up and walks about in the crowd, Darwin repeats that her species has very little time left. When she philosophically says maybe her extinction is God's will, Darwin replies, 'No, I don't think so.' Thus woven into these questions of life and death are explorations into religious issues, some quite provocative, but always approached tongue-in-cheek.

Using songs, faux lectures, and interactive activities with members of the public, Darwin and Mrs Dodo test the audience's knowledge and challenge them to engage in a scientific discussion more through actions than words.[18] When I saw *Darwin and the Dodo,* Darwin chose three volunteers from the local school children on a nature outing in the Chew Valley Lake Park and demonstrated evolution by putting three types of bird beaks on volunteers and explaining how the beaks evolved due to changes in food supplies, sending the *extinct* birds back into the audience.

At one point during the walkabout, they ask for help from the spectators who follow them to measure historical time with a long measuring tape. One spectator stands far from the rest of the audience holding the end of the tape at the 'beginning of time'. The physical distance between that person and the next ones who represent the appearance and development of life forms is significantly more effective than talking about millions of years ago as the temporal gaps between evolutionary events are depicted in spatial distances. Thus, in a simultaneously playful and serious way, they reclaim public spaces as the crowds gather around them, and they encourage the audience to bring debate into these spaces. As Jon Beedell explains: 'Street theatre must not play safe....Street theatre is not for wimps—it takes you by the balls, gets under your skin, invades your shopping bag—and goes home with you' (*In Situ*: 76, 82).

Democratic Performatives 67

Figure 5 Desperate Men, *Darwin and the Dodo* (Chew Valley Lake near Bristol, England, June 2011)

The walk-about characters in Ilotopie's *Les Gens de Couleur* (Coloured People) are quite gentle and playful, but they encourage the public to either accept or reject their difference through actions and reactions of the passers-by.[19] As they walk the city streets unannounced with their almost naked bodies thickly painted in shiny colours in shades of reds, blues, greens, yellows, oranges, and purples, they overturn notions of invisibility and simultaneously suggest the possible danger of hypervisibility of otherness. Each brightly coloured body seems to recognize the hazards of standing out from the crowd, of not blending in, and each is *instinctively* drawn to objects of the same colour. A sky blue body gleefully greets the blue train and looks despondently as it continues down the street, while the green, orange and purple bodies next to him do not react at all as it passes by. (See Colour Plate 4.) Deep blue bodies closely follow police in blue uniforms; red bodies wrap themselves around red letter boxes; orange bodies imitate the gestures of highway workers in bright orange vests or brave the traffic to sit next to orange cones; green bodies find their community among plants and grass and so seek out the parks, gardens, or any other green space in the city, even a window box; and purple bodies often wander dejectedly in search of likeness.

Les Gens de Couleur came about by accident, admits Françoise Léger, who, along with Bruno Schnebelin, has directed Ilotopie in Port Saint Louis du Rhône since 1980. The brightly coloured bodies were originally part of *L'Île aux Topies*, developed in 1985. At the end of the show, the actors had to cross the city on foot or on bicycles to get to the nearest shower. Although they assumed they were finished performing, the public regarded the trip through the streets with delight and very soon, the coloured bodies became an intervention apart from the other performance. *Les Gens de Couleur* continues to be performed well after the other show was disbanded, and it has toured around the world for over thirty years (Heilmann *et al.*, 2008: 66). The production challenges acceptable codes of behaviour in public spaces. Dressed in thick paint, the male and female performers wander almost nude through urban downtowns. While they do not flaunt their nakedness, (in fact, on the contrary, they act as though they are fully clothed), the city inhabitants whose everyday space has been invaded unexpectedly by these outsiders react quite intensely, sometimes with delight as such colour (and obvious theatricality) contrasts with the monochromatic architecture, but sometimes with disgust and anger. In Australia, a 'colored' couple were handcuffed and jailed. The incident was photographed by cameramen following the performers and shown on television. The arrest caused a diplomatic scandal and vigorous debates on censorship of the arts, apologies and excuses from the Minister of Culture, and finally a formal interdiction to perform (Heilmann, 2008: 66–8).

Les Gens de Couleur not only crosses a threshold of normative behaviour, it also plays with issues of racial difference (as the title clearly establishes) as it forcefully casts the city inhabitants in the role of insiders who must accept, reject, or pretend not to notice the outsiders. The vivid images of 'colored people' highlight racial divisions as the bodies are identified primarily by their colour. This simple, cartoon-like intervention vividly troubles discourses of assimilation as it pokes fun at utopian dreams of togetherness as the group of 'coloured people' try to form a community with the inhabitants as they wander through the city. It also suggests the potential problems of segregated communities as the reds cannot find a place in the world of the blues or yellows.

Street arts' dynamic and constantly shifting interrelationship of creative event, reception by an engaged audience, and location in an actual public space creates Rancière's 'aesthetic rupture' and initiates an affective response. The democratic performatives, experienced during street arts interventions regardless of scale and complexity, represent acts of dissensus in actual public spaces that can contribute to embodied knowledge construction of abstract concepts of democracy and citizenship. Whether verbal or corporeal, these small acts mimic democratic struggles for human rights and personal agency in face of societal controls (from surveillance cameras and increasing privatization of public spaces to norms of behaviour and actual laws) and reactionary forces (especially in the attempts by right-wing authoritarian movements to self-identify as populist democratic movements and to present democratic forces as reactionary[20]). The democratic performatives contribute to the circulation and thus increased awareness of a discourse of democratic practices as individuals begin to recognize previously unseen forces of social control and rehearse alternative possibilities. Once experienced in one site, the democratic performatives can spread to other sites: 'affective contagion'. Ernesto Laclau and Chantal Mouffe in their pioneering work on radical democracy, *Hegemony and Socialist Strategy: Towards a Radical Democratic Politics*, claim that the 'subversive power of democratic discourse' is its ability to reproduce itself in different situations or locations (1985: 155). Street arts thus join other forms of aesthetic social activism like protest songs, political cartoons and murals, documentary photographs and films, carnival, agit-prop or performative interventions by protesters. James M. Jasper, a sociologist who looks at social movements, also links aesthetics and democratic activities of resistance by equating the roles of artists and protesters in society as the ones who clarify moral and social issues and encourage the public to question normative beliefs and actions:

> "We all have moral intuitions, but someone needs to articulate these inchoate urges and sensibilities, develop them into specific beliefs, programs, and ideologies. In doing this, protest organizers are very much like artists, putting into concrete form new ways of seeing and judging the world, new ways of feeling and thinking about it....Like artists, [protesters] are offering us visions to 'try on' so we can see what fits. (1997: 369–70)

He equates the ability of both art and protest to create 'a separate world for its participants, in which they can do things they can't do in the quotidian world, establish modes of interaction, gain a taste of a just society, or simply dream' (1997: 376). All these activities contribute to a messy and yet potentially efficacious network[21] of these diverse, and yet interconnected, aesthetic-political acts of dissensus.

I am not claiming that the democratic performatives of street arts represent a panacea for social ills or will single-handedly reinvigorate democracy. I do think, however, that they represent a potentially powerful tool for social change as they suggest a way to engage in democratic discourse physically though affective responses and acts of the body in familiar public places. As spectators engage in acts of social disobedience or collaborative co-operation, even though within the frame of art, they consciously or unconsciously experience active citizenship. And the active citizen engaged in debate through verbal or physical statements in public spaces is the cornerstone of democracy.

3
Performing Democracy on a Grand Scale

The Sultan's Elephant in London

On Thursday, 4 May 2006, surprised Londoners discovered a large smoking wooden rocket embedded into the broken tarmac of Waterloo Place at the end of Regent Street. A small group of people gathered to investigate or take photographs, but many others just glanced and hurried by. This rather low-key and unadvertised event heralded the start of the large-scale durational performance of *The Sultan's Elephant*,[1] created by Royal de Luxe, one of France's most famous and oldest street theatre companies, founded in 1979 by Jean Luc Courcoult who remains the director. The spectacle was originally commissioned by and performed in Nantes and Amiens in 2005 in honour of the centenary of the death of Jules Verne, and it was brought to London in 2006 by Nicky Webb and Helen Marriage of Artichoke.[2]

On Friday, Londoners found a huge mechanical elephant, over eleven metres tall and weighing forty-two tons, *sleeping* in the Horse Guards Parade. On his back was a gazebo-like structure and on each side of his body were balconies with gabled French doors. *The Jules Verne: Free Illustrated Supplement*,[3] a gazette publishing new detailed instalments of the story each day, revealed that in 1900, a 'Sultan from the Indies' had commissioned his engineer to construct a mechanical, time-travelling elephant, large enough to house his court for several months so that he could find the little girl who haunted his dreams. The Sultan, his concubines and court entertainers emerged from the Elephant and were ceremoniously welcomed to London by the Lord Mayor of Westminster accompanied by many schoolchildren.[4] At the same time, the Girl (five and a-half meters tall) emerged from the rocket in Waterloo Place. Several actor-technicians needed to bring this mechanical puppet to life arrived on the scene on a large crane followed by a live band on a flatbed truck. The crane manoeuvred into place, opened the rocket, and with the help of the technicians in their long red velvet coats and knee breeches slowly lifted the giant little girl. As soon as her head with its leather aviator's cap and goggles appeared, her eyes blinked open and she looked over the hundreds of people below.[5] The crowd let out a collective gasp as she came alive. Gradually, the Girl (as she was unassumingly called), dressed in a green dress, white ankle socks, and brown strap shoes, was lifted free of the rocket and placed on the ground.

As the actor-technicians removed her goggles and aviator's cap, she shook her head back and forth to free her hair to the delight of the crowds. Theatre designer, Julian Crouch (who has worked on large-scale, site-specific shows with companies like Welfare State International and is now one of the Artistic Directors of Improbable) admitted:

> When they lifted the Girl out of the rocket, the crowd just gasped. Of course I work in 'the business' so I tried hard to stifle my own gasp, but by the time her flying-hat was off and she blinked, and shook out her hair, I was absolutely and completely lost. She was beautiful. But really beautiful. In a deep way. I must have stood with my mouth open....And mixed in there with my admiration was a little voice in my head that said, 'you could never, ever have made this'.
> (Webb, 2006: 21)

Every now and then, the Girl would glance at the technicians getting her ready for her walk in the London streets, and they would respond with a nod or a wave – simple but effective momentary exchanges that established her alive-ness, her existence independent of them. But mostly she looked at the people around her, seemingly making eye contact and smiling (although a smile was actually impossible). In these first moments, she developed a strong rapport with her public, and when she began to walk, the public happily followed. Each of her legs was moved by a choreographed *dance* of actor-technicians, flying red tailcoats, and ropes; her arms were controlled like a string puppet; her head moved up and down, left and right, and tilted; and her eyes blinked or could follow a person on the ground or a bird in the sky. No attempt was made to hide the workings of the mechanical figure, and while the skill of the puppeteers was fascinating to watch, it was the puppet's amazingly human movements bringing her to life that seduced the audiences. Spectators interviewed over the weekend tried to define her appeal: 'She's alive. It's fantastic. She's real. Completely real' and

'She's anyone's daughter' (Spectators in Artichoke's documentary, *The Sultan's Elephant*[6]).

Since the Girl and the Elephant came to life at the same time, but in different locations, it was impossible to see the first moments of both of them, but the inevitable emotionally-charged meeting between the two giant visitors took place a couple of hours later, and for the rest of the weekend, they toured the city, sometimes together, but most often going off in opposite directions, meeting periodically to be greeted by a London dignitary. The Elephant plodded slowly[7] through the ceremonial heart of the capital city along The Mall, Piccadilly, Regent Street and Haymarket stopping traffic, disrupting business as usual, and drawing crowds of over one million people.[8] He trumpeted loudly, flapped his huge ears,[9] blinked his long eyelashes, and sucked water into his trunk to spray the crowds. With every step he took, a cloud of dust arose around his huge foot. At night, he knelt down, closed his eyes and slept, but he never stopped breathing. Over the weekend, I spoke to a policeman, completely taken in by the event. When I asked if the Elephant were coming down Regent Street, he responded, 'Oh no, he saw Regent Street yesterday and so is off to see Haymarket today!' The Girl also went sightseeing through London, sometimes walking, sometimes on a scooter, and for three hours on the top of an unroofed London double-decker bus with 'Elephant and Castle' written on the front. Her tour took her far beyond the centre of the city.[10] People, unaware of the theatrical event occurring downtown, stared and pointed as she drove by and waved.[11] Her head turned and tilted as she flirtatiously blinked her eyes at the people around her. Photographs show drivers staring open-mouthed at the passing sight and pedestrians trying to run alongside the bus. At various times during the weekend, she knelt on cushions on the street or in St James Park and invited children to swing on her arms, and in the Horse Guards Parade, she sunbathed in a deck chair. (See Colour Plate 5.) At one point, she was handed a giant lollipop: as she held the candy up to her mouth and licked, she closed her eyes and her delight in the taste seemed evident on her face. At night, she dreamt of sewing and the consequences of her dreams could be seen on the city streets the next day as cars were stitched to the pavement – a whimsical sewing together of the fragmented urban fabric[12] or a more sinister expression of being tied down, stuck in the routine of urban life? Each morning, she showered in water sprayed from the elephant's trunk while the actor-technicians now in over-sized plastic ponchos and holding umbrellas helped her bathe. On Sunday, 7 May, she said goodbye to the Elephant as he tenderly touched her face with his trunk. The Sultan and his court waved farewell from his back. The Girl got back into her rocket, the tip was latched shut, and a fire was ignited underneath. Once the flames burned away, the rocket was opened to reveal that she had disappeared. Tears filled the eyes of many in the crowd.

The Sultan's Elephant was a large-scale intervention of extraordinary artistry and technical skills, but key to the success of this event was the enthusiasm of the audience to engage with the visit of the huge mechanical puppets both physically and emotionally in a variety of often contrasting ways. The *art* dominated the event, never receding behind the participation of the huge number of spectators, and yet the details of the scenario and the aims of the artists seemed insignificant in relation to the public's art-making and community construction (what Victor Turner called 'communitas', a sudden sense of social togetherness, belonging and equality). And the *set* for the performance – the ceremonial heart of London – played a paradoxical role in defining the nature of the fictional royal visit as the identity of the visitors acquired a unique significance in juxtaposition to architectural icons of the British Empire. *The Sultan's Elephant* arrived in London as a complete artwork, but it was rewritten through an interaction with both the city and its inhabitants. The audience's experience and understanding of the event and their own art-making were complicated and contradictory as onlookers and city officials alike participated simultaneously in a narrative of consensus and a counter-narrative of dissensus. The *texts* of these narratives circulated among the spectators as told stories, but also as physical actions and reactions. *The Sultan's Elephant* succeeded in using 'the medium of participation to articulate a contradictory pull between autonomy and social intervention' (Bishop, 2009: 255).

The narrative: consensus and participatory democracy

The Sultan's Elephant has been called 'magical', a once-in-a-lifetime event, and a transformative experience by audience members, journalists and city officials alike. Howard Jacobson of the *Independent* wrote: 'We were entranced. We have not stopped smiling or looking dreamy for days…. Last May we rediscovered the child in our self…and were a-quiver with enchantment' (Webb, 2006: 7). Spectator Elizabeth Kuyper admitted, 'What began as mild curiosity, ended up being a full obsession….I got nothing accomplished that I'd intended to, because I ended up following these characters around town as if I'd joined a cult' (Webb, 2006: 46). David Middleton from Nottingham wrote, 'Just wanted to say thank you. For the first time since the London bombs my daughter rang home with that sparkle back in her voice. She'd gathered with others to watch *The Sultan's Elephant*. It just made the difference' (Webb, 2006: back cover). And Lyn Gardner of the *Guardian* was even more explicit:

> If art is about transformations, there is no more transforming experience than *The Sultan's Elephant*....This is a show that disrupts the spectacle of everyday life and transforms the city from an impersonal place of work and business into a place of play and community.... This is about the giddy pleasure of interaction as girl and elephant communicate with each other and the audience, and the audience communicates with each other. (6 May 2006)

In restaurants and on the underground, I engaged in so many spontaneous conversations about Elephant and Girl encounters and overheard comments that treated the giant puppets as though they were alive: 'The Girl actually winked at me!' 'Did you see her pee in the middle of the street? I guess she couldn't really fit in the public loo, but she did look embarrassed.' 'The Elephant saw me trying to get really close with my camera and took aim with his trunk and soaked me!' 'He lowered his trunk and reached out to touch my outstretched hand.' Parents carried children on their shoulders so they could see, but I also saw several pet owners carrying dogs on their shoulders as they explained what was happening to them.

The success of *The Sultan's Elephant* to capture the public imagination is impossible to deny. Jill Dolan calls this type of experience a *utopian performative*: a theatrical moment that offers an affective sense of a better world. She explains that the utopian performatives are:

> small but profound moments in which performance calls the attention of the audience in a way that lifts everyone slightly above the present, into a hopeful feeling of what the world might be like if every moment of our lives were as emotionally voluminous, generous, aesthetically striking, and intersubjectively intense....Utopian performatives, in their doings, make palpable an affective vision of how the world might be better. (2005: 5–6)

The communal outpouring of affection for the giants created a utopian vision of urban life as well as a Debord 'situation' and a Lefebvre 'moment'. The liminal space of the theatrical event, simultaneously displaying the fiction of a visit of large puppets from elsewhere and the reality of their welcome on the streets of London, gave the crowds the opportunity to experience, both imaginatively and physically, the city transformed (albeit temporarily) from a place of anonymity and routine to one of community and surprise.

The utopian ideal of urban harmony was picked up by city officials as well who used the event as a way to articulate a unique socio-cultural identity for London. *The Sultan's Elephant* became a transformational moment that enabled London to present itself as a forward-looking, 'can-do' city, a city that can play and that can turn its streets over to the people. City official after city official eloquently and passionately equated the celebratory use of public space with ideals of consensus, cooperation and coherence – a narrative of post-political democracy in which, as Chantal Mouffe explains, 'partisan conflicts are a thing of the past and consensus can now be obtained through dialogue' (2005: 1).[13] Sarah Weir, Executive Director of the Arts Council London, emphasized the level of collaboration across many municipal agencies: 'This involved everybody....You name it, people have been involved—the police, the fire brigades, every single public service in London has had a hand in making this project happen. That's how big it is' (Artichoke's documentary, *The Sultan's Elephant*). Other officials highlighted the sense of community that the event fostered.[14] Tessa Jowell, Culture Secretary to IFACC World Summit on Arts and Culture, exclaimed:

> In London, over a million people were captivated by the story of a little girl and a time-travelling [sic.] elephant. Even now it seems incredible, but the spell that *The Sultan's Elephant* cast on those who saw it meant that for those few precious hours, everyone involved felt a sense of kinship and connectedness. Part of a single life-changing experience. And all in a single city. (*Artichoke News*, 2006: n.p.)[15]

David Lammy, Minister of Culture, added efficiency to this utopian narrative for cheering crowds of hundreds of thousands in Trafalgar Square with the Sultan by his side and the huge Elephant resting on his knees behind him (and still taller than the entrance to the National Gallery). He thanked Royal de Luxe 'for reminding us that we can have street theatre, that we can smile, that we can believe in magic, that we can believe in wonder. And that we can also put on a huge event like this'. And after the weekend, he marvelled that, less than a year after the London bombings, the city could 'come together for a celebration of culture and of wonder and of magic and of joy is really, really tremendous' (Artichoke's documentary, *The Sultan's Elephant*).[16]

The narrative of consensus and homogeneity that developed around *The Sultan's Elephant* offered a 'what if' model of social transformation that functioned on several levels. It created a social imaginary of a post-conflict democracy; it offered a way to ensure cultural and economic benefits to London by creating an urban identity of beauty and harmony that could act as a global model; and it highlighted the social usefulness of this ephemeral public art that created a public space where citizens could engage in participatory democratic activity and dialogue.[17] This narrative of cosmopolitan democracy free of partisan conflict certainly gave the audiences and city officials alike an ephemeral urban experience of community and a glimpse of a new paradigm of urban operation. But, cracks in consensus appeared even amid the euphoria since this spontaneous temporary community in London and, in fact, the notion of cosmopolitan democracy as well, are based on the existence of a like-minded public often intolerant of others who disagree with their views or experience. The acts of exclusion were evident on the street as drivers, impatient with the stationary traffic letting the Elephant amble by, were booed by the crowd. Exclusions were even more blatant online in the celebratory blogs. Individuals making disparaging comments, including a negative review by Michael Billington, received often witheringly dismissive responses or name-calling.

These acts of exclusion can be viewed in contrasting ways. The crowd relished their seemingly *revolutionary* reclaiming of the streets, yet they ignored the fact that street closures to traffic were an act that was officially sanctioned and well-controlled and that it functioned as a safety valve to promote social harmony. Thus while *The Sultan's Elephant* was an incredible, once-in-a-lifetime theatrical experience, its narrative of consensus was not intrinsically democratic as it created a space with one appropriate response[18] and promoted an unquestioning 'follow-the-crowd' passivity. As such, the acts of exclusion support Mouffe's claim that cosmopolitan democracy is not a triumph in the evolution of democracy and instead that it is wrong-headed and dangerous. She argues that consensus actually signifies a suppression of debate that is potentially totalitarian: 'Could it ever be more than the establishment of the world hegemony of a power which would have managed to conceal its rule by identifying its interests with those of humanity?' (2005: 6).

In contrast to signalling a budding authoritarian state however, these acts of exclusion can be understood as the first steps by an active citizenry to create a democratic public space that legitimizes debate. The potential for efficacy of *The Sultan's Elephant* does not reside solely in a narrative of consensus, but rather in the fact that on the streets of

London, the spectacle functioned paradoxically as a source both of consensus and of dissensus, as both safety valve and a radical democratic practice, and that contradictory pull is key to its lasting impact. The experience of the spectacle in the heart of London created a paradoxical collage that juxtaposed a narrative of consensus and cosmopolitan democracy with a counter-narrative of dissensus and radical democracy. 'Collage', explains Rancière as discussed earlier in the book, 'can be evidence of the hidden link between two apparently opposed worlds' (2006b: 84). Collage is necessarily political because it causes a rupture in the logic of the visible, the sayable and the thinkable. While the counter-narrative of dissensus tells a different story of the event, it was 'written' and shared by the same public that created the narrative of consensus.

The counter-narrative: dissensus and radical democracy

The optimistic narrative of consensus eloquently portrayed London as a city where 'utopian performatives' could safely happen on the street, but a counter-narrative of dissensus offered an opposing vision, a parallax, of democratic practices. Dolan claims that the power of the utopian performative, even though it cannot 'translate into a program for social action' (2005: 19), comes from its ability to provide 'a place to rehearse our potentially full and affective participation in a more radical participatory, representative democracy' (2005: 91). *The Sultan's Elephant*, as performed in the ceremonial and commercial centre of London in public spaces that up to that point had been reserved for events of 'national importance' (state, military and sometimes major sporting events), offered the huge audiences of over one million people that rehearsal space to practice the role of active citizen in a radical democracy. The text of this counter-narrative was not in the enthusiastic reactions of hundreds of spectators, but rather in the small actions and experiential shocks enacted and embodied by the people who followed the Elephant and the Girl through the streets. The huge audiences paradoxically lived and experienced the contradictory narratives simultaneously.

Ernesto Laclau and Chantal Mouffe in *Hegemony and Socialist Strategy: Towards a Radical Democratic Politics* introduced the argument that a society is not a functioning democracy when its public space delegitimizes debate and seeks compromise and agreement. Democracy is a form of social practice that challenges homogeneity and universality with charges of authoritarianism and that promotes mobilizations and pluralisms outside a single unified narrative. This radical pluralist democracy, writes Mouffe two decades later, promotes the 'creation of a vibrant "agonistic" public sphere of contestation where different hegemonic political projects can be confronted' (2005: 3).[19] Her ideas echo those of Foucault who claimed that 'where there is power, there is resistance' and that power actually depends for its survival on points of resistance (Foucault, 1990: 95–6). Modern democracy, Mouffe argues, draws on two opposing traditions: the 'liberal' tradition that emphasizes equal rights and individual liberty and the older democratic tradition[20] that seeks equality, popular sovereignty and a quest for a 'common good'. Radical democracy must combine the best of both of these traditions in spite of the fact that they are essentially contradictory and therefore will always be in tension – what she calls the 'democratic paradox'. In this radical democracy, disagreements and conflict (agonism) are sustained since their erasure signifies an imposed agreement or homogeneity of an authoritarian state.

Agonism, Mouffe claims, is:

> a relation not between enemies but between 'adversaries,' adversaries being defined in a paradoxical way as 'friendly enemies,' that is persons who are friends because they share a common symbolic space but also enemies because they want to organize this common symbolic space in a different way. (2000: 13)

The tension between these groups, just like the tension between the two forms of democracy, should not be silenced or even be 'a relation of *negotiation* but of *contamination* in the sense that...each of them changes the identity of the other' (2000: 10). A radical democracy or 'agonistic pluralism' establishes an arena that does not erase, destroy, or ignore other voices, but rather places them in an adversarial position as differing but equally valid positions, and it seeks to 'harness [conflict] in a productive way' (Mouffe, 2000: 9).

Similarly, Rancière finds democratic political activity in the disruption of the accepted connection between perception and meaning when ordinary individuals intervene in what is visible, sayable and thinkable. Rancière's concept of 'emancipation' in relation to perception, understanding, or knowledge (already discussed), echoes Mouffe's notion of equally valid, but often opposing, positions. Rather than a process of 'transference' of an intellectual object in its completed form from the 'knowledgeable' to the 'ignorant', emancipation relies on a process of 'translation' in which the object crosses the distance from one (sender) to another (receiver). This distance is between equals with different sets of knowledge skills – in the case of theatre, between the performers and the spectators. And as this object is translated, it becomes something different than what was sent, something that now belongs to the receiver and is repeated and expressed in his or her own words. Developing the concept of the emancipated spectator through a notion of critical pedagogy, very similar to that of Freire, Rancière seeks a theatrical space in which perception, awareness, or understanding can be altered not by a gift of the performance from the actors, director, playwright, or designers, but by an active spectatorship. Active spectatorship does not mean that the spectators become participants in the spectacle, but rather a community of 'translators' of the event.[21] The emancipation of the spectator means a 'blurring of the boundary between those who act and those who look' (2009: 19) as he or she 'translates' an experience into words or actions.

To locate these ideas in the discussion thus far of *The Sultan's Elephant*: the collective power of the spectacle is not just the experience of harmonious members of a utopian cosmopolitan democracy, but also the individual translation of a theatrical event in an agonistic relationship with aesthetic strategies and familiar sites, landmarks, and activities. The spectators who shared the experience that changed 'the way we saw ourselves, our neighbours, and our city', as Sarah Weir recognized, were like Rancière's 'emancipated spectator'. They helped to create a narrative of community consensus through a dynamic exchange between the performance event, its site, and their imaginative and affective reception, but they also developed a counter-narrative around the event. *The Sultan's Elephant*, as performed in the ceremonial centre of London in public spaces that up to that point had been reserved for events of 'national importance' offered the public the chance to disrupt and intervene in that tradition and to 'rehearse' the role of active citizen in a radical democracy as they participated in socio-political constructions of the city. Even though these democratic practices may not have been *consciously* understood, they were *unconsciously* implanted and actually experienced in the bodies of the spectators in real public spaces.

The text of this counter-narrative of dissensus was in the small acts of resistance and shocks of rupture as the familiar became strange. While on the street, the boundaries of these ruptures were almost indistinguishable, for the purposes of analysis, it is possible to identify three: the audience-constructed story of encounter across difference, the site-specific performance of Britain's colonial past at odds with the one told by the monuments, and the parody of an official state visit evident in the people's procession in the spectacle.

1 The audience-constructed story

Rancière claimed that an 'emancipated community is a community of narrators and translators' (Rancière, 2009: 22), and that emancipated community was evident on the street in the audience-constructed *story* of the unusual and spectacular visit. The intense emotional connection to the Elephant and the Girl certainly did not come from the flimsy *official* story that justified the sudden arrival of the two giants; in fact, many spectators had no idea there was a story at all. Told day-by-day in a detailed account in the free newspaper available onsite, the complicated narrative, written in the style of Jules Verne, focuses on a mythical Sultan from the Indies who travels through time in a mechanical elephant to find the little girl who visits him in his sleep and disrupts his ability to govern. The audience on the street, however, experienced and understood a very different story for which the Sultan's search was a mere footnote, dwarfed figuratively and literally by the two enormous puppets. The story that drew the crowds was the love that developed between the Girl and the Elephant, between two oversized travelers from very different worlds who, nevertheless, bonded quite publicly across difference. The *mechanical* wooden elephant escaped the role of time machine and mobile abode for the Sultan and his court in which he was locked in the show's written narrative and, like Pygmalion's statue, came to life through the intense love of his creator, only here the creator was the public. The Elephant, not as a dwelling but as a living creature, was the one to develop a rapport with the Girl. Their incredibly life-like movements enabled the spectators to personify the machines so that they could *see* their facial expressions change and could care about the puppets as though they were living creatures. It is 'as though the soul of a living elephant has migrated into this wooden one' (Webb, 2006: 8) wrote one spectator. The Elephant and the Girl both had what Joseph Roach has identified as *It*, 'that certain quality, easy to perceive, but hard to define, possessed by abnormally interesting people' (2007: 1).

The audience, enamoured of the Elephant and the Girl, were not particularly interested in the shenanigans of the Sultan whose costume iconography was both silly and provocative. Nor did they care about the antics of his court: his harem of five scantily dressed concubines, court entertainers and wrestling strong men, navigators busily studying huge maps, servants who constantly washed, waxed and polished the living quarters on the Elephant's back, and even a European explorer. Many of the spectators I spoke to thought these characters were decorative ornaments for the Elephant, much like his tapestries. The more the Elephant came to life, the more the Sultan and his court on the Elephant's back became puppets. His search for the Girl was beside the point; and, in fact, the Sultan and the Girl rarely interacted except when he waved at her from his perch on the Elephant. His more visible story was as a visiting *head of state* greeting city officials and shaking hands with the *native* population of contemporary Londoners. I will return to the Sultan's provocative performative narrative and its parody of an official state visit later in the chapter.

The spectators created a complex performance narrative in the meeting and deepening love between the Elephant and the Girl. The audience spoke quite openly about this scenario of an encounter of cultures as the many testimonies indicate, and the media mentioned this aspect as an example of socially responsible, efficacious art. This romantic and harmonious meeting of different cultures, time periods, and species, however, had quite an erotic aspect as well. In the initial meeting in the Horse Guards Parade, the Elephant used his long and flexible trunk to court the Girl, quite tentatively at first as he seemed to sniff the newcomer, but he soon wrapped his trunk around her.

Figure 6   Royal de Luxe, *The Sultan's Elephant* (London, England, May 2006)

Each morning he bathed her with water sprayed from his trunk, and when they travelled together, the Girl perched on his trunk as it rose between her legs. 'Now that's some first date!' exclaimed a young girl, who was standing next to me, to her giggling companions; other spectators whistled loudly. Yet this very public love affair was never crude, but always romantically ideal since both the Girl and the Elephant were real and not-real, alive and not-alive simultaneously, and this engaging existential ambiguity challenged natural categories and expanded their possibilities for public intimacy. Their visible love for each other was between the 'living' Elephant and Girl, both visitors to a new place for a few days who deeply enjoyed each other's company, but their erotic love remained pure and could be enjoyed by adult and child alike because it was between two large mechanical puppets. The London audience of *The Sultan's Elephant*, like Ranciere's 'emancipated spectator', participated actively in the construction of their own narrative of encounter across cultures, time periods and species. As a community of *interpreters* or *translators* of the event, the spectators created their own artwork, alongside that of Royal de Luxe, an act that places them on an equal footing with the artists in creating an original vision of social experience.

2 Site-specific performance of Britain's colonial past

Another complex and ambiguous element of the counter-narrative in the London production is its 'translated' site-specificity that satirizes and critiques Britain's colonial past, even though that was not the artists' original intention. The detailed plot of *The Sultan's Elephant* was created by Royal de Luxe to mimic one of Jules Verne's faux-authentic travel accounts and was distributed daily in written form in the free gazette. Like Jules Verne who plagiarized the images of explorers Henry Barth and René Caillié for his stories of fictional travels to exotic places, Courcoult and Delarozière copied the work of Jules Verne. Jules Verne was important in popularizing and raising interest in different cultures as he adapted the esoteric work of historians and explorers for fictional travel accounts for a mass audience.[22] Similarly, Royal de Luxe, within their large-scale spectacle, popularized the post-political narrative of a utopian cross-cultural encounter that did not result in the subjugation of one culture by another for a mass audience, a possible 'third way' to adopt the phrase of the May 1968 protesters.

The story clearly represented a parody of a European colonial expansion narrative. The exotic dignitaries on an enormous elephant arrive in the capital city unannounced and in force (one hundred and fifteen actors and technicians in addition to the Elephant) to conquer and subdue the *native* population, not through battles and weaponry, but through spectacle, empathy and ruptures in the links between perception and meaning. In addition, the foreigners are on a quest to find and tame the rebellious oversized Girl, whose dress and shoes, if not face, suggest a European affiliation.[23] She threatens the sovereignty of the Sultan by invading his dreams. The blatant exaggerations of the 'noble savage' in the Sultan's court made it difficult to take the *invasion* seriously. Nevertheless, the vivid imagery was a reminder of the cultural misconceptions of eighteenth and nineteenth-century Europeans of the *Orient* and simultaneously acted as a challenge to twenty-first-century audiences and their schizophrenic attitudes toward multiculturalism.

The parody of a narrative of imperialist conquest certainly is both meaningful and fraught within the French context in which it was created. The arrival of the Elephant, the Sultan and his Court in the ceremonial heart of London, metropole of the British Empire, however, added a layer of irony that far surpassed the production's plotline. The exoticized members of the Sultan's Court provided visual reminders of England's forays into India and the Middle East whereas the Elephant and the one black concubine referenced Africa as well.[24] In London, the subversion of a narrative of empire became apparent in the *détournement* of iconic architectural symbols of the British Empire. The Girl dwarfed Admiralty Arch when she filled the archway as she passed through, and the Elephant diminished the structure even further, both physically and metaphorically, since he was too large to fit through the openings. The National Gallery shrank as the Elephant stood in front of its entrance, and the lions around Nelson's Column looked like play toys for the Girl. The Horse Guards Parade transformed into the campsite for the two puppets who, for four days, *banished* the Queen's horses. During the durational performance, the juxtaposition of these monuments and the giant puppets seemed to challenge the assumption of colonial power of the British Empire and perhaps even mock contemporary England's reading of the past. This rewriting of familiar London landmarks was a constant source of laughter in the crowds. Rancière argues that the tactics of collage 'always work. But they work by turning on themselves, like the denigration of power in general taking the place of political denunciation' (2006b: 87). This 'politics of collage' is what is happening here.

Many spectators also recognized the spectacle's satire of the West's construction of the 'Orient', as described by Edward Said. Cultural authenticity was eschewed in favour of 'orientalism' (although not expressed in those terms on the street). The Sultan and his Court, from 'the Indies' (a fictional amalgamation of India, the Middle East and Africa, colonies so resonant in a British context), theatrically presented a chaotic collage of exoticized images recognizable from painters like Delacroix and Fromentin. Each 'oriental' costume of the five concubines was an overstatement of a stereotype highlighting the fabled sensuality of harem women. The Sultan's costume offered a provocative mélange of signals from several former British colonies. Like the women's costumes, none of the Sultan's clothing was accurate, just suggestive of styles and ethnic groups. He wore an Islamic-like turban that had an airplane crashing into one side and a guitar poking out of the other – certainly a reminder of 11 September 2001, but perhaps also a depiction of clash of cultures or a conflict of art and technology. His pale blue suit resembled an Indian sherwani and a long black horsetail whip dangled from his waist. He hung a curved dagger around his neck and carried a shark-like fish for his sceptre that he could manipulate so that it opened its mouth to bare its teeth. The image of the Sultan seemed calculated to evoke contradictory feelings about the exotic and primitive Other. The rest of the Court also challenged stereotypes in their over-the-top characterizations: almost-naked strongmen, a tatooed advisor to the Sultan wearing extensively embroidered clothing and a chain from his nose to his ear, a pirate-like navigator, French maids dressed in the recognizable black dress and small white apron, and the European explorer–ethnographer in checked trousers taking pictures and writing notes of everything the Sultan and his Court did. The visual iconography not only was a reminder of European imperialism and Eurocentrism with its skewed view of the colonies, but it also inverted a European sense of ethnic and cultural superiority.

3 Parody of an official state visit

The parody of colonial conquest sharpened in London through the satiric re-enactment of an official state visit performed by the Sultan and his court. This text began when a representative of official London, the Lord Mayor of Westminster, and *local natives* (children from twenty-seven primary and secondary schools) welcomed the Sultan, his concubines and court entertainers to London, not as theatre actors, but as a visiting head of state and his court. Or when, in front of the National Gallery, the Sultan and his entourage descended to street level to shake hands with and listen to speeches by Minister of Culture David Lang as well as the Deputy of London and the head of the Arts Council

London. The fictional characters inserted themselves into the actual ceremonial and official life of London, and the city officials entered the fantasy of the performance as they, as themselves in their official capacity to welcome visiting dignitaries, greeted the exoticized faux foreign delegation.

Yet another example occurred in an intervention within the larger spectacle that enabled the Sultan to perform the role of visiting dignitary ostentatiously and thus to parody the seriousness of such an event. One evening, the Elephant bedded down at the corner of Marlborough Street and Pall Mall, the street of exclusive private clubs. On that particular night, a private fund-raiser for a children's organization – the annual ARK charity dinner – was taking place at Marlborough House, but word of the Elephant not far away lured many of the guests in their elegant gowns, high heels and jewels or tailcoats, vests, and cravats into the street. The anomaly of such audience members amused the crowd in tee shirts and trainers who helped the elegantly dressed spectators climb onto walls and over railings. Later that evening, the Sultan and his concubines *crashed* the ARK charity party. While this visit by the Sultan was actually planned, the news of the *uninvited* guests eating, drinking, and toasting at the exclusive event spread rapidly through the delighted crowd over the rest of the weekend.

But, the parody of the state visit was most blatant in the procession of the Sultan, his court and his elephant along The Mall. This ceremonial processional route that runs the length of The Mall from Horse Guards Parade to Buckingham Palace is traditionally reserved for events of national importance. It is intriguing, therefore, to think about the procession of the mechanical elephant with exaggerated exoticizations of subaltern peoples of the British Empire on his back either as an event of national importance or, conversely, as an event significant enough in terms of art, cultural tourism, or enhanced urban identity to change tradition. On The Mall, the Elephant bellowed, sprayed the police and other city officials with water, and even stopped to pee gallons of malodorous liquid as the actor-technicians shrugged and waited for him to finish. Spectators laughed and were quick to comment on the Elephant's cheekiness to relieve himself so close to Buckingham Palace. The Elephant processed along The Mall with as much dignity as the Horse Guards,[25] but he would always turn up the narrow Marlborough Road before reaching the gates of Buckingham Palace. Navigation on this road was very difficult for such a huge creature, and rumours flew through the crowds that if the Elephant with the Sultan on his back as a visiting Head of State (fictional or not) arrived at the gates, the Queen,

Performing Democracy on a Grand Scale 87

who was in residence at the time, would be required to greet him – and that, she refused to do! Over the weekend the rumour began to be repeated with more and more certainty.

The Elephant and the Girl walked slowly through the streets in the heart of London, but they did not walk alone. In spite of the enormous size and potential danger of the creatures, the public could get very close. The only barrier separating the giants and the spectators as they travelled together through the city was a red and white striped plastic ribbon carried in a v-shape in front of the puppets by local volunteers[26] to create a fluid, flexible barrier rather than a fixed one that would have held the crowds rooted to one spot to watch a parade. With the constantly moving ribbon, spaces were open both ahead of and behind the Elephant and the Girl, and the many spectators took advantage of them to create a *people's procession* that hints at an ambiguity between utopian experience and site of resistance.

Figure 7 Royal de Luxe, *The Sultan's Elephant* (London, England, May 2006)

Significantly, the *people's procession* that created community and consensus was also a subtle, but effective form of 'an artistic occupation of the city and a reclamation of the streets for the people' (Lyn Gardner quoted in Webb, 2006: 104). Gardner's somewhat confrontational words hint at the role of active citizens adopted by the spectators. As much a part of the whole show as the processions of the giants, audience members changed their roles *from* anonymous rushing city dwellers reacting to, but not directing, situations around them *to* active inhabitants with enough personal agency and communal clout to determine how their city could work. City officials, law enforcement officers, transportation specialists, and others who gave permission and planned the event's logistical details also felt empowered by the event, and the experiential shocks that they felt encouraged them to begin to imagine using the city in very different ways.[27] And for Artichoke producers, Webb and Marriage, the intense and extensive collaboration of at least twenty-five London agencies from Transport for London and the metropolitan and park police to the Horse Guards to close the streets and take down traffic lights, street lamps, and other obstacles in order to make the event happen marked a paradigm shift in urban planning.[28] This was not a parade viewed by static spectators, but a people's procession (with the people being city residents and visitors as well as city officials). Its opposing sources of momentum of cooperation and confrontation thus drew attention to the tensions between cosmopolitan and radical democracy.

While not using those terms, Rebecca Solnit in *Wanderlust: A History of Walking* explores similar issues when she looks at the close connection between popular festivities that take place on the streets and revolutionary activity. Every festival, she argues, is 'inherently revolutionary...a triumph over alienation, a reclaiming of the space of the city, of public space and public life' (2001: 231). The loss of public spaces is ultimately the end of an engaged public that participates as active citizens in the processes of democracy. She claims that:

> direct political action in real public space may be the only way to engage in unmediated communication with strangers, as well as to reach media audiences by literally making news. Processions and street parties are among the pleasant manifestations of democracy, and even the most solipsistic and hedonistic expressions keep the populace bold and the avenues open for more overtly political uses. Parades, demonstrations, protests, uprising, and urban revolutions are all about members of the public moving through public space

for expressive and political rather than merely practical reasons.... Walking is a bodily demonstration of political or cultural conviction and one of the most universally available forms of public expression. (2001: 216–17)

Walking in the middle of the streets with the Elephant and the Girl not only enabled the urban inhabitants to experience the appeal of accessible public spaces, but also to walk in the shoes of an active citizen. While the engaged spectators may not have consciously associated their actions with active citizenship and establishment of a radical democracy, their small acts of resistance against urban rules and codes of behaviour on actual city streets and their altered perceptions of iconic landmarks created memorable *affects* as they implanted democratic practices in the bodies of the participants.

It is through walking with the giant visitors at the slow pace they set that the contradictions in how the city functions and what it represents, as exposed by the counter-narrative, begin to appear. This faux-delegation led by the Sultan eerily echoed a much more serious, but a similarly theatrical, state visit of four Indian 'Kings' to the court of Queen Anne in late April 1710. These four Kings were members of a delegation of Iroquois leaders who sought to ally themselves with England to protect fur-trading rights in French Canada. Roach, in *Cities of the Dead: Circum-Atlantic Performance*, unravels the significance of this 'performance-rich' official state visit where real alliances and power dynamics – a 'fateful geopolitical contest between nations and peoples' (1996: 121) were being played out on the public London streets and stages. I do not wish to suggest that the visit of a fictional Sultan in any way carried the national import of the eighteenth-century state visit, but it did cause an adjustment in official policy and create public memories that still circulate in the social imaginary. In addition, the activation of two contradictory narratives of consensus and dissensus challenged the understanding and use of public space in both the development of the identity of the city and in the procurement of 'rehearsal space' for the public to practice active citizenship. With *The Sultan's Elephant*, the agonistic space created by the parody of a narrative of the power of the British Empire provided an arena in which Londoners could become 'narrators' and critics of the ceremonial rituals of official visits by Heads of State. The parody clarified and mocked the theatricality of the real, and while the impact of these public memories on future state and military processions is impossible to assess, it is intriguing to contemplate.

The success of the Elephant in London resulted in a number of cities around the world trying to buy the show; however, rather than repeating the event over and over (an act that would most likely emphasize the 'show' side of the event over its more radical aspects), Royal de Luxe chose to dismantle the elephant and to use its body parts in new machines. Celebrating the event as a model of a cosmopolitan future through the narrative of consensus as well as accepting its challenge to opening public spaces to debate and revisiting errors and crimes of the past through the narrative of dissensus reveals the radical, and perhaps long-lasting, impact of *The Sultan's Elephant* on London's landscape.

4
Trespassing in Urban Places

Ephemeral public art

Louis Daguerre's *View of Boulevard du Temple*, one of the earliest photographs of Paris, taken in 1838 or 1839, reveals a disturbingly eerie avenue, empty at mid-day.[1] The image, taken by a nascent camera unable to capture movement because of a necessary exposure time of several minutes, depicts the physical city severed from its human activity. Only in the corner can one discern a man having his boots polished by a shoe-shine boy whose image is much less distinct. The blatant absence of bustling daily life in the daguerrotype vividly demonstrates that a city is not an inanimate framework; on the contrary, a city is a vibrant social structure animated by its users. The idea is certainly not new, and this chapter relies on its familiarity to explore street performances that play with tangling and detangling the intertwined relationship of spatial forms and social practices. Doreen Massey's often repeated definition of place as a "social space" is the starting point for understanding the affective impact on the casual passer-by caused by an ephemeral art intervention suddenly appearing in a familiar public space, a shock caused by seeing the spatial through a lens of alternative social practices. Massey elaborates that place is:

> the articulation of social relations which necessarily have a spatial form in their interactions with one another. If this notion is accepted, then one way of thinking about place is as particular moments in such intersecting social relations, nets of which have over time been constructed, laid down, interacted with one another, decayed and renewed....Thinking of places in this way implies that

they are not so much bounded areas as open and porous networks of social relations. (1994: 120–1)

In *For Space*, Massey challenges her readers to let go of the binary of *space* as abstract and *place* as local and lived or 'as closed, coherent, integrated, as authentic, as "home"' (2005: 6) as she develops the inevitable link between space or place and socio-political practices further. She lists three propositions that offer a way to think about the spatial and the political differently: (1) 'space as the product of interrelations; as constituted through interactions', (2) 'space as the sphere of possibility of the existence of multiplicity in the sense of contemporaneous plurality; as the sphere in which distinct trajectories coexist; as the sphere therefore of coexisting heterogeneity' and (3) 'space as always under construction' (2005: 9). Thinking about space in these new ways, she argues, can influence our understanding of the performance of the political.

The emphasis on the dynamic, constantly-changing characteristic of the spatial of Massey's third proposition, binding the spatial to the temporal, is particularly resonant with the performance interventions explored in this chapter. Space as process implies future possibilities, a 'radical openness of the future'. Drawing on Laclau, Massey claims that 'only if the future is open is there any ground for a politics which can make a difference' (2005: 11). She argues that this idea of the temporal has a parallel in the spatial: open space of multiple interactions that can lead to unimagined connections, constructions, and conceptions. This open space/place is never finished, but is a site of shifting social relations, 'an ever-shifting constellation of trajectories' that troubles our 'throwntogetherness' (2005: 151). 'What is special about place is precisely that throwntogetherness, the unavoidable challenge of negotiating a here-and-now (itself drawing on a history and a geography of thens and theres); and a negotiation which must take place within and between both human and nonhuman' (2005: 140) or within and between the city's architecture and infrastructure and its inhabitants. She sees 'places not as points or areas on maps, but as integrations of space and time; as *spatio-temporal events*' (2005: 130). This idea of place as a never-ending stories unfolding in socio-political moments within a larger spatial context speaks to the significance of public art, whether permanent or temporary, as it seeks to contribute to those stories and to affect some change (aesthetic, functional, symbolic, ideational, social, or political) in/on the 'social space'.

Art historian Patricia Phillips asks, 'Can public art offer experiences that shape insights on public life – the human condition?... What can public art reveal about the art/human dimension, public life and democratic culture, and the space of transactions and transformations?' (2003: 123, 132). She reminds us that while some people deliberately journey to see public art, it is most often experienced by the casual passer-by who is on the way to do something else and who has not chosen to view art. It seems counter-intuitive that an art form that may have the potential to 'shape insights', to transform our understanding of our world and our place within it, would rely on chance encounters with its audiences, so certain questions must be asked: What it is about surprise and unpredictability in familiar and everyday places that can heighten the aesthetic experience and insert the art moment into the body of the unsuspecting spectator? And how can that embodied aesthetic experience or affective response encourage participation in democratic practices? Cultural historian Malcolm Miles begins to answer when he explains that public art initiates a collision of responses to the artwork itself and to the surrounding city. Drawing on the work of Henri Lefebvre on the production of space,[2] Miles explores how art in public spaces creates two opposing spaces simultaneously experienced by the public: an aesthetic space (that represents a space of art and art appreciation) and a lived space that represents 'the space around bodies of city dwellers...replete with values, personal associations, appropriations, exclusions and invitations, and the shared and disputed issues of the public realm' (1997: 59). The 'aesthetic space' encourages an individual to assume the role of detached observer whereas the 'lived space' encourages some form of physical, social or emotional engagement. While the aesthetic space promotes the policy of democratization of the arts through its emphasis on accessibility, the lived space represents a 'form of street life, a means to articulate the implicit values of a city when its users occupy the place of determining what the city is.... it produces social processes rather than objects' (1997: 59). Public spaces are 'never successfully colonized as an art space' (1997: 15), insists Miles, so the viewer of public art must inhabit the opposing spaces at the same time, but that very paradox is what initiates participation in democratic practices as the viewer's actions have reality in both the aesthetic and the lived spaces (as discussed earlier).

    Phillips also tackles the question of the possible causal relationship between affect and active citizenship when she argues that public life is no longer defined by what people share, but rather by 'shifting differences that compose and enrich it. Public life is both startlingly predictable and constantly surprising...[and public art] can provide a visual language to express and explore the dynamic, temporal conditions of the collective' (1992: 296–7). Public art can play a significant role in the construction of the meanings and uses of these democratic public spaces and in making them sites of debate. Public art can intervene in the site, not only as an urban renewal and beautification project, but also as a disruption to urban power structures and policies of exclusion, privatization and gentrification. It can turn a familiar place into a place of social and critical engagement. Phillips dismisses the notion that public art is just art in public spaces and insists that 'it is public because it is a manifestation of art activities and strategies that take the idea of the public as the genesis and subject for analysis. It is public because of the kinds of questions it chooses to ask or address' (1992: 298). Public art thrives on exchange, disagreement, even volatility, and contrary to official goals, it must not seek consensus. 'Public art falters when it attempts to be for everyone', asserts Phillips (2003: 122). When it no longer creates dialogue and debate, when it is no longer *seen* and *felt*, it has ceased fulfilling its function and its potential as an aesthetic form of democracy. But the voyage from aesthetic experience to participation in socio-political life is not so straightforward as Rancière explained:

> There is no straight path from the viewing of a spectacle to an understanding of the state of the world, and none from intellectual awareness to political action. Instead, this kind of shift implies a move from one given world to another in which capacities and incapacities, forms of tolerance and intolerance, are differently defined. What comes to pass is a process of dissociation, a rupture in the relationship between sense and sense, between what is seen and what is thought, and between what is thought and what is felt. (2010: 143)

And it is in the creation of these ruptures that public art can play an important role.

The previous chapter looked at how a large-scale theatrical spectacle of ephemeral public art can create aesthetic and socio-political ruptures in urban narratives and counter-narratives simultaneously. This chapter looks at much smaller, more intimate street performances that intervene in urban places of public life and democratic discourse as they disrupt how city residents see, understand and relate to the city and to each other on a human-sized and personal scale. Each of the performance interventions discussed in this chapter, Compagnie Willi Dorner's, *Bodies in Urban Spaces*; the living statues of Liu Bolin and Desiree Palmen; Lili Jenks's, *PAPERGLUE-n-SCOTCH*; Jeanne Simone's, *Mademoiselle*; and Opéra Pagaï's, *Safari Intime*, uses a contradictory juxtaposition of image-event and place to cause a shock, and that affective response can lead to insights into the supposed neutrality, openness, freedom of action and accessibility of public spaces that mask restrictions and rules defining and regulating acceptable behaviour there. These interventions augment, contradict or confront the meaning and function of public spaces by adjusting the relationship between that social site and the public. Rejecting the notion of place as stable, the artists use visual and embodied languages to expose public spaces as sites of agonistic democratic processes. Phillips argues for an ephemerality in art in public spaces that reflects these dynamic social practices of public life. Rejecting the privileging permanence in public art, she claims:

> The temporary in public art is not about an absence of commitment or involvement, but about an intensification and enrichment of the conception of the public. The public is diverse, variable, volatile, controversial; and it has its origins in the private lives of all citizens.... A conceptualization of the idea of time in public art is a prerequisite for a public life that enables inspired change. (1992: 304)

Compagnie Willi Dorner, Liu Bolin, Desiree Palmen, Lili Jenks, Jeanne Simone and Opéra Pagaï raise questions and initiate debate about a range of aspects of social life in their ephemeral public art. They challenge assumptions about clear boundaries between buildings and bodies, public and private realms, and art and non-art.

One way to understand how these artists achieve their goals is to look at the ideas of the Situationists that proclaimed that traditional Art is dead and that art is now found in the city itself and its inhabitants.[3] They argue that the city must be reconstructed on a personal and emotive scale. Urban geography is not a study of city architecture, wrote Debord in 'Introduction to a Critique of Urban Geography' in 1955; it is a psychogeography that examines 'the precise laws and specific effects of the geographic environment, whether consciously organized or not, on the emotions and behaviour of the individual' (Knabb, 2006: 8). Later Debord wrote that psychogeography not only depends on observation and interventions, what he called *constructed situations* (Knabb, 2006: 39; discussed in Chapter 1), but on new forms of behaviour in experiencing the city, notably the *dérive* and *détournement*. *Dérive*, with its clear historical precedents in Baudelaire's *flâneur* and the practices of the dadaists, is a ramble determined by chance encounters and the walker's desires, 'a passional journey out of the ordinary through a rapidly changing of ambiences....Dérives involve playful-constructive behavior and awareness of psychogeographical effects, and are thus quite different from the classic notions of journey or stroll' (Knabb, 2006: 40, 62). A *dérive* relies on chance, but it is not a haphazard or unconscious stroll. On the contrary, it has its own logic as an individual walks through the city drawn by its attractions and thus more attuned to its sites and the reactions they evoke. The *dérive* merges the spatial and the temporal experience or superimposes a temporal moment onto an actual place. For the Situationists, the *dérive* offered an alternative way to figure out how to change the world – not through books, but through wandering.

Another key Situationist tactic for social transformation is *détournement* that uses disorientation and defamiliarization to propel an individual into a sense of confusion and uncertainty that, in turn, causes an altered view and understanding of the situation. An important Situationist writer, Raoul Vaneigem cautioned that 'the spontaneous acts we see everywhere forming against power and its spectacle must be warned of all the obstacles in their path and must find a tactic taking into account the strength of the enemy and its means of cooption. This tactic, which we are going to popularize, is *détournement*' (Knabb, 2006: 162). The underlying assumption is that every aspect needed for a new society exists within the current society of spectacle, so the way to achieve societal transformation is essentially to change how one sees the world in which one lives. *Détournement* is a process of that revision; it represents a transformation through a form of collage where ordinary, recognizable images are reassembled into new and startling creations. It does not rely on unique or original ideas or images, but rather re-uses familiar elements from daily life to modify their meaning. *Détournement* is:

> the reuse of preexisting artistic elements in a new ensemble.... Détournement has a peculiar power which obviously stems from the double meaning, from the enrichment of most of the terms by the coexistence within them of their old and new senses. And it is very practical because it's so easy to use and because of its inexhaustible potential for reuse. (Knabb, 2006: 67)

wrote the Situationists in 1959. For Guy Debord and Gil Wolman, this strategy 'clashing head-on with all social and legal conventions...cannot fail to be a powerful cultural weapon in the service of a real class struggle' (Knabb, 2006: 18).

Contemporary street artists who adapt these tactics often lead the audience on a *dérive* and construct situations or interventions that use and misuse, that manipulate and subvert, familiar, pre-existing places, objects and activities to produce new forms, meanings and functions. In so doing, they show that occupying public spaces can be a political act, a democratic act of resistance. These artists *trespass* into other people's spaces and bring the public with them. Together they infiltrate and reclaim urban territories and, even temporarily, change them. But, the 'détourned' memory is inserted into the bodies of the spectators causing an affective response. *Bodies in Urban Spaces*, Liu and Palmen, *PAPERGLUE-n-SCOTCH*, *Mademoiselle*, and *Safari Intime*, ranging from momentary interruptions to daily life to full-length performances, exploit the familiarity of the city locations and daily activities to intrude on quotidian routines. As a result, attention is drawn to what is overlooked, what has become invisible because of its familiarity, or what local inhabitants choose not to see.

Compagnie Willi Dorner, *Bodies in Urban Spaces*

'If we experience architecture as communication...then we ought to pay close attention to what is being said, particularly since we typically absorb such messages in the midst of all other manifold distractions of urban life', warns David Harvey (1990: 67). In 2004, almost as if in response to Harvey, choreographer Willi Dorner and photographer Lisa Rastl initiated a photography project that began to explore what urban architectural landscape could be communicating by interrogating possible varied and unexpected relationships between architecture and the human body. Trying to understand the place of the human body in the urban landscape, they photographed people that they had squeezed into small architectural voids in the cityscape between a wall and a drainpipe, in open archways or under furniture. Any place that was apparently empty was packed with living bodies moulded to fit neatly around each other to fill the architectural gap. The images offered contrasting messages of urban overcrowding versus tightly knit communities. With these photographs, Dorner and Rastl began to explore the intimate relationship between the body and the surrounding city structures. The visual nature of the photographs, however, seemed to limit the body/architecture relationship to one experienced through the eyes and to neglect the other senses since the images foregrounded stasis over dynamism. The city, however, is very much about moving bodies, about people rushing or strolling, finding short cuts and creating 'desire paths'. It is the movement over, around and through the city's obstacles that creates its unique character. That sense of movement does not just come from live bodies criss-crossing a static space however; it exists in the architecture itself. Architect Juhani Pallasmaa, in *The Eyes of the Skin: Architecture and the Senses*, writes, 'There is an inherent suggestion of action in images of architecture, the movement of active encounter, or a "promise of function" and purpose....As a consequence of this implied action a bodily reaction is an inseparable aspect of the experience of architecture' (2005: 63), and architecture historian, Beatriz Colomina calls architecture 'an event' (1994: 5).

Not surprisingly, during a residency in Barcelona in 2006, Dorner and Rastl transformed the photographic project into a live performance using twenty dancers, climbers, and circus artists. The performers assembled and disassembled a series of embodied sculptures as they created physical encounters with urban architecture. Since 2007, Compagnie Willi Dorner, based in Vienna, Austria, has performed *Bodies in Urban Spaces* in many cities in Europe and the United States.[4] For each performance, Dorner uses local dancers and circus artists to create the ephemeral sculptural and architectural pieces of public art made with human bodies. Bodies become parts of the urban structure, but simultaneously the urban infrastructure becomes an extension of the body, and the building and demolishing of the ephemeral sculptures both mimic and mock social life. The colourful, living cityscape made by the performers' bodies seems to negate 'the dullness, the monotony, and the tactile sterility which affects the urban environment' condemned by Richard Sennett in *Flesh and Stone* (1994: 15). The performers take the audiences on a guided *tour* of the city to reclaim or 'recolonize' overlooked or forbidden urban spaces (to adopt a term coined by Julie Pellegrin, director of Ferme du Boisson, a centre for contemporary art) and re-organize and re-form them into democratic public spaces by demonstrating their accessibility and by creating images that initiate comment and debate. The guided tour offers a contradictory message to its audiences as it highlights the obsession in modern living with speed as the runners use the streets to get quickly from one place to another and challenge spectators to keep up at the same time as it uses the momentarily stationary sculptures to point out what many city inhabitants miss as they rush so quickly through urban spaces.

The performance begins as twenty people, dressed in colourful sweat pants and hoodies, approach the waiting crowd, run through it, and disappear down the street. The audience follows and catches up at the first sculpture where several performers have carpeted a long flight of steps with their bodies or become human railings on a staircase or some other startling large image. They hold their positions for a couple of minutes and then run off to a new location. The spectators become new urban tourists of temporary living architectural sites or public art sculptures as they snap photograph after photograph and marvel at the image. The performers, sometimes alone, sometimes with several others, arrange their bodies to follow, contradict or mock the architecture and thus to disrupt its meaning. The images insist on a symbiotic relationship between the human body and the architectural object and reject as unnatural buildings without bodies or bodies without buildings. In *Atlas of Emotion*, Giuliana Bruno explores geography as 'a terrain of "vessels": that is to say, it is a place that both holds and moves' (2002: 207), an embodied terrain that has a special relationship with human bodies. 'As Merleau-Ponty has shown,' she continues, 'the relations between bodies and space is such that "our body is not in space like things; it inhabits or haunts space.... Through it we have access to space." In the natural world, an actual "mimicry" can exist between organism and environment' (2002: 208). The bodies in *Bodies in Urban Spaces* perform that mimicry as brightly coloured clothing inhabited by a momentarily still, but warm and breathing (actually usually panting since the performers run from one sculpture to the next) body tucks itself into the architectural crevices. The bodies fit neatly and intricately together, but suddenly the colourful urban landscape begins to move, deconstructs, and is off running with the spectators following the pieces of living architecture that were able to break away. It is almost as though we spectators have entered a fantasy book where the bricks and boards of the urban landscape come alive and try out different geographic locations and different configurations to find the most congenial.

After leaving the first sculpture, the spectator finds much smaller ones scattered along the way: two dancers on their knees in a garden with their faces to the wall of a building as though they are climbing vines trying to attach themselves to the smooth stone or a clump of dancers in a doorway creating a colourful mosaic-looking door with their intertwined bodies. (See Colour Plate 6.) Others fill the hollow metal framework column on one side of a large gate; one is in a tight ball wedged into the gap between a telephone box and a building looking as though a child threw this ball and it got stuck; others wrap themselves around a one-way sign as they humorously contradict its directional instruction with their heads pointing the opposite way. (See Colour Plate 7.) One performer flattens himself to look like a diagonal line on the side of a building with the drain pipe holding him in place; several close an opening in a brick wall with their bodies or fill the forks of trees; another connects two pieces of drain pipe, one about one-half

Figure 8 Compagnie Willi Dorner, *Bodies in Urban Spaces* (London, England, October 2009)

metre to right and above the other, through a body bent at right angles in two places. In one startling sculpture, a performer places his body to contrast with the frame of a metal tube for locking a bicycle.

In a flower box, bodies look like plants trying to grow. Several make a brick pillar taller by kneeling on hands and knees in a tight wad so only their bottoms can be seen. These amusing sculptures with the bodies tightly tucked into small spaces make audiences laugh and applaud, but the merging of living bodies and inanimate buildings also forges an intimate human/environment connection. And the ephemerality of this living architecture challenges the permanence and stability of the city itself.

While many configurations are delightful, humorous, and whimsical, others, as in most fantasy, reveal a darker side of urban life. The performers' faces are rarely visible in the living sculptures and thus comment on urban anonymity or perhaps even urban populations as faceless statistics. In each sculpture, the bodies are upside down or contorted in some way, suggesting discomfort or dislocation in the urban landscape. The more sinister images of tangled bodies elicit a silent

Figure 9 Compagnie Willi Dorner, *Bodies in Urban Spaces* (London, England, October 2009)

response, instead of applause, as they evoke impressions of urban violence. A pile of bodies, upside down or contorted, with legs and arms protruding from the pile, is wedged into a dead-end corridor made by the meeting of two buildings or, as in the London production, placed in the middle of a vacant lot as though it is just the beginning of what will become a much larger pile. It echoes images of corpses washed into a tight urban space by a flood or executed prisoners thrown into an empty space in a concentration camp.

But this image and several others also evoke a feeling of human beings in the urban environment as the detritus of contemporary society. On a balcony, the bodies are flattened against the metal railing as though discarded pages of a newspaper, and others seem to be pouring out of a large drain pipe. Another human sculpture reveals just spread legs protruding about two feet above the ground from the edge of a building far down a narrow alley. It looks as though the body has dived into the space to get away from something terrifying or has been hurled with great force and is wedged into a tight spot. In a laundrette, the bodies are thrown in the corner as though they are rejected old clothing. In the London production, a body is flattened around the corner of a building (held in place by a tall pole) about two metres above the pavement with arms and legs splayed out so that the body makes something like a large X. A sign to the left and the right of the body reads 'Underground. This way to the air raid shelter.'[5] The resonance of a nuclear attack with the body now fused with the wall is disturbing.

The final sculpture of *Bodies in Urban Spaces*, while varying in form from city to city, uses all the performers to celebrate the interconnection between urban inhabitants and their environment, but the intervention as a whole leaves a more nuanced impression of this relationship. Since the architecture of a city represents its cultural history, the insertion of living bodies with concealed faces into the architectural gaps offers a haunting testimony to the existence of groups of anonymous city dwellers conveniently erased from historical records or excluded from urban spaces. The living sculptures suggest a hidden text of the construction of the city although the details of that text are not revealed. And the temporality of the sculptures as they are built, remain for a moment, and then disappear seems to imply waves of groups of people whose presence is briefly acknowledged, but then concealed. While in some of the living structures in *Bodies in Urban Spaces*, the urban architecture seems to embrace or protect the human bodies, the interventions often expose a troubled, even confrontational, relationship between the organic and inorganic parts of the urban body. *Bodies in Urban Spaces* in its many manifestations specific to the city in which it is performed, asks the urban residents not only to see their city with new eyes, but also to reflect on the impact of the environment on the people and the people on the environment, to consider who or what fills the gaps, and to understand the symbiotic relationships between constructed urban practices and affective urban landscapes.

The living statues of Liu Bolin and Desiree Palmen

The living statues created by Liu Bolin from China and Desiree Palmen from the Netherlands, also experiment with links between body and architecture and between visibility/invisibility and location. Although they did not know each other's work when each one began, they both developed a form of camouflage art where they use their bodies as blank canvases painted to mimic the surroundings so that they become *invisible* in the urban landscape. Their actual bodies are the works of art, fading into the physical surroundings and thus commenting on the increasing anonymity and dehumanization of the individual in the contemporary city. But conversely, as their bodies fuse with the architecture, the artists embody the public spaces, bring the city to life and forge a living link to previous inhabitants and users of these spaces.

While both artists create their living statues in actual public spaces, the live intervention on the street is a means to another intervention in a public space not restricted by geographic or temporal limitations as the artists post photographs of their *disappeared* living statues online. Here the camera eye enhances the human eye so that the viewer *sees the invisibility* from a perfect angle and unhampered by the slightest movement as the image is frozen in time. The fleeting temporal moment of invisibility is 'preserved' in the photograph, and the photograph 'preserves' that paradox in a single image depicting the impossibility of *being-there* and *not-being-there* simultaneously. 'What is preserved' explain Deleuze and Guattari, 'is a bloc of sensations, that is to say a compound of percepts and affects' (1994: 164). As with many interventions already discussed, the artists seek to initiate an affective response as the perceptual shocks make the viewer aware of how much is *not* seen.

Liu Bolin,[6] based in Beijing, began painting his body to blend in with a carefully chosen background in response to the government's demolition of the artists' colony, Suo Jia Cun, in which his studio was located, in 2005. He claims that this closure had a direct impact on his art as he decided to use his own body as a silent signal to protest his enforced *disappearance* as an artist. Each living statue requires a team of artists and several hours to paint Liu so that he merges with the landscape and thus inserts his presence into his surroundings and highlights the problematic relationship between the two. The *trompe l'oeil* is then photographed, and the living statue is dismantled. The *performance* exists on multiple levels: watching the process of construction, noticing the invisible statue by accident on the street, and enjoying the photographs online. In *Hiding in the City* and *CCTV* that he has created in the UK, France, and Italy, as well as in China, his entire body is painted to disappear against an urban landmark: a London telephone box, graffiti art, a concrete barrier in a street, a grocery shelf full of cans, a tall fence, a cannon, a steam shovel, or a train engine, to name just a few. His interventions and the subsequent photographs posted online highlight his own invisibility. As spectators walk by and suddenly *see* him, they acknowledge his artistic voice that refuses to be silenced, and when they visit the numerous websites with photographs of his camouflage art, they engage in small democratic activities that support his protest against censorship.

In most of his statues, Liu stands upright, seemingly in defiance of the forces trying to erase him, and even in his seated statues, his posture is vertical and angular, indicating strength and force. Liu made an artistic choice to *camouflage* his face, and his apparent gaze, even sometimes from behind closed eye lids, offers a silent but aggressive challenge to those who choose *not to see* him. Simultaneously, his gaze gives the impression of an eye that is always there watching even when one does not see it – a kind of embodied surveillance camera. Liu's aesthetico-political protest through camouflage mocks, challenges and makes visible the invisible anonymity and silenced voices in easily recognizable contemporary cities where he has installed his statues.[7]

Desiree Palmen,[8] based in Rotterdam, claims that, 'Camouflage is effective in attracting people's attention' (De La Boulaye, 2010: 38, my translation). She often creates her living statues for the eye of a surveillance camera using invisibility to draw attention to the loss of privacy and the hypervisibility of urban residents whose activities are constantly captured in video. But, in addition, the stationary performance in front of the camera captures footage of the hidden rules and *self-control* that govern public spaces as people glance at her, but pretend not to notice, or regard her as an obstacle to avoid. While the *eye* of the surveillance camera can barely see her since it has the ideal viewing perspective for her camouflage, passers-by can more easily see her living statue and sometimes their appreciation of the joke she is playing on the camera is evident in their reactions. On her website, she includes a video, *Old City Suit*, of her living statue intervention using a surveillance camera in Jerusalem in 2006–2007. She appears motionless as she blends into the stone street. Adult passers-by try not to see her as they walk around her, and this *not-seeing* draws attention to normative codes of *not getting involved* that signify citizen passivity and apathy. A child, however, is fascinated and imitates her position, gently touches her, and points her out to the camera. He thus metaphorically confirms her civic right to occupy a public space.

Palmen's living statues rely on a range of bodily positions, but in each position, her body is curved or hunched rather than straight or angular. She bends her spine and looks down as she blends with a city street, or she drapes her body over a table disappearing against a pile of books and papers. The curvilinear lines of the position of her body and her bowed head suggest a gesture of subservience. Unlike Liu, Palmen hides her face, a choice that she insists reduces the human aspect and thus emphasizes a particular social issue. In a project she simply calls *Camouflage*, she highlights the invisibility of the homeless who live their lives on the streets by painting her sleeping body to dissolve into a park bench or red leather seat on a train. Her camouflage of a couple locked in an embrace painted to disappear against a park bench draws attention to the plight of the homeless compelled to engage in intimate activities in public spaces as it blurs the boundaries between public and private space. The passer-by on the street who stops and stares at these figures or the spectator who views them online is simultaneously placed in the contradictory positions of *voyeur* staring at the Other and *activist* refusing to look away. The apparent invisibility and subversion of signs of political power achieved by Liu's and Palmen's living statues encourage the passers-by to see the geographic site and human presence within it in new ways and to be aware of watching and being watched. But the photographs posted online move the art beyond the street. Using their bodies as aesthetic dissensus, Liu and Palmen link art and politics in a single image, ephemeral on the street, but much more lasting online.

Lili Jenks, *PAPERGLUE-n-SCOTCH*

PAPERGLUE-n-SCOTCH is not a single show, but rather a series of momentary interventions on a range of topics, some quite playful, others more provocative, organized into several varied thematic collages, for example, *Apocalypse, Parts 1, 2 and 3*; *La Mecanista*; *Perdre le Nord*; or *La Disaparicion*. Each intervention takes place in a public space, but it is caught by a hidden camera and appears spliced together with several other interventions on YouTube as 'street stop motion' or video.[9] French-American Lili Jenks, like Liu Bolin and Desiree Palmen, uses her body to play with and *détourne* familiar urban locations for multiple groups of onlookers. Some see an impromptu intervention live but separate from a larger narrative context; others see the video that connects the interventionist moments into a linear or collage form but miss out on the disruption in a public space. Her live interventions always occur in public spaces or in privatized public spaces, like supermarkets, billboards, or highways, without official permission although she jokes that she often gains authority when she dons her yellow construction worker vest and hardhat. She does not try to gather an audience for her interventions, but will engage with passers-by if they stop to ask her what she is doing. For a passer-by, part of the thrill of the live intervention is the danger, not only in terms of watching her trespass but also the physical risks she takes as she climbs onto roofs or up billboards or navigates traffic in a busy intersection to lay out a graffiti-like installation. The interventions are never announced, and even if Jenks is part of a festival, the interventions take place outside of the designated festival area and thus surprise or confuse those who see one of the provocative isolated moments. Each intervention, lasting from a few minutes to several days, is ambiguous, so that it initiates some sort of participation, interrogation or reaction by the public who chance to see it. Sometimes the interventions reference socio-political issues, but, more importantly, these small disruptions are themselves political acts of social disobedience. They represent a form of trespass as Jenks mounts or climbs into spaces that are 'off-limits' – billboards, street lamps, roofs of buildings, or other *private* public spaces – and thus draws attention to the spaces themselves and to unexamined codes of appropriate behaviour.

In a series entitled *La Mecanista*,[10] created for MiramirO festival in Ghent in 2010, her starting point was to insert human labour back into our increasingly computerized and mechanized society. Using cranks created out of cardboard and light switches made from string, Jenks becomes *la mecanista* who climbs onto a billboard with computerized moving images and sets up a cardboard crank that she holds on the side of the billboard. As the image changes, she turns the crank. And when the image falters, she attaches an 'Out of Order' sign.

Or she sits in the open window of an emergency vehicle with her crank held onto the roof to ensure the working of the flashing light on top as it drives down the street. In a car park, she places her crank next to the barrier bar and when someone takes a ticket, she turns her crank

Figure 10   Lili Jenks, *La Mecanista* (Ghent, Belgium, July 2010)

to *raise* the barrier. One driver sat waiting for her to turn her crank so he could enter the car park and, after close to a minute, he asked in a rather annoyed voice to please let him in. She said, of course, but that he needed to take a ticket first. At the festival in Ghent, she collaborated with a city worker who had the keys to turn the street lights on and off. One evening, Jenks climbed an old beautiful art nouveau lamp on one of the bridges, held a light switch on the side, and *performed* turning the bridge lights on and off. (Of course, the lights were really manipulated at the control box just far enough away to seem disconnected to the seemingly impossible actions by Jenks.) Several passers-by stopped and asked her how she did that and whether they could have a go. One teenaged boy laughed delightedly when he too turned off the bridge lights. On a narrow street, she climbed to the roof of a low building, tied a string around a street lamp and used it to turn all the lamps on the street off and on. Since the master switch operated by the city worker was several buildings away, a group of young festival-goers spent quite a while puzzling about how a silly string could affect all the lights. Jenks makes no attempt to disguise the rough home-made quality of her cranks and switches, and, in fact, exploits their obvious uselessness as a real piece of equipment to draw attention to the unseen labour that keeps the city running. While clearly her absurd crank is not controlling the lights, billboards or barriers, the useless tools raise questions about what and who does all the work.

Jenks uses humour to win over the spectators and to defuse their automatic defences against her bizarre actions. Their laughter seems to release their reticence to reflect on and tackle serious issues. In the series called *Perdre le Nord* (that plays with a somewhat literal translation, Loss of the North [Pole], and a more colloquial expression, To Lose One's Head), she presents an Eskimo trying to survive in the urban environment after her natural habitat has melted because of global warming. She fishes in a manhole on the street where she catches nothing and in the frozen food section of a grocery store where she hooks boxed fish. She skis down a long flight of stone steps, and in an attempt to get a break from the warm weather, she climbs into the open freezer holding frozen vegetables in the grocery store. In another series again intervening in the debate about the environment, Jenks confronts the increased use of automobiles that not only pollute the air of the cities but also discourage debate about these issues as people sit isolated in their own cars. For this intervention, she ripped the life-sized image of a car off a billboard and mounted it on cardboard. She then *drove* along the sidewalks, through outdoor cafés, and into shops (carrying the car in front of her as though she is seated in the driver's seat as she walks through the city). When no one stopped her from driving through a clothing store, she chose some trousers and a blouse and drove out the front door quite deliberately. Only then did a sales clerk run out to retrieve the clothing. In another set of interventions, she focused on the ephemerality and fragility of our cities by writing *disappeared* in chalk (in various languages) in a way that the word disappears: on the top row of bricks of a wall that is being demolished, on a pole barrier to stop cars from entering a space that sinks into the ground, on the hand rail of an escalator that becomes hidden as it reaches the top, on the pavement just in front of a street cleaner with a powerful hose or in a place with a great deal of pedestrian traffic. In one image, some of the letters remain on a street grill, but it looks as though the other letters had fallen into the hole.

The three parts of *Apocalypse*[11] involve an extensive back story about the end of the world, but the interventions experienced on the street propose an alternative possibility. The original inspiration for the project is a violent and vivid comic book designed by Paco Carrion, and some of the frames are inserted into the videos in a similar fashion to the actual interventions inserted into daily life on the street. Jenks explains that she wants to use the street and its everyday activities to explore apocalypse and to highlight that the end of the world is always near. The main character of *Apocalypse* is Pita, a pregnant young woman whose long hair has fallen out because of the nuclear disaster. Pita appears throughout the city as cardboard silhouettes sometimes quite large and other times very small. Jenks pastes a huge Pita onto the streets of an intersection so that cars and trucks must drive over her pregnant belly or attaches a tiny Pita onto the railroad tracks for trains to crush. In other interventions that explore the baby she is carrying, Pita's belly is placed over an open manhole so that the worker ascends from under the street through her, or Jenks curls up in a foetal position in her womb so people must walk around or step over her, or the paper silhouette in placed so that a tall palm tree is growing in her body in place of a baby. The images are disturbing and ambivalent, and people often stop and ask questions as they try to understand. In Part 3 of *Apocalypse*, entitled *Merry Crisis*, the interventions are so *real* as to represent forms of invisible theatre. While the story is about a starving businessman who has survived the disaster, the interventions juxtapose the contradictory images of a well-dressed man in a business suit and an exaggerated stereotypical image of a homeless individual. The businessman carrying a briefcase suddenly digs around in a rubbish bin, climbs a skip full of trash to retrieve a large cardboard box, jumps the underground turnstile, or scatters the pigeons eating bird seed thrown onto the pavement so he can scoop up the seeds to eat. He sleeps on the steps just outside the door of the Bank of Spain until an actual security guard makes him move or stares into restaurant windows until the diners shoo him away.

It is very difficult for the general public to see all the interventions on the street even in a single series since they may take place far away from each other or several hours apart, and even if all interventions were seen, they would not create a coherent narrative since their order on the street is determined by logistics rather than dramaturgical structure. Thus, each intervention experienced live leaves a sense of uncertainty about its meaning, its purpose and its theatricality. Although a more complete version of her work (a thematic collage) can only be fully appreciated in its video or stop motion form, each single intervention viewed by a passer-by in a public space draws attention to a provocative social issue that makes people on the busy street stop and stare, or it pokes fun at various social practices that, in turn, makes the public aware of normative behaviour as they are confronted with unexpected or deviant activities. In the series called *Besòs*, she tries to kiss a person sitting next to her in a moving subway car, thus not only trespassing in a public space, but also invading a stranger's private and personal space. In another called *La Eva-Lucion*, she challenges the public with her nudity as she walks dressed just in a fig leaf along a busy highway to the grocery store.[12]

Jenks collects and inventories these multiple interventions, or 'accidents' as she calls them, to initiate a revision by the public of the narrative of the city's social structures and official policies. She manipulates ordinary objects and locations overturning their function or mocking their seriousness. Her playful forays challenge the utility and value of these items and aspects of daily life, and as they lose their original purpose, even momentarily, they teeter on the threshold of art and non-art. As a cement-mixer becomes a giant milkshake blender, even as a temporary visual gag as in *La Mecanista*, its status changes and it acquires the strangeness and ambiguity of an aesthetic object. The whimsical collages and transformations delegitimize the accepted significance and function of the objects or locations through humour rather than commentary. In the many variations of *PAPERGLUE-n-SCOTCH*, Jenks seeks to reclaim and *détourne* public spaces through her momentary interventions that insert art into domains of non-art and that muddle the distinctions between fiction and reality. And her concealed recording of that appropriation and then the placement of the new narrative in the very public sphere of YouTube act both as a comment on official recordings of activities in public spaces through surveillance cameras and as a subversive challenge to the encroaching attempts to control these spaces.

Jeanne Simone, *Mademoiselle*

Jeanne Simone, a French urban dance company founded by Laure Terrier in 2004,[13] creates improvised choreographies that aesthetically intervene in a public space to slow the pace of urban life by inviting city inhabitants going about their daily business to engage in a brief unexpected interpersonal, and often somewhat intimate, relationship. In *Mademoiselle*, created in 2010, Terrier plays with points of intersection between two audiences: intentional spectators who gather specifically to see the show and accidental spectator–participants who become a part either of the show or of the intentional audience in the course of their daily activities. And she then focuses the attention of these two groups with porous boundaries on everyday routines that result in urban isolation as disconnected individuals rush past each other without seeing others with whom they share the space. Through her spontaneous interactions with various people she meets, she overturns that isolation by forging impromptu playful encounters with strangers. The goal is to create connections, even if transitory, as a way to rewrite social relations and spaces in the city. This revision can only be made with Terrier in collaboration with the city dwellers who find themselves participants in the art-making. In *Mademoiselle*, a relational strategy based on surprise offers passers-by a chance to experience a new form of city life.

The piece does not begin with highly visible images and scenes or other obvious signals marking the start of a performance. Instead, *Mademoiselle*, like Jeanne Simone's earlier pieces *Le Goudron n'est pas meuble*[14] and *Le Parfum des Pneus*, begins quietly, almost invisibly with a recognizable daily routine and gradually transforms an impersonal space into an intimate social place, even if only momentarily, and ordinary activities briefly become aesthetic ones and then fade back into ordinariness. The studied performance of ordinary activities slowly begins to map the geographic site and its expected spatial practices as the performers become what Julie Pellegrin calls:

> bicoleurs who appropriate and manipulate, inventing ways of using or occupying existing form. They produce other forms, unwanted

forms that limpet onto the totalitarian regime of functionality and create deviations, short-cuts or accidents. Alien to the systems they infiltrate, yet difficult to tell apart, they melt into the scenery the better to subvert it. (2008: 73)

Terrier is the young woman, the *mademoiselle*, who lives and works in the neighbourhood.[15] When I saw the intervention on the rue Daguerre in Paris in 2010, Mademoiselle *worked* as a waitress in a small sandwich shop with an eating ledge and high stools in front of the plate glass window and a few tables outside, and in Béthune in 2011, she worked in a bakery. The character's performed job depends on the performance site, so she can work at any somewhat routine job that provides her with a logical reason to move around. She chooses a place with large windows so that the performance of her job can be framed as her actions become more *performed*. A second actor, a Man, in street clothing but with a fashion statement that makes him noticeable with his sunglasses and cap, watches her from a distance, non-menacing, but observant. His identity is a mystery, but he has spoken briefly with each member of the intentional audience who is gathered at the meeting point before the show asking them to follow him quietly and not to move ahead of him when he stops. He seems to inhabit the world of the spectator and the world of Mademoiselle simultaneously, creating a 'porosity between play and reality' (Terrier).[16] Why he watches is less important than the role he plays to guide the spectators' gaze as they delve deeper and deeper into the young woman's social and interior life. He frames the daily activities of Mademoiselle so that we too can watch, not as a voyeur, but as a witness or an engaged onlooker. Terrier says that he gives the intentional audience a taste of a 'hidden viewing point', a spot where one can observe both Mademoiselle and the pedestrians, shoppers and merchants going about their daily business with whom she interacts. He keeps the audiences who come to see the show at a distance so as not to disrupt these encounters. From this 'invisible' vantage point, the viewers are directed to experience Mademoiselle's private moments of exchange with a stranger passing by within the public space. And it often takes a minute or so before the passer-by realizes that he or she is *performing* an encounter, but the invitation to share a private moment in public is so appealing that few turn away. But the Man's *rules*, act in contradictory ways: they offer a privileged vantage point so spectators watch, but 'without being seen'; they provide a vicarious, and thus somewhat titillating, experience of human contact; and they give the audience permission to behave anti-socially as onlookers are

Figure 11 Jeanne Simone, *Mademoiselle* (Béthune, France, June 2011)

encouraged to stare. Thus the audience is straddled between a sense of privilege and a kind of deviance, guided by the blatant and intense staring of the Man.

When the man leads the intentional audience to the first viewing point of Mademoiselle in the role of employee, the intervention is well under way as Terrier interacts with unsuspecting audience-participants who lift their trays as she wipes the table or pay her for a baguette (depending on her *job*). She blends into her workplace; she is the invisible waitress or salesperson not seen by customers unless she is too slow or makes a mistake. But Mademoiselle gradually becomes visible as she begins to exaggerate her role at work. In Paris, she gazed dreamily out the window for a long time until a couple vacated an outside table. She reluctantly picked up the tray to clear the dishes, but then wiped the tabletop for a very long time as she clearly wiggled her bottom in rhythm to the motion of her hand. She lifted the tray, but dropped a napkin. Instead of reaching down to pick it up, she choreographed a bend while balancing the tray. As she got to the door of the sandwich shop, she started to enter and backed away, an action she repeated several times as she kicked the napkin into the shop. One could watch and just think that she was just a bit odd, but within a range of normality. And, in fact, several young girls giggled at her and whispered as they walked past, creating layers of *audience* spectatorship.

The slight narrative story line follows Mademoiselle as she finishes the last few minutes of her shift, does a bit of shopping, plays with people she meets and goes home, but within that simple and yet tightly structured plot is space for what Terrier calls 'instantaneous scripting'. Each performance is improvised within these parameters and in response to the particular place and the reactions of the public as her bodily interventions into everyday life change its daily rhythms, startle passers-by with whom she develops a brief intimate relationship and affect onlookers who vicariously experience a friendly encounter with a stranger.

After Mademoiselle leaves work, she begins her stroll home but her posture and gait become more and more stylized as she walks backwards, adds some dance steps, lies down on the pavement or explores the street from various heights, sometimes on tip-toes, sometimes crouching as she walks. In Béthune, she left work crawling out of the

Figure 12 Jeanne Simone, *Mademoiselle* (Béthune, France, June 2011)

shop with a large Madeleine in her mouth as though to highlight the positives of her job (the pastry) and the negatives (standing on her feet and moving around the tiny shop quickly to serve customers who do not really see her). She physically expresses the burdens of service employment and contrasts that exhaustion just moments later with her skipping and dancing in the street as she gets away from work.

Rue Daguerre in Paris is a pedestrian market street, so as Mademoiselle playfully makes her way home, she dances with shoppers, establishes a warm eye contact with a fellow pedestrian, plays with a child, or asks passers-by to lift her so she can see the feet of the cow on the roof above the butcher shop. She lies down in the middle of the pedestrian street, sticks her face into potted plants and takes a deep breath, or traces the outline of a parked van or other objects that are obstacles affecting how we move through the space. Suddenly the impact of these obstacles on the use of the public space becomes very obvious. Mademoiselle performs daily life in both a physical and a psychogeographical city of closeness and interiority, and her physical contact with strangers draws attention to expectations of distance and detachment.

In one of the performances, she caught up with the fishmonger who was returning to his shop. She took his hand, smiled, looked directly in his eyes and followed him into the shop. There they danced as he told her about the fish. Suddenly, she picked up a large whole fish and danced out of the shop with it as the man called after her, but you need to pay for that and then laughed and shook his head. Mademoiselle cuddled the fish, held it high above her head like a protest sign, introduced it to passers-by and finally freed it by allowing it to escape into the Paris sewer system. (See Colour Plate 8.) She helped a man put his groceries in the boot of the car as she climbed in to arrange the sacks in an orderly and artistic fashion, and she stopped a convertible sports car, climbed in and asked for a short drive down the street. In a clothing shop, she chose a bright green dress, took off her own shirt and wiggled seductively into the dress in full view of the street. She modelled the dress in recognizable poses but moved from one to the next very quickly. She *showered* in the mist spraying the vegetables in the green grocer and then bought a large head of lettuce, shared some of the leaves, danced with it to the delight of a child who joined in, and eventually planted it in flower box. In one performance, she chatted with a man sitting on a blanket with a cup in front of him. His possessions were in plastic bags behind him. As they sat together on his blanket, he whispered in her ear and she nodded yes. He jumped up and went into a nearby café. She watched his belongings and encouraged people to drop a coin in his cup. He returned in a few minutes and thanked her. The intersection of art and non-art was vividly displayed. The intervention ends as she wanders off way down the street disappearing in the crowd.

In *Mademoiselle*, the performer 'becomes a user of public space just like anyone else' (Pellegrin, 2003: 73) except that she also reveals a revised story of the space through her engagement with it and with the people who use it. Audiences observe and accompany Mademoiselle on a dérive where, as Debord explains, 'during a certain period [they all] drop their relations, their work and leisure activities, and all their other usual motives for movement and action, and let themselves be drawn by the attractions of the terrain and the encounters they find there' (Knabb, 2006: 62). Mademoiselle experiences the city viscerally and reinvents it according to her personal desires. But, as with psychogeographic excursions, she is clearly affected by the geographic and social environment and, as witnesses, the spectators experience similar effects. Trained as a dancer, Terrier uses dance as a response to the place, but it is not the dance itself that interests her. She uses 'dance to reveal and to enter into discussion with the bodies next to me in a particular place: the non-dancing body, the spectator, the passer-by' (Terrier). Her moving body, she believes, overturns the public's expectations of movement and interaction in the space and gives permission for other bodies who just happen to be there to re-inhabit and take over the public space – 'a transgression, certainly, but also an authorization', she says. The physical poetry she uses to develop Mademoiselle's story and to interact with her surroundings and her neighbours does not blur the boundaries between interior and exterior physical space as in Opéra Pagaï's *Les Sans Balcons*, (discussed in the Introduction), but between interior and exterior self. Terrier offers her body as a site of experimentation with a more connected form of urban living as she confirms the viability, if not necessity, of human contact. As the audience follows her journey, the boundary between her imagination and her physical actions is blurred. Could she (or we) really act like that or are we, the spectators, in her mind seeing how she would like to engage with her surroundings? Is an encounter with a stranger possible and how can that change contemporary social life?

Terrier prefers to perform unannounced and so, even in a festival setting, she changes locations and does not reveal the performance place until an hour before the show starts. Consequently, most of the *audience* is not expecting to see a show. This unsuspecting public is a crucial element in the performance's transformation of the public space from a place of isolation into a space that encourages human connection grounded in the senses. The space is no longer a transit point or busy intersection, but a participatory performance site as she uses stylized and choreographed movements to slow down and play with the people going about their daily activities. In this performance space, it is very hard for the unsuspecting public to remain passive since they are drawn into the action, and often the spectatorial role of the intentional audience is unexpectedly transformed into unanticipated acting as well.

While the specific activities performed in the intervention may not sound very exciting, it is thrilling to watch the subversion of a busy commercial space as it *becomes* a performance space. Each performance relies on the particular inhabitants with whom Mademoiselle engages and the specific characteristics of the space (its geography, its rhythms, its activities, its codes of behaviour) that develop into unique performative moments that question assumptions about urban life through her intentional performance of human behaviour. Why, *Mademoiselle* asks, should we avoid eye contact with a stranger? Why should we not dance in the street or stick our noses deep into the flowers? As she draws attention to both an actual physical landscape and an emotive imaginative one, she asks if there is a clear demarcation between the two. And as she convinces adults involved in their daily activities to stop for a moment and 'play', she inserts art into daily life in very personal and individual ways. Art merges with the urban fabric and social relations to create simultaneously a sense of urgency since the art is so transitory and a feeling of timelessness since it is so recognizable.

Opéra Pagaï, *Safari Intime*

Safari Intime, by Opéra Pagaï also relies on a strategy of intentional performance of everyday life to explore various facets of the urban landscape as audiences walk around an actual neighbourhood peering in the open windows to watch what goes on inside these private spaces.[17] The real-life inhabitants have relinquished their homes for the duration of the four-hour performance. Their front rooms, gardens, and cars become quasi-peep-show theatres with scenes of everyday life, and their neighbours *perform* the neighbourhood alongside the professional actors. (See Colour Plate 9 showing a group of spectators staring into the front room at two men watching and commenting on a documentary on the mating rituals of large African mammals.) The artists use the site of a residential neighbourhood to interrogate the demarcation between public and private space, and they focus attention on the window as the key sign of that porosity. The window marks a dividing line between the outside and the inside, and, as such, it represents a border between public and private space. With the window closed, the two realms are kept apart, but with the window open, public and private begin to merge. Explaining that apparent joining together, architecture historian Beatriz Colomina argues that the open 'window works in two ways: it turns the outside world into an image to be consumed by those inside the house, but it also displays the image of the interior to that outside world'. That display, she insists, is a way of 'represent[ing] our domesticity' (1994: 8).[18]

Safari Intime exploits that dual function and liminality as private domestic spaces transform into public stages on which performers (professional and amateur actors as well as local inhabitants) enact private, intimate moments of daily life for the onlookers. They perform domesticity. There are approximately twenty-five vignettes scattered around a neighbourhood creating interwoven private and personal stories about a small community, but these private stories also reveal the close link between individual and domestic concerns, on the one hand, and public or social issues, like domestic violence, teen peer pressure, anti-social behaviour and crime, on the other. This interconnection between public and private realms raises ethical concerns revolving around conflicting interests of private morality, individual rights and the common good. *Safari Intime* thus challenges what Chantal Mouffe calls 'a false dichotomy between individual liberty and rights on the one side and civic activity and political community on the other' (1992: 230) by satirically constructing a neighbourhood community in which these tensions are played out in individual lives intimately in private domestic settings and are displayed in the greater public arena simultaneously.

In *Safari Intime*, the scenes of ordinary life vary from city to city as a particular neighbourhood suggests certain moments either through its spaces or through requests and ideas from the inhabitants. Sixty people participate in the show, but only a few are professional actors from the company. The rest are local actors and inhabitants from the neighbourhood in which the performance takes place, performing themselves and their actual or imagined neighbours. Thus the show is particularized to each community. The actors work with the neighbourhoods over a period of months, first to win their trust and interest in the performance and get permissions to use their homes and later to work with local participants on the individual scenes. During the art-making process, neighbours get to know each other beyond a 'hello' in the street as they grapple with issues important to them personally and to the community. The vignettes in *Safari Intime* wedge themselves as small slices of life into the performed community, but into the actual one as well. Often, community inhabitants, who originally refused the request to stage a scene in their home, but begin to see the event as a community activity once the final rehearsals begin, offer their front rooms or *stage* their own scenic moment as they leave their shutters open and *perform* their evening chores or have a small party.

The show is set up as a 'safari' where the visitors are able to observe the 'mammals' (who happen to be human beings) in their own habitats. Before entering the neighbourhood, the spectators join a lecture already in progress about the specimens they are going to see: humans going about their daily lives in their private milieux. After a few moments while the lecture continues, a guide leads a small group of visitors into the neighbourhood, explains the social rules of etiquette on the safari, and shows them the first specimen. The spectators are then free to wander at their leisure. Some of the scenes on display through open windows, in gardens, cars or garages or even on street corners are almost static moments – a mother nursing her baby, a woman colouring her hair, a man working late at the office, police in a car at a stake-out, teenagers smoking and drinking on the street corner, a student practicing a piece of music, a man concerned with his body image as he dresses and undresses in front of a mirror. Some create mini-narratives. A man on the toilet transforms this most private place into his private *public* space as he pretends to be a DJ using a coca-cola bottle as his microphone and a toilet paper roll as his headset, but he shifts backs to the intimacy of absolute privacy as he scratches his bottom and then sniffs his fingers. The spectators groan or turn away in disgust, but, for me, the awareness that I had invaded someone's private space, that I had been caught being a 'Peeping Tom', could not be avoided.

Other tableaux vivants offer less provocative, but equally intimate, mini-scenes like an argument between a mother and her adult daughter about marriage or a mother and her teen-aged son on where he is going that evening, a piano lesson, two men excitedly watching television on the sexual behaviour of mammals, two women chatting about the sexual behaviour of men, a man working on his car, a passionate love scene in a garage, the flashlights of burglars stealing from an empty house when the family is on vacation, or a family going through the evening routine of cooking dinner, helping with homework, and vegetating in front of the television. Sometimes it is impossible to tell who are the actors and who are the actual neighbourhood residents who did not give up their homes. When I saw the performance in Sotteville-lès-Rouen, two neighbours were chatting over the wall separating their gardens, but when I approached to listen in to their conversation, I received withering looks. Some of the tableaux give the impression that activity is taking place elsewhere in the house. Others, in homes with two front windows in different rooms, allow us to watch the activity as it goes from one room to another. When I saw *Safari Intime* in Chalon in 2007, I watched a family bedtime routine as the parents talked in their bedroom and the two children played in theirs, but there was constant moving back-and-forth as the children came to jump on their parents' bed or a parent went into children's bedroom to quiet them. By *following* the family members as they walked through their home, the spectator was cast in the role of voyeur–intruder. In another tableau, several windows of apartments in a highrise were illuminated to reveal parallel activities of several households or to expose some moments of unusual behaviour – everyday life framed by the window.

Some of the scenic moments are made up of several vignettes scattered through the neighbourhood, but that the spectator can weave together to tell a story. One of the first scenes reveals a man on the phone in the corner of a garage. He gets more and more agitated, seems to freeze and finally

Figure 13 Opéra Pagaï, *Safari Intime* (Sotteville-lès-Rouen, France, June 2007)

120 *Contemporary Street Arts in Europe*

rushes off. I assumed that I had witnessed a lover's quarrel and move on. Later, through another window, I saw a woman providing telephone sex, and then I understood that first scene. In another interconnected series of scenes, a married woman is having an affair with another woman. The first moment the audience sees is the postman opening and reading a letter. Later we see other scenes: the two women making love in a trailer, the husband breaking dishes as he reads and re-reads many blackmail-like looking letters taped onto the cupboards, and finally a man in a basement room cutting and pasting letters and words to create the accusations on the cupboards. (See Figure 13.) The spectator constructs the narrative.

The vignettes sometimes reinforce expectations as they blur boundaries between private domestic issues and public policy responses as in two linked scenes: a wife in her new home answering the phone and getting more and more frightened and a block away, her estranged husband sitting in a van on his mobile phone, clearly stalking and threatening her. Other vignettes purposely play with audience expectations as they challenge gender roles and stereotypes. In another set of paired scenes, two women sit in a garden drinking wine and discussing sex while their husbands are in the kitchen at a nearby house discussing children and domestic duties.

At each of the 'scenes', a small tongue-in-cheek, explanatory panel, similar to those seen at a museum or in a zoo, offers an ethnographic analysis, in pseudo-scientific language, of the moment of human behaviour being observed. As I watch a postman opening and reading letters he is going to deliver, I read: 'Hubert, 49 years. Postman of Social Ties. As with ants and bees, humans developed a complex system of communication. Certain messengers, recognizable by their blue outfits, receive the responsibility of transmitting information from the community. So, a series of determined signals are exchanged confidentially between members of the tribe.' Watching a moment of sexually charged courtship, I read, 'Quentin 21 years, Justine 27 years. Nuptial parade. Having focused his attentions on a female, a young male separates himself from the tribe. He begins a lengthy choreography that ends only when the female accepts the coupling.' Or the panel close to the window revealing a transvestite applying make-up explains, 'Jose, 23 years. Hermaphrodite, nocturnal molting. Although genetically male, certain individuals experience a hormonal conflict causing gender ambiguity. This difference, like all others, is not accepted by the tribe. So these individuals must wait for nightfall to metamorphose.'[19]

The interwoven scenes and the explanatory panels purposely play with the audience as they challenge expected demarcations between art and non-art. An audience may come across an ambiguous panel, and nearby, often somewhat hidden, is a homeless man who may be a performer or not. Unlike the other marked scenes in which the 'inhabitants' do not acknowledge the spectators staring at them, this man not only speaks to those who stop and look, but aggressively attacks their snoopiness. In another supposed scene but with no panel, spectators can watch an older couple eating a small supper slowly in complete silence, but it is not clear whether they are part of the show or not. Many people glance in, but then look away. Reactions vary from embarrassment at being caught staring into someone's window at a private moment to irritation that the local inhabitants would be so exhibitionist to confusion over art and non-art. The scenic moments startle viewers who are compelled to acknowledge their voyeuristic pleasure. In Rennes, I watched the rehearsal for a scene between an interracial couple in which the husband was playing a computer game and totally ignoring his wife while she did all the chores around the house from folding his laundry to setting the table for dinner. She gradually became angrier and angrier, slamming the forks down as she set the table in the dining room and then stomping into the living room to see if her husband had even heard her. They began to argue loudly. (See Figure 14.)

Suddenly I became aware of someone behind me. As I turned, the woman who had stopped to see what was happening made a racial slur about the inevitable breakdown of relationship of such a couple and then suddenly shifted gears and belligerently told me to mind my own business.

It is crucial not to underestimate the significance of the actual geographic location in this performative dialogue of public and private. The tableaux vivants and even the dislocated narratives would have been meaningless and incredibly boring if they were not in actual settings – real private homes, cars and trailers. The company tries to make no changes to the rooms viewed from the street, so they are recognizable to neighbours and seem lived-in to an outside audience. The reality of the location makes the audience aware of their spectating as they are cast in the role of voyeurs peeking through doors and windows. Sometimes that voyeuristic role was *invisible* in the performance, but sometimes shutters were slammed shut in our faces...but was that part of the performance or *real*? The show's site in an actual neighbourhood bestows an authenticity on the private domestic moments put on display, but the public performativity of these moments connects private actions of domestic life to public acts of civility and community.

Figure 14 Opéra Pagaï, *Safari Intime* (Rennes, France, July 2009)

Looking at the private/public division from the perspective of radical democratic citizenship, Mouffe explains:

> The distinction private (individual liberty)/public (*respublica*) is maintained as well as the distinction individual/citizen, but they do not correspond to discrete separate spheres. We cannot say: here end my duties as a citizen and begins my freedom as an individual. Those two identities exist in permanent tension that can never be reconciled. But this is precisely the tension between liberty and equality that characterizes modern democracy. (1992: 238)

Safari Intime exploits the hidden stories of urban life not only to expose most people's fascination with the secret lives of their neighbours, but also to explore these private/public tensions. Audiences are both seduced and repulsed by the intimate moments that they watch with interest and by their apparent inability to turn away. The spectators *trespass* as they gaze into private lives, but the framing of that voyeuristic pleasure within a theatrical event, a 'safari', encourages the gaze to shift from elicit Peeping Tom spying to a whimsical form of ethnographic research. Even though humorous, satiric and theatrical, the scenic moments are also recognizably real, and they highlight that private, individual choices and sociality in public life are reflections of each other. *Safari Intime* offers a ludic 'thick description' of a neighbourhood that analyses human behaviour from a supposedly objective, scientific perspective as it highlights the context and the interpersonal connections that explain supposedly inexplicable actions. Art infiltrates the realm of the social and the social becomes the art.

Each of the interventions discussed in this chapter performs urban places using a site-specificity that is both locational and discursive. The locational paradigm assumes site to be an actual geographic location that becomes the starting point for an aesthetic and experiential exploration of the socio-political, historical and symbolic meanings of a particular place. Deutsche explains that in this locational site-specificity, 'the newly acknowledged reciprocity between art work and site changed the identity of each, blurring the boundaries between them, and paved the way for art's participation in wider cultural and social practices' (1996: 61). And these interventions participate in the wider context as they use the site discursively. The discursive paradigm of site-specificity gets to the heart of the role of public art in the social context of contemporary cityscapes and communities as a field of knowledge is physicalized, in part, by the place. Miwon Kwon explains:

> 'the distinguishing characteristic of today's site-oriented art is the way in which the art work's relationship to the actuality of a location (as site) and the social conditions of the institutional frame (as site) are both subordinate to a *discursively* determined site that is delineated as a field of knowledge, intellectual exchange, or cultural debate. (2004: 26)

She continues, site:

> is now structured (inter)textually rather than spatially, and its model is not a map but an itinerary, a fragmentary sequence of events and actions, *through* spaces, that is, a nomadic narrative whose path is

articulated by the passage of the artist...the site textualizes spaces and spatializes discourses. (2004: 29)

The next chapter explores how street interventions use the notion of discursive site in more depth specifically in relation to the interchange between the discourse of the role of the outsider, the Other, in a democracy and the exploitation of particular types of geographic sites to draw attention to public assumptions, exclusions, and prejudices.

5
Subversive Imaginaries: Performing the Other

We/they and public art

Chantal Mouffe identifies the 'real challenge facing democratic politics' in the twenty-first century as 'not how to overcome the we/they relation but how to envisage forms of construction of we/they compatible with a pluralistic order' (2005: 115). For Mouffe, that constant tension of inclusion and exclusion, of opposing viewpoints acknowledged and debated, implied in the notion of *the people* in a democracy is exactly what keeps democratic politics alive. 'This "agonistic pluralism" is constitutive of modern democracy and, rather than seeing it as a threat, we should realize that it represents the very condition of existence of such democracy', argues Mouffe (1993: 4). The pluralism debate is often framed in terms of we/they, insider/outsider, or citizen/other identity conflicts. In their pioneering work on radical democracy, Laclau and Mouffe stated that 'the presence of the "Other" prevents me from being totally myself' (1985: 125). Mouffe develops these ideas further in *The Democratic Paradox* where she uses Derrida's concept of the 'constitutive outside' to clarify the significance of the we/they conflict and the resulting democratic antagonisms. Something outside, she explains, is not outside a 'concrete content', but rather it challenges the 'concreteness' itself. It is not just a case of opposites, but rather an indeterminacy of both leading to agonistic tensions. 'In this case, antagonism is irreducible to a simple process of dialectical reversal: the "them" is not the constitutive opposite of a concrete "us," but the symbol of what makes *any* "us" impossible' (2000: 12–13).

Rosalyn Deutsche draws on these ideas of identity as provisional and dislocated. She claims that 'identity comes into being only through a relationship with an "other" and, as a consequence cannot be internally complete' (1996: 274). The Other exposes the instability of one's own identity, and that threat decentres any sense of self. It is no wonder that tensions and antagonisms arise, and those conflicts are played out in the Lefortian democratic public space. In analyzing the sources of prejudices leading to exclusions of the homeless, Deutsche writes 'Disorder, unrest and conflict in the social system are all attributed to this figure—properties that cannot be eliminated from the social system since, as Laclau and Mouffe argue, social space is structured around an impossibility and is therefore irrevocably split by antagonisms' (1996: 277–8). This Other (whether the homeless, the disabled, the poor, or the foreigner) thus is not just someone who is different, but rather becomes the embodied site of disruption and loss of social order. To change that perception of the Other, Deutsche asserts that it is necessary to show that conflict, or antagonism, is integral to democracy and its corollary, public space; it 'is not something that befalls an originally, or potentially harmonious urban space' (1996: 278). Democratic public space, according to theories of radical democracy, denies the possibility of social unity and harmony; therefore, the Other is not the source of disunity, just a manifestation of democracy.

Public art, rather than suppressing that inherent antagonistic character of public space as a site of debate, must stimulate controversy. As Deutsche insists, public art is 'a practice that constitutes a public, by engaging the people in political discussion or by entering a political struggle' (1996: 288). The street interventions that perform Otherness, discussed in this chapter, strive to engage the public in the debate about the role of the Outsider in the city through experiential shocks that can lead to questioning and reshaping assumptions and through democratic performatives that enable spectators to rehearse alternative encounters with the Other. And, these interventions take place in actual public spaces, Lefortian sites of democracy, where negotiation about what is acceptable and what is not takes place, public spaces that imply a set of relations (i.e. individual to others, individual to place) and power dynamics. The *sites* of these interventions are locational in that they take place in actual geographic public spaces, but they are also 'discursively determined sites' circumscribed by ideas about and attitudes toward who should and who should not have access to the public space or, in other words, about the role of the Other in a democracy. These interventions performatively animate the agonistic democratic public space (as described by Lefort and Deutsche) as spectator–participants engage in debate about the Other through words and actions. Onlookers are thus confronted with an embodied version of Massey's claim that space is the sphere of 'coexisting heterogeneity. Without space, no multiplicity; without multiplicity, no space. If space is indeed the product of interrelations, then it must be predicated upon the existence of plurality. Multiplicity and space as co-constitutive' (2005: 9). It is this multiplicity, the opposing reactions to an encounter with the Other, that are the core of these interventions. They use varying strategies that are often uncomfortable, disturbing or controversial to provoke affective responses to Otherness, to startle the spectators into recognizing their own attitudes and expectations by casting them either in the role of insider confronted with the outsider or in the role of outsider facing indifference or hostility, and to compel both an action and a critical awareness of the significance of that action. These interventions represent a form of transitory public art that troubles the space with displays of difference and disorder. While they draw attention to the presence of the Other in the public space, they test the assumption that the disturbance is caused by the Other by putting the focus on the reactions of the public – the 'insiders'.

Compagnie Kumulus, *Les Squames*

In the early nineteenth century, the area around Gare Montparnasse, now in the fourteenth arrondissement of Paris, was largely rural. Yet, the opening of the train station in 1840 transformed the area by developing a vibrant commercial life with lively markets and street vendors hawking wares and showmen exhibiting all sorts of freaks of nature or exotic Others. In the twenty-first century, Place Raoul Dautry, the large square just in front of Gare Montparnasse, echoes the nineteenth-century fairground atmosphere with vendors selling clothing, DVDs, food, and various other flea market items, one of the few carousels in Paris, and a tiny theatre in a stand-alone building that gives the impression of an old peep-show. It was here that I saw Compagnie Kumulus' *Les Squames* – an unannounced performance intervention in late May 2007. *Les Squames* echoed the history of the site by presenting an exhibition of oddities to amuse, provoke, upset, and even disgust the unsuspecting audience who were placed in the role of spectators gawking at the exhibition of the exotic Other.

Les Squames is a performance intervention posing as an actual exhibition of a 'newly discovered tribe of creatures—part-human, part-monkey' – in a large cage set up in the square for public viewing. It fit into the quasi-fairground space in front of Gare Montparnasse perfectly. The controversial intervention was the French street theatre company's first show, originally created soon after Barthélémy Bompard founded Kumulus in 1986 and first performed in 1988. Like Guillermo Gomez-Peña and Coco Fusco's *Two Undiscovered Amerindians Visit*, first performed in Madrid in 1992, *Les Squames* compels passers-by to confront their attitudes and assumptions about difference. As Diana Taylor explains in relation to the Gomez-Peña/Fusco piece, it 'put the viewer back into the frame of discovery' (2003: 63)[1] where the spectator assumes the normative privileged position – the 'we' – observing, commenting on and evaluating the 'they', the exotic Other. Both these interventions mimic the staged exhibitions of actual, so-called *discovered* native peoples or other oddities or monstrosities at the great fairs, primarily in the seventeenth to the nineteenth centuries. Both Compagnie Kumulus and Gomez-Peña and Fusco play with the contrasting responses of fear and fascination that viewing the Other evokes, and they test the limits of credulity of supposedly well-informed audiences in the twenty-first century with exaggerated performances of a *fictional* alterity. These faux-exhibitions not only highlight and exploit the continuing spectatorial pleasure received by gazing at the Other, but they expose how many in the crowd accept without challenge the stereotypes of the primitive Other.

When I arrive at the square in front of Gare Montparnasse, curious onlookers have already stopped near the empty cage to read the small sign announcing the Squames, a previously unknown primitive tribe discovered in the 1970s in the mountainous regions of central Europe. 'For these humanoids, man and civilization are their greatest enemies', it explains. Another small sign displays a Neanderthal-like creature with an open mouth in a red circle with a diagonal line through it, thus cautioning against feeding the Squames. The cage floor is covered with long strap-like pieces of black rubber. Platforms of different heights fill the corners, and bungee-cord harnesses and a rope hammock hang from the roof. Crowds and commotion about one block away announce the first siting of the nine Squames led on leashes, three-by-three, by the three guards. The unruly, almost naked creatures, with bodies darkened and smudged, teeth yellowed, and hair plastered down in a wax-like substance, pull at the leashes as they lurch along in a hunched monkey-like fashion. They run toward astonished passers-by and grab a jacket, a hand or a bag if they can get close enough. If a spectator is just out of reach, they whimper or snuggle close to each other refusing to move. Sometimes they make faces at the people staring at them or imitate a surprised spectator by pointing and dropping their mouths open. Their behaviour is unpredictable and somewhat aggressive, and it feels dangerous since only a long leash protects the public from the creatures. When the creatures arrive at the cage, the guards thrust them inside, and the Squames are then displayed for the next four hours. (See Colour Plate 10.)

Once the Squames are safely locked in the cage, the guards begin to explain details known about the tribe to the crowds that have gathered. One of the guards explains to the curious spectators that the Squames are usually naked and their skin is tough and can withstand the elements. For the exhibition however, the organizers thought nudity would be too shocking, so they had to find garments. They tried all sorts of fabrics, but the Squames could only tolerate rubber loin clothes. She admits that it 'took a while to realize that the penis tubes had to be open' for the males. A guard tells me that 'the peasants hunt the Squames for their skins, so just a few remain. They are caged for their protection.' Another explains that the tribe is a gentle and close-knit family unit. But the game-keeper (in overalls and carrying a broom to 'sweep up the mess made by the Squames') pokes at the creatures in the cage with his broom to agitate them so that they show a more *dangerous* side. The Squames play with the audience, making faces and reaching out, but if a spectator gets too close to the cage, a Squame grabs a bag or a jacket and holds on tightly so that the spectator has to call for help from the guards.

At feeding time, a guard enters the cage with a large platter of raw vegetables that the Squames quickly devour. The Squames use monkey-like sounds to communicate and are very physical – caressing each other, playing with their own and each others' genitals, or piling on top of one another. And the guards do not hesitate to point out their 'anti-social' behaviour. The artists thus *perform* incredibly oversimplified and exaggerated stereotypes of the Other as a bestial, sexualized object that is potentially threatening, but simultaneously stimulating. Rather than trying to promote acceptance of the Other, the installation seeks to provoke a disturbing encounter that maintains a level of tension between the passers-by, the content of the faux-exhibition, and their response to it. These critical images act as a way to interrogate the credibility threshold of passers-by to accept these manipulated visual signifiers of the exotic Other as real.

The Squames were on display, but the viewing of them was guided by the very official-looking guards who offered innumerable details about the tribe with a professional seriousness. (In Colour Plate 10, one of the guards has just pointed out that the Squames may look quite human, but their animal nature is evident in their lack of inhibitions to engage in intimate acts as others watch, and she directed the

130 *Contemporary Street Arts in Europe*

Figure 15 Compagnie Kumulus, *Les Squames* (Paris, France, June 2007)

woman's gaze to two Squames fondling each other.) The guards gave an 'authenticity' to the exhibition, and their commentary seemed to give permission to gullible spectators to reveal their fears and prejudices against the Other and express assumptions of their own superiority. I was amazed when I saw it in 2007 at how many people believed it was real. When I said to some fellow onlookers that it was a show, one woman assured me that it was real because the uniformed guards were so knowledgeable. It seemed that many viewers longed for the authenticity of this primitive Other comfortably (at least for the spectator) contained within a cage. One woman, however, was furious that creatures so human were caged and exhibited, and she railed against the guards and the other spectators for over ten minutes. The guards and the Squames responded as though she were creating a disruption at an actual exhibition. The guards tried to calm her and keep her away from the cage saying she was agitating the Squames. The Squames reacted by hiding under the rubber, cuddling close to one another and rocking back and forth, or howling. Floriane Gaber writes that at the initial performances in the late 1980s, spectators 'took [the show] at face value and attacked the guards or demanded that the authorities stop the "show"' (2009a: 103). At the end of the performance, a closed truck pulled up and opened its back door; the cage was opened and the Squames jumped out in an orderly fashion and walked upright to the truck. The truck door was closed and it drove off. Most spectators realized that they had been duped and laughed, embarrassed at their gullibility; others were angry; some just hurried away. Many with whom I spoke were quite shocked at their own attitudes toward the Other that had surfaced in their agreement with the guards' assessments of the Squames' bestial Otherness.

The performance was much more about how the public reacted to and interacted with the caged *native* tribe and the guards than about anything the performers actually did.[2] The very pointed use of the cage was not only for shock value – although it certainly accomplished that. Its clear visual reference to caged wild animals at a zoo made it a signifier for the potential for danger from the creatures on display and, simultaneously, for their exoticism. The cage performatively and sarcastically confirmed the belief that these *primitives* could be safely contained for our viewing pleasure and that we could learn about their life style by watching their ordinary activities completely decontextualized from a native habitat. This provocative intervention exploited the fear and fascination with the Other and implanted that encounter into the bodies of the spectators as they came face-to-face with their feelings of superiority, compassion or disgust. The significance of the intervention existed in the spectators' embodied experience of a key fundamental question posed by democratic societies: what is the place of outsiders in a democracy? *Les Squames* offered one possible cynical, tongue-in-cheek response, but it did so in order to shock the public into recognizing and questioning unexamined assumptions about the Other, about the we/they tension in a democracy that Mouffe explains as the need to determine who belongs and who does not (2000: 36–59). In addition, with the emphasis on the anti-social behaviour of the Squames, the 'reading' encouraged in the intervention suggests that *citizenship*, and of course its opposing category of *foreignness*, is increasingly defined in terms of normative behaviour. That definition opens the door for the distance between citizen and foreigner to be framed in moral terms of right and wrong or good and evil. The participatory form of *Les Squames* arouses a powerful affective response to this disturbing Other, and that somatic reaction to the faux-exhibition is physically felt, whether the viewer thinks the Outsider is real or not. While one's response can be intellectually analysed at a later time, the on-site reaction is powerfully immediate as it compels the spectator to confront his or her 'feelings' about Otherness.

The intense visceral reaction of such an experience grows out of what I have chosen to call *metaphoric memory*. Street interventions that perform the Other often develop a *memory* in the mind of the spectator. This memory is not just of the show, but rather of the spectator's affective experience of Otherness. While that experience occurs within the frame of a performance event, it is actually felt in the spectator's body, both physically and psychologically, during the show and is recollected by the body later. 'What is remembered by the body is well remembered', writes Elaine Scarry on pain and physical violence (1985: 152). In addition, it is experienced in a familiar public space that the passer-by associates with everyday activities. Thus what is experienced in the aesthetic space thus acquires an uncanny reality making metaphoric memory possible.[3]

Pascal Laurent, *Melgut* and *VitupErrance*

Pascal Laurent, one of the directors of Friches Théâtre Urbain in Paris, France, has developed two solo characters that rely on anti-social behaviour to push passers-by into a position of choosing to reject him. In the late 1980s, he created an exotic character who appeared in urban centres unannounced and often unwelcome.[4] Melgut, a hunched character on one-meter stilts, dressed head-to-toe in flowing red robes, seems to come out of nowhere and tries to blend in with unsuspecting pedestrians who suddenly find a foreigner – disoriented and scared – in their midst. He tries to be as invisible as the normal inhabitants of the town, but his physical difference clearly sets him apart. Although the spectators force him to engage with them, Melgut is always the outsider. He has entered the public's space, and his precisely enacted awareness of that intrusion firmly places the crowds that surround him in the role of insiders who easily become intolerant of his difference as his behaviour in response to their attention becomes more erratic and aggressive.

While some spectators try to connect with Melgut by, for example, offering a cigarette, he gets the audience to laugh at his surprise and over-reaction to the gift and thus turns the act of kindness into a way to mock the Other as someone who does not know the behavioural codes. Some moments of connection with the *insiders* happen as Melgut touches someone's head, leans on someone's shoulder, or allows people to hold his hand, but that connection makes him feel cornered, so he frightens the crowd as he rushes into their midst in an attempt to get away. Sometimes, he pushes the connection too far and so turns the crowd against him. In one show, an unannounced performance intervention in June 2002 near Saint-Germain-des-Prés in Paris, a crowd of children surround him, pulling at his robes and grabbing his hands. Suddenly, he lifts one child up and swings her around three or four times. The others are stunned; some want a turn, others back away, but Melgut takes off across the street, stopping traffic. (See Colour Plate 11.) His actions dramatically convey the image of being hemmed in and terrified, and his escape that leaves him trapped among the cars encourages the crowd to follow, to *chase* him. While Melgut brings the outsider's feelings of isolation, fear, anger and longing into sharper focus as he highlights the impossibility of assimilation for some newcomers, he also forces the audience to experience how easy it is to discriminate against someone who looks and acts different since his actions do not really allow 'us' to accept the outsider: he harangues us too fiercely, he invades our space too aggressively; his mercurial temperament is too frightening. Melgut offers a hyperbolic characterization of Otherness, and while that characterization is offensive as it embodies and reinforces negative stereotypes, it also exploits extreme exaggeration to dispel any possibility of being construed as an accurate portrayal and thus shifts the focus from the content of the piece to the experience of the spectators reacting to this encounter with the Other. Melgut balances precariously on the line between being so outrageous that he is just entertaining and being the source of biting social critique.

In *VitupErrance*,[5] first performed in 2011, Laurent abandons the visual signals of the outsider so evident in Melgut's red robes and stilts and blends more easily into the crowd at least at first. Like Melgut, this new character just appears in urban centres unannounced and often unwelcome. In this piece, Laurent says he seeks the fine line between intervention and scandal as his character tests the boundaries between real life and performance. Everyday life is at the heart of the intervention, but the quotidian provides the lens through which to view larger social and political issues. In *VitupErrance*, Laurent explores the point where people stop being tolerant toward someone whose behaviour is different or erratic and experiments with what kind of actions cause fear, anger or disgust. But he also plays with the moment that invisible theatre becomes visible as he measures how much he needs to exaggerate his movements, his words or his reactions before an unsuspecting audience realizes they are watching a show.

Laurent begins the performance intervention dressed quite well in a suit and leather shoes, pulling a small black suitcase. The start of the show is unannounced and invisible, and the people with whom he interacts for the first few hours as he walks around the central town square think that he is an older man, perhaps a little distracted or disoriented, but someone looking for something – from his sunglasses to an inexpensive place to stay for the night. Laurent asks people where he can find the Centre Départemental d'Hébergement that can help him find a hotel, but this Centre is fictitious. People tend to be helpful as they try to search for it on their iPhones or take him to the nearest bar to ask the owner, but, of course, no one knows the place since it does not exist. As they search, Laurent's character begins to tell them little anecdotes about himself, how he has lost his job, how he has no place to live. It seems strange since he is well-dressed, but some people sympathize. He wanders around this public space asking for help and telling tiny stories for about three hours so that he becomes a familiar figure in the square. The character's autobiographical anecdotes are punctuated with complaints about human pettiness and selfishness or about elusive social services. While he begins gently, his criticisms against today's world from the railroads and industrial growth to American superheroes and profit motives become more caustic. He begins working with groups of two or three and then tries to gather larger groups of ten to twenty to participate in tiny ten-minute *shows* that many may not recognize as a performance intervention. Some people listen, some argue, others walk away, and still others ask him to leave. In one bar, customers threatened to call social services, so he thanked them for their time and help and left.

Rather than clearly establishing his Otherness from his first appearance as he did with Melgut, in *VitupErrance*, Laurent gradually alters his behaviour and his costume as he shifts from ordinary activities to obvious performance.[6]

The more obvious *show* begins as Laurent starts to command the space with his life stories punctuated by harangues. He begins this

Figure 16 Pascal Laurent, *VitupErrance* (Paris, France, September 2011) Photograph by Juliette Dieudonné (Courtesy of Friches Théâtre Urbain)

section mimicking the iconic panhandler on the Paris metro whose pitch begins by thanking the crowd for their time, patience and generosity and moves to telling them his life story. Laurent's character starts with expressions of appreciation that logically lead to why he is asking for help. He reveals personal details of jobs he lost because of changes in the industry and the economic crisis and moves into a critique of contemporary capitalist society that devalues the human being in favour of commerce. Each part of the meandering narrative reveals a personal anecdote accompanied by mimed actions, and as his narrative becomes more heated, he begins to take off the nice suit jacket, tie and shirt. He plays with the tie as a noose. He pulls an Australian greatcoat and a rumpled bowler hat out of his bag. In his new persona, he makes direct and often biting or cynical comments about the state of the world and accuses the people who just stand there and listen of shirking their responsibility. And just as suddenly as he started, he abruptly leaves.

His character could be a former successful businessman now down on his luck, but his behaviour identifies him as an unpleasant, and potentially dangerous, Other – an old man exhausted by life and powerless against society's forces, but furious at civic injustices and frightened by the steady descent into barbarism in today's social world. His Otherness, visually quite subtle in *VitupErrance*, is located in his attitudes and his tirades that become more frightening though his accusatory finger-pointing, the highly expressive emotions shown on his face, and his exaggerated glee, surprise, deep confusion or anger. The public's experience as they helped, ignored or mocked this old man before he appeared as a character is vividly remembered in the spectator's body, and Laurent echoes the gestures of kindness and those of hostility in his tirades. Like Melgut, this character arouses a visceral response in the spectators as they encounter Otherness. The invisibility of the beginning of the performance makes the initial audience reactions to an *actual* Outsider who then reveals himself as a *performed* Outsider, and this ambiguity and deception walk a fine line between acceptability and scandal, but the character effectively creates a metaphoric memory of Otherness in the spectator.

Osmosis Compagnie, *Transit* and *Alhambra Container*

The massive eighteen-wheel truck (or articulated lorry) with its two trailers (one with open sides, the other completely enclosed) dominates the square in front of the Hotel de Ville in Chalon-sur-Saône (2005) all through the day. The performance, *Transit*, begins only when the sun sets. In the dark, images appear on the sides of the closed trailer – rural roads, urban streets, a beach, the mountains, abandoned lots, open fields. Sometimes still photographs, sometimes video footage, the images can linger or switch very quickly to create a dizzying sense of speed or urgency. A lone figure appears in the open trailer. Ali Salmi dances the voyage of a refugee on his clandestine journey from Afghanistan to the port of Calais and on to England. Created in 2004, *Transit* is one of several choreographies developed by Salmi and Osmosis Compagnie, based in Forbach, France, as an homage to his familial memories of their migration from Algeria.[7] Each one is based on actual experiences and stories, recounted and imagined.

Inspired by the photography of Ad van Denderen's *Go No Go*, *Transit*[8] narrates the hazards of the exile's voyage through movement both of the dancer's body and the images projected on the sides of the trailer. The dancer uses the floor of the trailer, but also its walls as he tries to run up them only to be thrown back down, its ceiling as he dangles upside down, and its roof. (See Colour Plate 12.) The dance acts as a metaphoric discourse on the movement of migration. Sometimes the projected images provide a loose narrative line as the dancer-exile travels through various geographic locations and his body responds to the sites. Sometimes the images change so rapidly that one just gets a sense of speed or chaos. Other times they generate a sensation of travel through videos of fast-moving cars or trains as seen from the side of the road or, in contrast, through videos of rapidly changing landscape as though observed from the window of a moving vehicle. But the projected images do not just establish geographic locations. Real-time images of Salmi's moving body are also often projected much larger than life on the trailer walls. Sometimes the image is seen in the space of the other trailer as he dances so that he dances with an enlarged version of himself; sometimes it is superimposed on an image of a place so he is both in a geographic location and a *no-place*. His dance with his double visually expresses the migrant's tension of self and Other in one body (Salmi, 2012). This real-time footage of his dancing body focuses attention on his emotional states as he travels. Although this performance technique clearly allows the standing crowd to see facial expressions and energetic movements of the dancer's body that seems small at such a distance, it also creates an impression of entering the dancer-refugee's mind. I found the *sleeping dance* particularly evocative as the exhausted exile tries to grab a few moments of rest as he lies on the trailer floor, but his body writhes and thrashes. His actual body in the trailer gives an impression of movement caused by the jolts of the mode of transportation, but the enlarged projection of the exact same movements seems to reveal his inner turmoil.

Transit's companion piece, *Alhambra Container*,[9] created in 2008, focuses on the moment of arrival of the refugee in the unknown and often hostile destination. My affective responses to this piece were even more intense than to *Transit*. When I saw the show in Aurillac in 2008, I walked to a large parking lot on the outskirts of the city as the sky was beginning to darken. A small audience surrounded this open empty space. As with *Transit*, the show begins as the sun sets. In the dim light, three fork-lifts arrive, each one carrying a large shipping container, iconic symbols of gobalization and international transportation. We move out of the way as the fork-lifts rumble into the open area, deposit the containers in a somewhat circular formation at some distance from each other and back away. Silence and darkness descend until suddenly spotlights are shone on the doors of each container and then an image of the face of a singing Mahgrebi woman fills the container's end and her voice dominates the space. After a few moments, the doors open and a dancer leaves the safety of the container – an exile at the moment of arrival in the new and unknown land. As can be seen in Figure 17, the performer-exile inhabits the liminal space between homeland and new land at this moment as the image of home in the singing face is still projected on his body, but he must take that first step away.

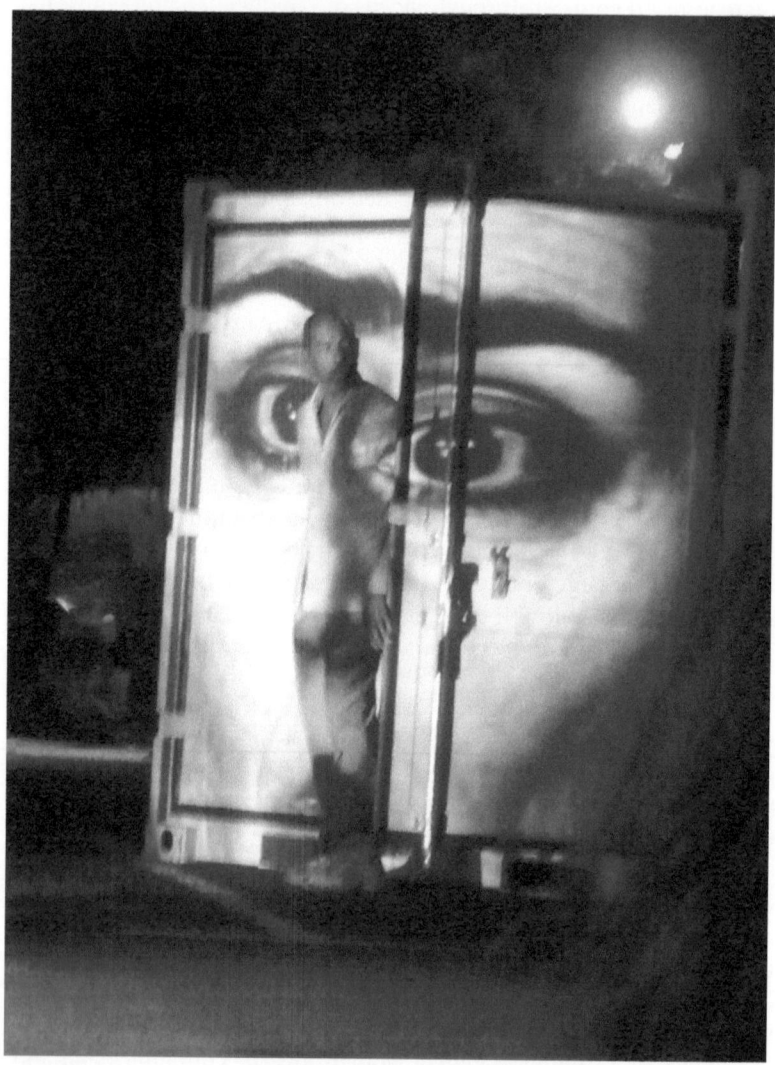

Figure 17 Compagnie Osmosis: *Alhambra Container* (Aurillac, France, August 2008)

The voices and images on the container's doors continue moving between Mahgrebi songs and calls to prayer as though they are the haunting memories of the home as the newcomer explores a new environment through dance – running, reaching, lunging and hiding until he falls exhausted. The image of the face grows larger and larger until all one can see is the mouth ominous and oppressive, then the image goes black. Now the forklifts join the choreography, sometimes aiding the newly arrived exile, but often acting as aggressor or oppressor. One exile rides on the prongs high above the fray; another is chased by a forklift. One powerful choreography between the female dancer and a forklift depicts the rape of the exile as she is trapped and metaphorically penetrated by the forklift's prongs.[10] *Alhambra Container* is actually danced by nine dancers: three human, three forklifts and three containers as the forklifts move the containers around the space with or without dancers in or on them. At one point, a forklift carrying a container holding the human dancers spins slowly in the centre of the parking lot, and at another point, the human dancers on the roof of one container are suddenly trapped by the prongs of the three forklifts. The choreography powerfully expresses the refugee's challenges of arriving in and adapting to a new country, but at the end of the dance one refugee successfully makes the transition as he sheds his old shirt for a new one. A forklift drops the old shirt into a container. Its doors are closed, and the show ends. *Transit* and *Alhambra Container* use a monumental oversized aesthetic to reveal small and intimate human reactions to the chaos around them (Salmi, 2012).

In these two choreographies by Osmosis Compagnie, the spectator adopts the role of *witness* to the experience of exile. Exploring the role of witness, Diana Taylor argues that transferring memory from the one who experienced the event to the witness:

> involves the shared and participatory act of telling and listening associated with live performance. Bearing witness is a live process, a doing, an event that takes place in real time. ...In performance, behaviors and actions can be separated from the social actors performing them. These actions can be learned, enacted, and passed on to others. The transmission of traumatic experience more closely resembles 'contagion': one 'catches' and embodies the burden, pain, and responsibility of past behaviors/events. (2003: 167–8)

As witness, the spectator 'catches' the condition of exile that, in turn, establishes an overlap between embodied knowledge and memory and makes metaphoric memory possible. The idea of metaphoric memory here is not just that the movements of a performer are actually remembered, but the affective response caused by witnessing a performed experience of exile creates a memory of the *experience of exile*. Spectators interpret a scene not just through perception of visual signs, but also through understanding and deciphering what a character is thinking about or doing with these signs,[11] and this engagement with enacted motivations enables the spectator to feel empathy. That engaged empathy activates various forms of metaphoric memory and embeds the experience of Otherness in the spectator's body. 'Embodying other's emotions produces emotions in us, even if the situation is an imagined or fictitious one.... In other words, emotions generated through simulation change how people think' (McConachie, 2008: 67, 69).

Back to Back Theatre, *Small Metal Objects*

Back to Back Theatre, based in Geelong, Australia, but performing all over the world, offers audiences another opportunity to witness the experiences of the Other, and it intensifies empathy by using actors who *are* the Outsider they perform. On its website, the company explains that it devises work based on the experiences of its ensemble of 'actors perceived to have intellectual disabilities, a group of people who, in a culture obsessed with perfection and surgically enhanced "beauty" are the real outsiders. This position provides them with a unique and at times subversive view of the world'.[12] In *Small Metal Objects*, the actors create a distinct form of intervention by offering a unique perspective from which to observe an intense personal moment unfolding in a public space and by casting the spectator in the role of witness–voyeur seeking out and overhearing what usually remains private. For this intervention, the act of viewing is formalized as the audience sits on a bank of seats facing a public space filled with ordinary pedestrians going about their daily activities. When I saw the show in Sydney, Australia in 2007, the audience faced the entrance to the ferries in Customs House Square at Circular Quay. Each spectator is given a set of headphones, and as a softly-spoken conversation between two friends nervous about an imminent rendez-vous begins, audience members search through the crowds of commuters rushing to catch a ferry to see who is speaking. After several minutes, the players in this drama become visible in the crowd. Steve and Gary are two men who would usually either be ignored or stared at because of their disabilities: the invisibility/hypervisibility conundrum playfully explored in *Les Gens de Couleur*.

They wait for the man with whom they have made some kind of deal. One wants to get coffee, but for some reason, his friend becomes rooted to his spot, unable or unwilling to move. The high-powered executive arrives and becomes quite angry when whatever he was promised by Steve and Gary is not available. Steve and Gary will not leave to get it since one of them stands immobile in the crowd, and his friend will not leave him alone. Why the young man will not move is never explained, and what the executive wants from them is never revealed. The executive calls a partner, and together they try cajoling, threats, and humiliation to get what they want, but to no avail. The executives show no respect to these disabled outsiders who are just a means to an end. As most of this exchange takes place well back in the station, sometimes the actors are obscured by the crowds although we can hear their softly spoken conversations through our headphones. After the executives finally leave, Steve and Gary wander off disappearing among the crowds of ordinary commuters.

The narrative of *Small Metal Objects* is less important than what it reveals about attitudes toward the disabled Other. The failed transaction between Steve and Gary and the two executives is played out among the crowds of ordinary commuters heading home after work and not intending to see or participate in a performance. And yet, these unsuspecting people form the setting within which this private moment unfolds; they are both performers creating the world in which the encounter takes place and spectators watching or trying not to watch the encounter. When I saw the performance, most of the people hurrying by glanced at Steve or Gary and quickly looked away, especially when one just stood there frozen to the spot. Even when the female executive offered sex to the stationary and clearly frightened man, the people in the crowd pointedly looked the other way as though they were trying not to hear so that they did not have to get involved in what was obviously a power play. In Figure 18, one can see the woman trying to get the young man to react through words and physical contact (on the left-hand side of the photograph). In the performance, his discomfort and fear were obvious, but, as the photograph reveals, all the people around this incident are pointedly looking away, except for the toddler in the stroller.

The action took place deep enough in the public space that ordinary passers-by noticed the dramatic moments, seemingly actual moments, before they noticed the bank of seats with spectators staring into the crowd. Thus the reactions we witnessed were those we often either ignore or perform ourselves everyday. The position in which *Small Metal Objects* placed the audience was particularly disturbing as we watched

Figure 18 Back to Back Theatre, *Small Metal Objects* (Sydney, Australia, January 2007)

the unsuspecting commuters, not yet aware that they had become performers, glance with disapproval, even disgust, at the Other. We recognized those familiar judgmental looks and were forced to acknowledge them as something we too could give or we could pretend that we were better than that and we would...what? Intervene? *Small Metal Objects* forced the spectator to recognize attitudes and prejudices toward the Other normally submerged and to acknowledge an equally submerged desire not to get involved.

Community art-making: Compagnie Kumulus, *Itinéraire Sans Fond(s)* and *Les Rencontres Internationales de Boîtes*

In 2003, Compagnie Kumulus again tackled the issue of Otherness, but in a form quite different from that of *Les Squames*. In *Itinéraire Sans Fond(s)*[13] and its companion piece *Les Rencontres Internationales de Boîtes*,[14] Kumulus used collaborative creation with various community groups to develop original pieces that look at issues of displacement and exile. The collaborative process was a source of inspiration for *Itinéraire*

Sans Fond(s) that was then devised into a participatory performance by the artists, but in *Les Rencontres Internationales de Boîtes*, the collaboration is the core of the intervention. Both pieces started from the premise that the characters had ten minutes to leave their homes and could only take their most important mementos that could fit into a shoebox. It is around the items saved in the boxes that the characters weave their stories of exile full of memories of intimate moments and lost homelands, family, and friends. *Itinéraire Sans Fond(s)* was developed over a two-year period that included not only improvisation and collaborative writing, but also a five-week journey to the Balkans and Turkey, areas ravaged by natural disasters and war that resulted in millions of displaced people. The entire ensemble travelled by bus, stopping at five locations for research, discussion, and collaborative performance workshops with local artists and communities. After the tour, Compagnie Kumulus reworked the material to create an imagined experience of displacement, not a documentary based on authentic voices of refugees imitated and reproduced by the actors. The show opened at several street theatre festivals in the summer of 2003. While *Itinéraire Sans Fond(s)* has an overall narrative trajectory, it does not have a single storyline that the audience can follow, but rather presents several separate narrative threads that sometimes intersect, sometimes coalesce. No one spectator can see all since the characters' narratives overlap.

The site of the performance is an open, isolated spot on the outskirts of a city, just after dark. The audience waits nearby until two military-like guards with harsh expressions appear, gruffly regroup the spectators often separating men from women, and order them, in an incomprehensible language, to follow silently into the darkness. Leading the group to a gate in a chain-link fence that surrounds the large barren area, the guards force the participants to halt, photograph each one, and then thrust them into the heart of the camp. The only light is from a few campfires, some bare light bulbs, and an occasional flashlight; the only place to sit is on the ground or on an institutional size can of vegetables. In these first few moments, the spectator experiences sensations of confusion, anxiety and discomfort. Unlike the interventions discussed in this chapter thus far, *Itinéraire Sans Fond(s)* casts the spectator in the role of the Other, not only as one of the refugees clearly established by the hostility at the entrance, but also as Outsider within the refugee camp itself. The experience of displacement cannot help but enter into the spectator's body.

The refugees already in the camp are huddled around the fires, often alone, sometimes in pairs. Their torn and dirty clothing shows the effects of travel, and their faces reflect extreme fatigue. At first indifferent

144 *Contemporary Street Arts in Europe*

Figure 19 Compagnie Kumulus, *Les Rencontres Internationales de Boîtes* (banlieue near Paris, France, June 2007)

to the arrival of the newcomers, the refugees sit in silence or softly exchange memories, fears, or angry words with a neighbour. No one speaks the same language although every now and then one can hear words like, 'accident', 'champagne', or 'Brooklyn Bridge'. The spectators gradually enter into the rhythm of the camp as the actors confront them with 'What's your name?' 'How much money do you have? Show me!' and 'Why did you come here?' or begin to share their stories through the contents of their boxes. Multiple 'scenes' occur simultaneously, and the spectators drift from one story to another as they learn about the characters' past lives from their mementos. One refugee opens his box to reveal an item wrapped in a dirty cloth. As he narrates his story in an invented language, he unwraps the object with great care to reveal a human bone. It is all that remains of his brother. After a few moments, he rewraps the bone slowly and lovingly. Although the actual words are incomprehensible, the story is clear. (This story was also used in *Les Rencontres Internationales de Boîtes*. When I saw the piece, the woman standing next to me gasped at this moment when the small bone was revealed and told me later that this story was her story as well. See Figure 19.)

In a woman's box is a small child's dress and a stuffed animal. Another box opens like a book and inside is what looks like a small stage with cardboard cut-outs of a man and a woman. Above them is a tree branch. The scene could be of a wedding, and on the other side of the box is a photograph of two young children. Another box is full of stones. One man animatedly talks about the shop he left behind that sold sodas, jams, face creams, and fruits. Now he doesn't even have 'a nail to hang his hat on'. One young woman dreams of going to America and asks everyone for information and help; another's elegance seems out of place as she reveals the pathetic remains of her wealth. A young couple has an intimate moment as they bring their keys together as though in a kiss. A woman shows a photograph of a missing man and asks the public if anyone has seen him. One woman cannot speak and can only communicate by writing invented words on bits of paper. One character offers to cut the hair of the new arrivals for a small fee. Spectators gather around a character to hear a story, inspired by the treasured items in the box, of a home burned to the ground, a marriage ceremony interrupted, a garden or shop destroyed, a family member killed, a woman raped, or of the beauty and music of the homeland. Some listeners leave after just a couple of minutes to find a different story; others stay a long time with one character singing or dancing together. Sometimes the actor/character gets up leaving the circle around him and joins another circle to listen to a fellow refugee's story thus blurring the distinctions between actor/character and audience member. At a certain moments, several refugees join in song as one plays an accordion. At other times, tensions break out as a man repeatedly slaps a woman who had been speaking loudly and then walks away. When she starts to cry, an audience member comes to comfort her. While the various groupings may seem random, the interactions, especially between actor and spectator, are tightly choreographed.

Toward the end of the piece, some of the refugees begin to play music and dance, encouraging members of the audience to join them, but the moment of happiness is suddenly interrupted by a gunshot. The audience is led out in silence. As they exit, they see their photographs, taken just before entering the camp, pinned onto the fence. Director Bompard says:

> It is violent, but we live in a violent world. The reaction of the spectators is always astonishing. They are more shocked to see violence in the theatre than on television!...In theatre, there is no screen, and the emotions, the reactions are stronger, more alive. When a spectator leaves having lived something, moved, profoundly touched, we have done our job.[15]

While clearly the experience of *Itinéraire Sans Fond(s)*, even when it is uncomfortable and disturbing, does not match the daily experiences of the refugee, it does implant metaphoric memories of discomfort and distress associated with exile into the imagination and body of the spectator.

In 2004, the company built on the work used to create *Itinéraire Sans Fond(s)* to develop another community-based piece, *Les Rencontres Internationales de Boîtes* that has been performed since 2004 in numerous cities throughout Europe and Africa. These 'rencontres' or encounters increased interaction with the public and stretched the boundaries of traditional performance significantly as the goal was an encounter more than a performance. For the event, each community participant works with an actor over a few days to create a shoebox of objects for a character. Often community members draw on their own experiences or on stories of family and neighbours. Once the participants complete their boxes, people from the larger community are invited to the meeting of the boxes. An actor and a community member sit face-to-face across a table and share their stories with each other through the objects and then move on to another face-to-face encounter.

Each story is told three or four times as the audiences move among the tables to listen. Like the shoeboxes in *Itinéraire Sans Fond(s)*, the boxes made by community participants are evocative and vividly narrate a lost life: a box full of feathers and a single egg, one stuffed with all different sorts of buttons, one with dirt and a broken sandal, another with medical supplies. In one very full box are children's crayons, string, paper scissors, tape – things needed in a classroom. Another has military medals,

Subversive Imaginaries: Performing the Other 147

Figure 20 Compagnie Kumulus, *Les Rencontres Internationales de Boîtes* (banlieue near Paris, France, June 2007)

and one is like a small shrine. Through these two shows, Kumulus seeks to provide audience–participants with an experience of being the Other. Compagnie Kumulus places the public in the center of the experience emotionally and spatially, and that physical experience creates affective responses and metaphoric memories that help the public understand exile. However, these interventions, while establishing dialogue and community participation, wobble between a social practice that retains a sense of unease and outsider-ness and one that erases inherent tensions in an attempt to establish connection. The metaphoric memory of Otherness, therefore, can offer contradictory signals.

Few of the street theatre performances that explore Otherness offer facts or background information or even workable solutions to real-life problems; rather they propel the spectator into the world of foreign-ness. The significance is not what the performances say about the Other, but how they say it. The spectator plays a key role not only in the intellectual process of the construction of meanings, but in the practical process of quasi-role-playing in the actual show as he or she enters the performance in a variety of ways and thus inhabits both the imaginary and actual worlds simultaneously. It is the public who penetrates the barrier between the everyday and the aesthetic experiences and, as a result, *experiences* somatically, emotionally and even spatially the issue of Otherness. This experience of the insider/outsider conflict lures the spectators into affectively experiencing the hardships of the Other and their own unexamined prejudices. Thus it offers a different experience of the issue, an aesthetic one to be sure, but also an embodied one, and it thrusts the debate into the democratic public spaces.

For Chantal Mouffe, the belief that the *we-they* conflict will be resolved through dialogue leading to consensus is not only misguided, but dangerous.[16] Consensus, she claims, is simply a form of exclusion. The social world is pluralistic, and with pluralism comes disagreement and conflict so the we-they distinction will not fade away through negotiation. For her, the Other is a political adversary, not an enemy, so that some form of political association based on a 'common bond' may exist even when the two parties are in conflict. For the street interventions that perform Otherness (discussed in this chapter), that common bond is the performance of our humanity. Political theorist, Zillah Eisenstein, writes that 'The homogenizing of a person as different, both institutionalizes and hardens difference; it distances and dehumanizes the "othered." Those who are "othered" become abstractly different, with almost no human content to who they are' (2004: 62). But that is not the end of the story either for Eisenstein or these street performances. Eisenstein claims that:

> Thinking without our skins and with our bodily desires and needs promises a possibility for recognizing human connectedness. Once one recognizes the human claims of one's bodily needs for food, shelter, love, privacy, and sexual autonomy they subvert the isolated self. These are shared meanings of what it is to be human. Each body demands food and can experience hunger.... Differences, of any kind are translatable because human differences are also connections. Only when the self is visioned as completely autonomous and individual do differences become totally distinct and separate. Humanity transcends and articulates polyversality simultaneously because no individual is ever completely different or totally the same as another. This is why I can know differences that are not my own; I can push through to a connection that allows me to see variety—even if in translated form through my own experience which is never identical with any other site. (2004: 53, 61)

6
Community Performance: Community Performatives

Witness/N14: it began with an eighteenth-century map

Witness/N14 began with the discovery of an eighteenth-century map. In 2005, Sarah Harper, the Artistic Director of Friches Théâtre Urbain, a professional street theatre company located on Rue de Toqueville in the seventeenth arrondissement in Paris, began to research the nineteenth-century industrial space in which the company has been housed since the late 1990s. L'Avant-Rue, as it is called, is an evocative space with skylights in the roof several meters above the concrete floor, dates carved into the beams, and brick remains of what could have been a kiln, but its history is obscured by contradictory memories and imagined stories. An old map, drawn by Nicolas de Fer in 1705, revealed that the building is located on the ancient axis between Paris and Rouen, linking the two cities for over one thousand years. Part of the axis follows the ancient Julius Caesar Causeway, and centuries later when France created the *route nationale* system, a large part of this route became the N14, a one hundred and seventeen kilometre road passing through the banlieues of Paris, farmland, woods, towns and small cities. It was one of the major connectors between Paris and the north until it was replaced by the motorway. In the early years of the twenty-first century, although its presence is evident, the Route d'Asnières/N14 is fragmented, with some sections of the old road disappearing under fields and others falling into disrepair in the banlieues.

The discovery of the map aroused Harper's curiosity in the N14's stories and memories and inspired her to discover its traces, its layers of history and legends and its contemporary identity. While the project began as a place on a map, it gradually evolved into what Massey calls 'spatio-temporal events'. Massey encourages abandoning the idea of place and space:

> as on the surface of a map....If space is rather a simultaneity of stories-so-far, then places are collections of those stories, articulations within the wider power-geometries of space. Their character will be the product of these intersections within that wider setting, and of what is made of them. And, too, of the non-meetings-up, the disconnections and the relations not established, the exclusions. All this contributes to the specificity of place. (2005: 130)

It is the idea of 'stories-so-far' that became the focus of Harper's search. Beginning in December 2006, Harper walked the N14 alone, guided by chance encounters as she sought people, images, sounds, and stories linked by their being situated along the route. Harper explains:

> The shopkeeper in Levallois led me to his friend in Asnières who took me to a *pétanque* game where I met a village official who pointed out the local historian who introduced me to an archaeologist. The archaeologist showed me the route's ancient traces and introduced me to a pomologist, who spoke to me about the history of steam engines, and to the director of a natural park, who sent me a *bande dessinée* by Jean Ferlier, the local historian of Vexin. (Harper, 2007b: 6, my translation)

All the people she met shared a story of the N14 – 'how it was before...it was better, it was worse, it was narrower, more important, straighter, full of potholes; it passed through villages, there were roadworks, it is no longer used, but even so it is used, it was better before, it was worse before, it was, it was...' (Harper, 2007b: 6, my translation).[1] Harper began to perceive the ordinary road through the eyes of historians, archaeologists, city officials, and inhabitants as well as through her own artist's eyes, thus giving her an aesthetic/socio-historical *double vision*. As she explored, she asked: 'What are the route's historical traces? What is its contemporary character? Who are my neighbours? What are the boundaries (real and imagined) that separate us and what are the links that bind us?'

Harper's initial act of solitary walking before the artistic community performance project had any form or structure connected her to the geography of the N14 through a physical and emotional awareness of place on a human scale and slow movement through it. 'To feel the place and take the time to meet the people, I chose to walk. Walking is an act of resistance', she claims. Relying on the Situationist strategy of a *dérive* with its chance encounters enabled her to enter the stories of the route as her physical body became the receptive site of the embodied geographies and narratives of the N14. The drawn map of the old route thus became an embodied itinerary of conversations and exchanges, no longer linear, but rather multidimensional, a network of unexpected introductions and interpersonal connections. The *dérive* enabled Harper to conduct a social psychogeographical investigation of the route and to discover urban ambiences and 'distances that actually separate two regions of a city, distances that may have little relation with the physical distance between them' (Debord, in Knabb, 2006: 66). For Harper, walking became an aesthetic protest against the reduction of public space, an emphasis on speed, and the alienation of contemporary life as she sought to unearth the traces revealing the forgotten links between anonymous neighbours. 'My search for treasures began on my street', she wrote in the *Dossier Artistique* (2007b: 5, my translation), and for the next year, she walked slowly – usually around ten kilometres in a day – soaking up impressions, chatting with people she met, stopping for coffee. Several days later, she would begin the next stage of the journey at the exact spot she had stopped. In 2007, with Juliette Dieudonné, a photographer, and Erwan Quintin, a sound designer (*créateur sonore*), Harper walked the length of the route again collecting stories, images, sounds, memories, found objects and videos. They gathered what they saw and heard 'without judgment as to what is important and what is not important', explained Harper. 'We have nothing to do but to be there, to witness.' In the Dossier Artistique, she elaborates:

> Equipped with digital cameras, recorders, video cameras, but also notebooks, we gathered material from our walks and conversations with the inhabitants, people who work along the route, and others. The route and the people we meet there are the heart of the process; they are the core of the creation. An individual is a history in and of him or herself, a part of the memory of the route and the way it is used. (2007b: 5, my translation)

In 1958, Allan Kaprow wrote that artists 'will discover out of ordinary things the meaning of ordinariness. They will not try to make them extraordinary but will only state their real meaning. But out of this they will devise the extraordinary and then maybe nothingness as well' (1993: 9). As Harper, Dieudonné, and Quintin gathered seemingly random bits and pieces, the idea of a 'démarche artistique' began to form, a creation that transformed the bits and pieces of found sound, objects, texts, and images into a series of walking performances, but the real focus of this project remained the dialogue and art-making process with the many varied communities.[2] Harper writes

> *Witness/N14* is definitely an artistic creation, but it is equally a cultural project attempting to establish new relationships between art, environment and people. How can we make visible the lingering links between cities and villages that were connected by regular traffic in the old days?...The inhabitants and the shopkeepers along this Paris-Rouen axis became the unforgettable figures in a story without past or future, but as testaments to the historic layers from which we are made. (2009:5, my translation)

Witness/N14 began as a site-specific inquiry and grew into a community performance project lasting many years and involving several disparate communities. *Community performance*, as it is used in this chapter, is a social practice: a socio-artistic process and event created in collaboration with a particular community or communities.[3] The term 'community' is deeply problematic in its implications of homogeneity, so I use it with trepidation to identify a group of people whether neighbours or strangers, similar or dissimilar, who, even temporarily, choose to work together for a common goal even when these partnerships among various community groups or between the groups and the artists are fraught with unmet expectations, misunderstandings and ethical questions. The collaborative process itself is the creative act of cultural intervention, an aesthetic experience that challenges conventional perceptions and assumptions about art and art-making, interrogates the spaces of and for art, and questions both the dialogues that result in a kind of connected and contextual aesthetic knowledge and even the nature and worth of such a collaboration. The *performance* is as much the choices that a particular group makes about what to exhibit as the performance installation itself. Although inextricably linked to various kinds of social work and grassroots activism, a community performance's emphasis on an artistic sensibility sets it apart from these other activities, but it shares their goals of constructing a critical and embodied awareness of the complexity and seriousness of the issue. As a consequence, the resulting art can act as a provocative socio-political and ethical critique that remains open, indeterminate and fluid responding to the dialogue that the art and the art-making sets in motion. As the complex project of *Witness/N14* began to take form, it was not focused only on a collaborative social art practice, but also on the construction of an *engaged public*, a participatory audience of engaged citizens composed of the artists, the community participants and spectators who came to enjoy the results of the art-making collaboration. All these groups engaged in dialogue, and in art and knowledge construction, and, through these activities, the audience/participants also engaged in democratic practices of freedom, equality and agency.

Grant H. Kester calls this kind of community performance work 'conversation pieces' in which the 'artists have adopted a performative process-based approach. They are "context-providers" rather than "content-providers"' (2004: 1). Kester describes the dialogical aesthetic that leads this work in ways that sound like Freire's pedagogy of the oppressed and Rancière's 'emancipated spectator'. He explains:

> In dialogic practice, the artist, whose perceptions are formed by his or her own training, past projects, and lived experience, comes onto a given site or community characterized by its own unique constellation of social and economic forces, personalities, and traditions. In the exchange that follows, both the artist and his or her collaborators will have their existing perceptions challenged; the artist may well recognize relationships or connections that the community members have become inured to, while the collaborators will also challenge the artist's preconceptions about the community itself and about his or her own function as an artist. What emerges is a new set of insights, generated at the intersection of both perspectives and catalyzed through the collaborative production of a given project. (2004: 95)

The communities are not simply a source of inspiration that the artist takes away and manipulates, but rather they play a key role in the aesthetic dialogue – what Jan Cohen-Cruz has termed 'theatre as call and response' (2010). The *art* is the community art-making process *and* the community performing itself.[4]

As a site-inspired social practice performance project, *Witness/N14* really is a dialogic aesthetic process between the professional artists and the many and varied communities along the Paris-Rouen axis. This artistic process is punctuated by six community walking performances (artistic *dérive* or *parcours*) to exhibit the shared art-making. These *parcours* are specific routes that are actual and metaphoric simultaneously. They represent the logical and necessary aesthetic moments in the developing relationships, not only for the artists, but more importantly for the various community members who contribute to the work and aspire to share their artistic creations with neighbours and strangers. Each parcours occurs only once along a section of the Paris-Rouen route, sometimes up to ten kilometres long. Three parcours have taken place at the time of this writing: *Parcours 1: D'Ici-Là!* (9–13 April 2008, along the block of Rue de Tocqueville on which Avant-Rue is located and inside Friches Théâtre Urbain's artistic space), *Parcours 2: Au-delà du périph* (15–18 October 2009, from Levallois through Clichy, Asnières, Quartre Routes to Gennevilliers—seven kilometres), and *Parcours 5: Un pas de côté* (28–30 May 2010, from Bord'Haut de Vigny to Cléry en Vixen – ten kilometres).[5] (See Colour Plate 13 with images from each of these Parcours.) The fragmented form of the artistic interventions, both temporally and spatially, parallels the fragmented N14 itself, but it is the links found in the stories, people, and locations that fascinate Harper:

> What link can one find between disassociated and displaced communities, between places without a shared history, people who are strangers to one another? In seeking these links, I want to retell the local histories in the context of the Paris/Rouen route. By doing that, I try to reconstruct a **mythic unity** of the axis. I seek to construct a heterotopia, a myth of the Route d'Asnières/N14 from Paris to Rouen, from Rouen to Paris....The story of this route exists, but it is not a single story. It is fractured and jostled by millions of other stories that transcend the banality of its spaces and everyday ordinariness....By placing the route at the center of all the stories we create a unity of place. (Harper, 2007b: 7–8, my translation)

Each of the three parcours that have taken place was characterized by a particular social issue inspired by the geographic locations, by the conversations with people along that section of the route and by the artists' personal reactions to what was seen and experienced there. The community participants and the artists manifested that broad issue (for example, the demolishing of the old buildings and neighbourhoods to make way for urban renewal in Parcours 2) in a range of art activities in their shops, hotels, cafés, streets and wasteland spaces located along the route. The artworks explored the social issues from a variety of perspectives and attitudes. Thus each parcours consisted of several stages offering a 'puzzle of a history told in different forms, a reflection of our urban life' (Harper): fragments of videos on small screens in windows or projected on the facades of buildings, sound montages and live music by local (often amateur) musicians, photographs of all sizes and films in which the roles are played by the local inhabitants, live performance by community members themselves who act as guides to the neighbourhood, and messages – written ones in buses and trains, sound messages in 'mailboxes' or in hidden boxes with motion sensors, or narrative messages spoken or whispered by the inhabitants. The many stages of each parcours represent what Claire Doherty has labelled a 'new situationism' where 'situation' or context is the 'impetus, hindrance, inspiration and research subject for the process of making art' (2004: 7). In *Witness/N14*, the art project originated with the artist, not the community. Harper acted as catalyst and facilitator as groups explored social issues through art, but her presence was crucial to the completion of Parcours 1, 2 and 5. And yet, at the same time, the art project only came into being through the collaboration between the professional artists and the local inhabitants in the artistic process. *Witness/N14* is not a project structured to resolve social ills or repair fragmented communities; rather it uses the art-making to interrogate collaborative practices. What happens when connections are made across difference, distance and time, asks Harper.

Parcours 1: *D'Ici Là!*

As I walk up Rue de Tocqueville, cross Boulevard Pereire, and step onto the bridge that goes over the railroad tracks, I see a table with bright yellow maps. People are gathered around it asking questions and trying to understand the performative 'carte topographique' that offers an 'itinéraire de randonnée', a story of a walk rather than a grid of streets. I listen at the first speaking letterbox to a witness of this disappearing route, a voice documenting it. I pass by a streetlamp wrapped in yellow tape, barely noticing it until I see a large photograph of the same streetlamp I just passed. It is transformed into an art object. I pass the boulangerie, hairdresser, le pressing, and épicerie, each with a television with a different video playing tucked in among the products or displayed in the window. (See Colour Plate 13a.) As I take a photograph of the television peeking out among the vegetables, the owner asks me to wait until she puts on some lipstick so she can be in the photograph too. The day that I take this picture, she and the hairdresser have exchanged videos so I can see her daughter's hair being styled in the shop down the street on a screen between the pears and the melons. I ask her how well she knows the hairdresser, and she says with a little laugh that they are great friends now, but she didn't really know him before. The travel agent features a hand-drawn silhouette of the Rouen cathedral and a parody of a travel video. On my way to the corner café, I pass large windows filled with various texts, a Japanese restaurant with photographs of Rue de Tocqueville, and a bar that was closed down just a few months before with texts commenting on the construction going on inside. Another bar, Le Rond-Point, plays a video that highlights the international gastronomy available on this block of rue de Tocqueville, and when I ask if I can take a photograph, the owner very excitedly turns the snapping of a photo into an event as I must wait until the café's kitchen appears in the video. Then I can take the photo with the owner next to the small screen. (See Figure 21.)

As I open the door to enter the darkened space of Avant-Rue, I am bombarded by so much visual stimulation. Six large video screens, each with a different video, hang at various angles around the space. (See Colour Plate 13b.) I am drawn to one of an old woman on a rural section of the N14 walking toward the camera. She gets closer and closer and then passes with a brief glance at the photographer.[6] She continues on her way, but now the camera videos her receding figure from the back. Another video transforms a seemingly banal block of the N14 in Clichy into the imagined setting of a film noir. There is also a live drummer and guitar player; a reconstruction of a bar on the N14 that offers snacks and drinks; several large photographs of people met along the route whose recorded voices can be heard in the headphones in front of them; a sound-mixing table to create personal sound montages from the sound and music recorded along the route; an 'I was there' corner where I can get in costume and have my picture taken in front of a large screen that displays the photograph of my choice taken along the route; a small room set up like a bus offering three different moving vistas on three walls of the room to simulate multiple views that could be seen through the front and side windows of the bus. I go upstairs to find a walking machine facing a large warehouse-type door. As I walk toward Rouen, the scenery projected on the door changes in front of me. If I walk all the way to Rouen, the door rolls up revealing balloons, flashing lights, and several screens with videos of different parts of the city. There are books to read, foot massagers, informational videos on walking, a chair with shoes on its feet, and more. I am disoriented.

The exhibition lasts from Wednesday through Saturday for several hours each day, and on Sunday, about ten spectators walk from Avant-Rue along the old route as far as Sannois. There are no installations along the way yet, but almost six hours of walking, collecting images and found objects, chatting with local inhabitants, seeing the scenery through different eyes, and 'watching' oneself observing is profoundly moving. As I walked as a fellow 'artist-ethnologist' of Witness/N14, I became hyper-sensitive to smells and sounds, to sights through open doors and windows, to possible links between images. I spoke to people that I would usually pass by. I noticed a 'pink theme' along one stretch of the Route d'Asnières. I took photograph after photograph of shop windows advertising exercise equipment, shoes, pedicures, or Chinese medical treatment 'in pink', of a pale

Community Performance: Community Performatives 157

Figure 21 Friches Théâtre Urbain, *Witness/N14, Parcours 1: D'Ici-Là!* (Paris, France, April 2008)

pink wedding dress that hung in one window, and of a spa, a restaurant, a beauty institute, and a pharmacy painted or highlighted with pink, until suddenly the pink stopped. I have no idea what I would do with the observation, but it was quite exciting to see what I would have overlooked if I had travelled the route just as a way to get from one place to the next. We finally arrived at the final destination for the day, a small gazebo in the middle of a round-about in Sannois, where we chatted sheltered from the rain as we waited for a ride back to Paris.

D'Ici Là!'s very detailed and complex performance installation on the street and in Avant-Rue was the first somewhat exploratory parcours of *Witness/N14*. Harper explains: *D'Ici Là!* is 'conceived as a point of departure for *Witness/N14*, a parcours on the street of rue de Tocqueville and a virtual 'stroll' to Rouen inside Avant-Rue proposed by visual and sound installations created in collaboration with the shopkeepers and inhabitants' (2009: 6, my translation). Although more contained geographically and more theatrical than later parcours, *D'Ici Là!* introduces artistic conventions, like establishing links between neighbours through multiple art forms created collaboratively and through walking as a dramaturgical form of the event, that become more prominent in later parcours. In this first parcours, Harper began to experiment with ways of working that expanded her theatrical palette to include alternative forms of art-making, art work and spectatorship that made boundaries between artist and audience (or performer and onlooker) permeable so that an individual could shift from one role to another during the event or even occupy two contradictory roles simultaneously. Equally, the art-making process and the art work are not clearly distinguishable entities. Suzanne Lacy identifies this type of socio-aesthetic practice as 'new genre public art': the 'source of these artworks' structure is not exclusively visual or political information, but rather an internal necessity perceived by the artist in collaboration with his or her audience' (1995: 19). She argues that in this type of work, the 'strategies of engagement are an important part of its aesthetic language' and the 'relationship [between artist and community] *is* the artwork' (1995: 19, 35).

Clearly, questions around participatory art-making processes are key to this type of social art project,[7] but equally important questions revolve around spectatorship. Who is the audience in this work? Or who is not a member of the audience? What do the audiences see and experience? And what do they take away? As demarcations between spectator and participant fade, the 'spectator' can appear in many guises. Harper confirms that her community collaborators are both co-creators and local spectators enjoying the *art* of their neighbours. They are an informed and engaged audience, knowing the neighbourhood but seeing it with different eyes and altered perspectives. For them, the *détournement* is both experiential and perceptual as their shop windows become art galleries, as letterboxes *speak* their messages, as they *walk* to Rouen seeing sights along the way without leaving Avant-Rue, and as they watch their neighbours *perform* the roles they live in daily life. This *audience* understands and appreciates the art-making process and simultaneously continues that process throughout the event. Nevertheless, that complicit audience is also keen to share their aesthetic collaborations with others, those Harper calls 'tourist–spectators' – visitors who have come to *site-see* and who experience walking the route and hearing its stories as a geographic and aesthetic destination, a 'show'. This public participates in a *randonnée artistique* that not only enables them to envisage the route's stories and memories filtered through artist-community collaborative perspectives, but also to create their own aesthetic narrative. It is unlikely that many tourist–spectators will see everything since the installations occur over a period of years. However, what the spectator finds or chooses to view determines yet another level of participatory audience experience as the spectator writes the *script* of his or her show.

As a tourist–spectator walks along rue de Tocqueville trying to find each of the sites of *art*, it is abundantly clear that the showing of the actual artistic products – the videos on small television screens in shops, restaurants, and among the fruit and vegetables, the photographs, the handwritten and printed texts covering windows, even the sound boxes – paled next to the demonstration of the artistic process of collaboration with the local public. This display of process was made visible not only in the product itself (video, photograph, sound montage, etc.), but in the surrounding *territory*, the environment that included the placement of the product in a particular window, restaurant, or shop and the consequent proud explanation by the resident or shop-owner as to when the video was taken, who was featured, or how he or she contributed to its creation or in disappointed comments that other shops or restaurants feature too prominently in 'their' video. In one case, on rue de Tocqueville, the video was remade to give the café owner a greater role in the artistic decisions about how his café would appear. Harper never relinquishes her artistic presence or authorial role in *Witness/N14*, but she also does not impose it on the art-making of the local inhabitants either. Instead, the collaboration is a give-and-take that interrogates the role of aesthetics in this form of community performance. Like the agonistic debate of a radical democratic society, Harper and her neighbours use art-making as a metaphoric public space that legitimizes aesthetic–democratic debate about the art certainly, but also about individual and community agency as well as aesthetic and socio-political intervention. Together, artists and community collaborators are *citizen artists*, and as such begin to participate in active citizenship.

Witness/N14 is obviously not just the performance installations and interventions in which a public new to the project participates at the various locations along the N14 (although it certainly includes them); it is not just the aesthetic product. Instead, it is a souvenir of the intersections of body, place, and stories. The exhibition of the findings of this relational aesthetic process does not encourage passive spectatorship; on the contrary, it compels the audiences, both community collaborators and tourist-spectators, to participate. It is what Massey calls 'the event of place' (2005: 140) where people, practices and places are all in flux, all constantly changing, 'becoming'. A goal of interaction is evident in the initial questions Harper asked as she first walked the Paris-Rouen axis, and it continues to be an essential ingredient in the work as a whole as she insists that her local collaborators are simultaneously the subjects of the art, the performers and its audience as they perform themselves live, in video, in recordings and in murals, photographs or other visual art works for and with each other and the tourist-spectators. This socially-oriented aesthetic practice of *Witness/N14* encourages the various publics to participate in the artistic intervention as co-creators of embodied places characterized by their unique identities, the relations of the people who live and work there, and their histories – Massey's concept of place as social relations in space/time, not geographic locations with boundaries and fixed identities.[8]

The exhibition inside Avant-Rue was more recognizably *Art* than the interventions on the street; however, it taught the tourist-spectators how to see and appreciate the display of artistic process when they went back outside and, more importantly, how to participate in the art-making process. This indoor performance exhibition of *D'Ici Là!* foregrounded interactivity between spectator and art and allowed audience members to become actors and creators of their own *show*. Harper explains that the installation is animated by and with the presence of the public. At each stage of the exhibition the public must activate the works themselves, implicating them in the research and in the choices. The spectator looks at large portraits of people met along the route and then chooses which interview(s) to listen to, mixes recordings of found sounds and music into unlimited combinations at the sound table, or dresses in a costume and poses in front of a screen displaying an image of a location along the N14 of the spectator's choice for a photograph that proves, 'I was there!'. But, I believe the interactive strategies of the performance installation do more than allow a spectator to participate in the artwork. In some cases, they shift the frame of performance to include the spectator both as *deliberate protagonist* in a self-composed drama and as *accidental protagonist* in a drama composed by a fellow spectator. When the accidental protagonist suddenly realizes that his or her ordinary actions are a performance for the person watching, the disconcerting realization 're-frames the theatrical', to use Alison Oddey's phrase:

> I am not outside the frame looking in, but rather inside embracing the contradictory, the co-existing emotions of human experience, ambiguity and the colliding of intertextual elements, which both dislocates and displaces my expectations of seeing towards a way of viewing differently... I become the image subsumed. I perform the work. I witness my own gaze. (2007: 1–2)

I want to call this altered role of the tourist–spectator *spectagonist*: spectator and protagonist in one body acting in and watching a self-composed show and also becoming aware of the gaze of others as one inadvertently *performs* in a drama composed by a fellow spectagonist. Here, the public does not just participate in the creative process. Without the public, (both collaborators living and working along the N14 and audiences new to the project), the artwork with its transmutations of spectatorship does not exist. The walking performance is the spectagonist's embodied experience of the route guided and influenced by the vision of the artistic collaboration certainly, but as the spectagonist is an 'emancipated spectator', it is still his or her own story. One obvious example of the concept of spectagonist occurred in Avant-Rue around a video screen playing a film that could be viewed from both sides. The lighting on one side turned people close to the screen into silhouettes *performing* for an audience on the other side. My gaze was directed to this *performance* by the very clear silhouette of the drummer as he played. As I watched him and the spectators listening to him, walking past him, or making unheard comments, I realized that I, too, am a protagonist in a 'shadow play' for the spectators on the other side of the screen. (Colour Plate 13b shows the drummer with the lighted screen behind him.) What happens in terms of audience reception and awareness in Avant-Rue within a clearly aesthetic setting is then taken out onto the street. Here, the real world inserts itself between moments of performance. I carried the role of spectagonist onto the street, I realized, as I gazed through the window of the coiffure at the video of the hair stylist blow-drying the long hair of a young girl and at the same hair stylist inside actually blow-drying the long hair of another young girl. I was in my research mode and made a mental critique of the juxtaposition. Suddenly, I became aware of my reflection in the large mirror inside revealing me *performing* the role of *art critic*. And, I saw the hair stylist and the girl smiling as they watched me in the mirror watching them – a very unsettling experience. They were the performers in my scenario, but I was the performer in theirs. On the Sunday walk, that reframing of the theatrical occurred often as I watched myself and the other walkers performing the role of artist–ethnologist and was aware of them watching me. We were all spectagonists. The disorientation that I felt gazing in the hairdresser's mirror resurfaced as I noticed that the photographer, Juliette Dieudonné, was taking pictures of me taking pictures, just like those on the blog, of a glove or a sock abandoned on the street. I was the accidental protagonist suddenly aware of my performance and the accidental spectator amused at the seriousness with which I played my role.

Parcours 1: D'Ici Là! of *Witness/N14* certainly engaged the inhabitants of Rue de Tocqueville in the art-making process, but Harper's strong artistic vision provided the tourist-spectator with a vivid participatory experience of seeing geographic places as embodied social spaces of community and of creating his or her own community-specific script with ordinary found objects and sounds as well as with local community members. The importance of this outside public remained very strong in this initial foray into social art. In Parcours 2 and 5, that emphasis shifted much more to the local participant-spectators along the route and to the collaborative art-making as a way of establishing links not only between isolated pockets of inhabitants but also between various communities and the social services and institutions that support them. The tourist spectator is an invited, but outside, observer of a longer relationship, only parts of which have been chosen by the art-makers to share. Parcours 2 and 5 shifted the location of the performance event both temporally and spatially as the artistic process with the various neighborhoods was the art work. It is very difficult to document this work in photographs since they cannot capture the dynamic exchange between artists and local inhabitants. The photographs just look like people talking, so visual records tend to prioritize the installations that actually represent just a small portion of the artwork.

The performative event in which the community member becomes artist parallels the process of developing a critical awareness of the socially constructed nature of one's lived world, introduced by Paulo Freire (as discussed earlier in the book). Freire claims that the hallmark of oppression is a passivity and an unthinking acceptance of one's reality and that to be fully human, to be an engaged citizen, one must be active and reflective. As oppressed peoples develop a critical awareness of their social reality and begin to understand what they can do to change it through their own actions, they assume a pro-active position rather than just waiting for help from the outside:

> We become capable of imaginatively, curiously, 'stepping back' from ourselves—from the life we lead—and of disposing ourselves to 'know about it.' The moment came when we not only *lived*, but began to *know* that we were living—hence it was possible for us to *know* that we know, and therefore to know that we could do more. What we cannot do, as imaginative, curious beings, is to cease to learn and to seek, to investigate the 'why' of things. We cannot *exist* without wondering about tomorrow, about what is 'going on,' and going on in favour of what, against what, for whom, against whom. We cannot *exist* without wondering about how to do the concrete or 'untested feasible' that requires us to fight for it. (1994: 98)

In *Pedagogy of the Oppressed*, Freire examines an educative process resulting in personal and/or community empowerment that he calls 'problem-posing education', a process which emphasizes communication where all involved are 'jointly responsible for a process in which all grow' (1989: 67). Traditional education, explains Freire, resembles banking in that the teacher deposits information into the mind of the student and thus discourages original thinking and simultaneously passes on traditions and prejudices. In contrast, problem-posing education uses dialogue as the tool that enables the speakers to 'perceive critically *the way they exist* in the world *with which* and *in which* they find themselves; they come to see the world not as a static reality, but as a reality in process, in transformation' (1989: 71). Through dialogue, the participants investigate other people's thinking so that they can achieve a critical perception of the world rather than accept an imposition of the values and beliefs of the more powerful or numerous. One voice does not perpetually hold the privileged position, but instead multiple voices share the authority and enrich the world view. Freire writes, 'Whereas banking education anesthetizes and inhibits creative power, problem-posing education involves a constant unveiling of reality. The former attempts to maintain the *submersion* of consciousness; the latter strives for the *emergence* of consciousness and *critical intervention* in reality' (1989: 68).

Parcours 2 and 5 of *Witness/N14* so blurred art and life boundaries that many of the installations were missed by the outside public, but not by the local community members who participated in the process that paralleled problem-posing education advocated by Freire. These art projects balanced community and social activist needs with aesthetic demands in the collaborative process. The tourist-spectators who walked the routes to see the various installations and to engage in conversation with the artists and community participants seemed to be late-comers to the art event that really happened during the art-making process. In Parcours 2 and 5, the performers are the community members who are in their shops or hotels sometimes eager to talk to the tourist-spectators, sometimes annoyed at their disruption to business. And the tourist-spectators enter the art-making process as they engage in conversation with community members who then can *perform* special activities, like pointing out unique aspects of the neighbourhood, narrating its history, or explaining an exhibition they set up in their window. But they can also *perform* the role they live in daily life with the tourist-spectator as co-performer.

Parcours 2 offers a 'directed' dérive[9] through northern banlieues of Paris, and Parcours 5 offers one in a more rural setting through villages but also on an abandoned stretch of the N14 that runs right next to the motorway. Here, weeds poke through the cracks in the pavement. Walking these two parcours after the first one on a Paris block gives me a better sense of the entire route so that I can appreciate its changing character from an urban setting to a rural one. Seeing the N14 on foot guided by the vision and perspectives of the artist-collaborators, both from Friches Théâtre Urbain and the neighborhoods and towns along the way, challenges the walker to see beyond the banalities of this old road and to experience the ordinary in new ways as bits and pieces of found sound, objects, texts, and images coalesce into many site-specific installations.

Parcours 2: *Au-delà du périph* and Parcours 5: *Un pas de côté*

Parcours 2 begins at a small booth ('agence de voyage') in a courtyard near rue Victor Hugo in Levallois, a stretch of the route that is dominated by office buildings, businesses and banks. I pick up a psychogeographic map of the seven-kilometre dérive. In the corner of the map just above a tiny picture of the booth, I can't miss a large photograph of a well-loved child's stuffed animal with colourful patches to cover holes and long arms to replace original ones.

The performative map not only provides the route of the walking performance and the spots along the route where there are performance installations and exhibitions, but it also highlights some of the areas where there is extended interaction with local inhabitants or buildings that no longer exist

Figure 22 Friches Théâtre Urbain, *Witness/N14, Parcours 2: Au-delà du périph* (October 2009)

with short descriptions, photographs and drawings. At the top of this piece of the map, for example, is a red box, the shipping container that shows the film created with the local inhabitants as writers and actors (described below). Near the booth, I approach the first sound installation hidden in a letterbox. As I lift the lid, I hear 'One day in March 2007, I took a photo of a little notice that said "Charlotte has lost her doudou in Levallois Perret" accompanied by a photo of the worn toy.' I listen to the imagined stories of Charlotte's lost treasure created and narrated by local children who invent what could have happened to the stuffed animal as she began her adventure. An adult voice interrupts with questions asking: Did Charlotte ever find her doudou again? Did she cry a lot? Is the doudou now loved by another child? As I continue along the street looking in the windows of shops and businesses, I see images of the stuffed animal next to bits of text, drawings and photographs revealing traces of history along this stretch of the route as though it is guiding my journey: in Magasin Cycles et Sport Alex Singer, I learn about Singer's innovations to the French bicycle and in Garage Renault, an installation explains the impact of the automobile on the evolution of the Paris-Rouen axis. I don't realize it at the time, but the loss of a loved stuffed animal parallels the saga of the loss of treasured buildings and communities that may look worn, ugly, and in disrepair to outsiders, but are significant to those who live with them. This theme ties the disparate stages of Parcours 2 together.

After completing the walk along this short piece of the route transformed by the perspective of the stuffed animal, I walk quite a way without any installations, but the re-enchantment of the urban spaces experienced earlier remains as I see parts of the ordinary street differently. I pass under a railroad bridge into Clichy, and I enter a totally new imaginative space, and for the tourist-spectator, the most theatrical. In front of me is a huge poster for an old film noire, 'Le Monte-Charge'. A little further along I find a phone box with a pool of blood inside, and as I approach the telephone rings. I pick it up to hear an enigmatic message by a voice clearly upset and frightened, and just up the street in the Stop-Bar I can watch the old film on a small television. Suddenly the scene I have just seen, seems to be happening live in front of me as two men enter the bar, argue and run off with one chasing the other. That theatrical presence and other installations evoke the film as I enter dirty bedrooms in a run-down rooming house that was actually used as the set for the film, glimpse a woman in a red dress in the distance, and hear eerie sound tracks in a restaurant are actually performed by the local inhabitants. Like the child's lost doudou, they reference what is lost – a transitory moment of fame when this section of the street was full of activity and excitement as the setting for the film. A bit further on, the next installations in Clichy are the actual buildings marked for demolition or empty lots where other buildings have already been torn down. One sound installation, a recording by local inhabitant and activist, explains that the whole block is being demolished and 'renewed' in spite of its rich history and neighbourhood gathering places.

As I cross the River Seine into Asnières, I can sense that the Parcours is shifting in focus to foreground a much more obvious presence of the community collaborators as I am met by a local historian who tells me so much about the area's past and present.

The Carrefour in the centre of the town has not changed much in one hundred years, and the installations along the way highlight the interdependence of the commerce and the route. Here I meet Madame Prago in the news agent/haberdashery. She has been at the shop since her stepmother bought it in 1932 and prides herself that it has not changed in all these years. In between the sales of newspapers and of needles, thread and buttons, she tells

Figure 23 Friches Théâtre Urbain, *Witness/N14, Parcours 2: Au-delà du périph* (October 2009)

me that she works from seven in the morning to nine at night, that she is an important fixture in the town, and that I should go so someone else can talk to her! What a formidable performance of herself! I am served mint tea by Mohamed, the manager of Hôtel de la Poste (a major stopping point on the Paris-Rouen axis one hundred years ago) and taken to peek into two rooms: in one, a sleeping weary traveller – a human-sized foot snoring loudly in the bed – and in another, the bits and pieces left by a writer. (See Colour Plate 13c.) At the bookstore, the owner, M Lenore, has organized a 'book signing', specifically for Parcours 2, with authors who have written about walking, the anatomy of feet, and pilgrimages. I ask M Lenore about this project, and he happily recounts the neighbours and city officials supporting it that he has met, the meetings where he began to see his ordinary block with eyes attuned to its aesthetics, and the small events he has organized in response to the project. He offers me a gift of the poster he designed to announce the book-signing. I leave reluctantly because I can see from the map that I have a long walk ahead of me, and my feet are already tired.

The final two major stages of Parcours 2 really highlight the art-making of the community members. A shipping container at Quatre Routes has been transformed into a small cinema showing 'Au Port des Quatre Routes', the film on the neighbourhood written and performed by the inhabitants who came together for this event. They often met in the cafés at this crossroads before the area was razed to the ground, again in the name of urban renewal. The film was shot on site and reveals the particular international character of this part of the route as it narrates a story of displacement when local inhabitants learn they must move because their apartment building is being torn down. A bit further on in a small grocery, Afric Quatre Routes, the owner displays a video of himself selling his vast selection of African vegetables. And in the final stop, I have a coffee and listen to local teen-agers who are accomplished rappers.

Seven months later, I return to France to participate in Parcours 5 along a semi-rural section of the N14 where the inhabitants all told Harper the same story: the young people are fleeing the area because of rising house prices and no work. The villages are transforming into long distance suburbs of Paris where the new inhabitants travel a long way to work all week long and spend the weekend resting rather than investing in village life, so 'the life of the village is dying'. Again, loss is a predominant theme. The parcours begins near a derelict factory where over 600 people worked until it was closed just two years before. I pick up my map and walk past the few houses in the village of Le Bord'Haut de Vigny. The inhabitants sought to present key moments in village life in large 'staged' photographs: an Easter treasure hunt, an autumn walk, the 'past' when one of the houses was a brothel, the oldest couple in

Figure 24 Friches Théâtre Urbain, *Witness/N14, Parcours 5: Un pas de côté* (May 2010)

the village. One inhabitant has turned the front of her house into a museum gallery revealing the history of the village in old photographs and memorabilia that she explains with enthusiasm to everyone who stops to look. On the window sill are small toy cars and trucks to emphasize the significant impact of the opening of the Motorway on the tiny village that is never visited now that the N14 is no longer used except as a local road.

I meet one of Harper's collaborators who invites me into her home and offers me coffee. She talks about the project and how much it revived the village that relished celebrating their special moments and exhibiting their special talents, like wine-making. On leaving the tiny village, the walkers take a little detour to walk the Julius Caesar Causeway through the fields. I travel this section of the parcours with Harper's mother and father who have come for the performative event. In their seventies, they set a fast pace along the path enjoying the scenery but confused about the 'theatre'. Both professional actors, they question me about this social art form. I try to explain that in this parcours the artistic process is the art work, and the tourist-spectator is the outsider allowed to see only small pieces of the collaborative art-making. Suddenly we come across a series of children's drawings nailed onto posts.

Harper had worked with the children at the local school and asked them to draw the road that they would like to walk. Their imaginative responses blowing in the breeze acquired an eerie significance that offered a vision of a world not bound by adult logic. The road was their road, and we tourist-spectators could only get a glimpse. While we learn about the villages and the impact of the abandonment of the N14 for the motorway, the real art, even for the tourist-spectator, is in the moments in the chance encounters with pieces of community art or brief conversation with the inhabitants.

At a picnic prepared by the collaborators – another form of their art-making as they prepared 'typical' dishes from local products – I watch testimonial-videos of many of the collaborators. I continue on toward Cléry-en-Vexin, the final stop. These last four or so kilometres are dotted with many small installations – a series of playful scarecrows (See Colour Plate 13d), graffiti art by the local young people, trompe l'oeil photography of the area, two pup tents with the large sleeping foot and the objects of the writer seen in the hotel rooms in Parcours 2, a word puzzle spread out over a large space, and an 'outdoor café' (some chairs on the side of the road and juice).

Figure 25 Friches Théâtre Urbain, *Witness/N14, Parcours 5: Un pas de côté* (May 2010)

Local activists had copied the idea of a performative scarecrow and had placed two additional ones protesting various governments policies that affected the area in the centre of a round-about. In the final village, the villagers created life-size cardboard cut-outs of themselves and videos their village life – a time suspended – and Cedric Rosseuw shared his garden of flowers, vegetables and his paintings.

As it develops, *Witness/N14* is becoming a very complex, multi-layered project that braids together aesthetic vision, social activist impulses, community empowerment and democratic practices in public spaces to explore and reveal historical resonances and contemporary realities of a road that has lost its national significance as the major connector between Paris and Rouen, but retains its local importance to its inhabitants. *Witness/N14* encourages its tourist-audiences to understand sections of this road from the local perspective. While the artistic fragments that these outsiders see encourage an awareness of individual and community identity on the part of this audience who comes to see the public event, even more interesting and significant, I think, is the socially engaged art that happens through the collaborative artistic process between artists and their neighbours and neighbourhoods. Much of that community-specific art may be invisible to a spectator who comes to walk for a couple of hours along the N14, but for the communities involved it not only forges important intersections between art and activism, aesthetics and social issues, but also develops interpersonal relations among neighbours who were unknown to each other before the project. Thus the several parcours of *Witness/N14* push the idea of the democratic performatives for their multiple audiences in interesting ways. The form and process of *Witness/N14*, inseparably intertwined, firmly embed the project in the realm of socially engaged art. And while it has an existence as aesthetic object, the artistic originality of *Witness/N14* comes from its performative investigation into the conceptual and political links between corporeality, connection across difference, landscape, and mobility.

Walking is the key dramaturgical tool used by Harper, Dieudonné, Quintin and their collaborators along the route. But walking also leads to an embodiment of geographic place by transforming spatial location into embodied experience as the body must necessarily feel the natural surroundings (the weather, the inclines and broken pavement, the fatigue and sore feet). Walking connects body and place, as both geographic location and Massey's social relations. The act of walking, not only on the part of the artistic team and the community collaborators, but also as a performance strategy for the tourist-audiences at the public events, represents a political act of 'taking back the streets' and of insisting that public spaces remain public. Rebecca Solnit wrote:

> Walking is only the beginning of citizenship, but through it the citizen knows his or her city and fellow citizens and truly inhabits the city rather than a small privatized part thereof. Walking the streets is what links up reading a map with living one's life, the personal microcosm with the public macrocosm, it makes sense of the maze all around. (2001: 176)

While it is clearly hyperbolic to assume walking the length of the N14 will lead to radical democracy, the walker does claim his or her right to reclaim and occupy the public space for dialogue, encounter and art. Artist Krzysztof Wodiczko insists, 'Public space is where we often explore and enact democracy' (Phillips, 2003: 33). In *Witness/N14*, that public space is reframed so that it is not just defined by its function, but also by its possibilities, by its Deleuzean 'becoming' that does not transform it into something that already exists, but into something not previously imagined. Here the public can engage with social issues by helping define them, so as the lost stuffed animal in Levallois becomes a metaphor for loss of interpersonal connection along this stretch of the route dominated by office buildings, businesses and banks, it also offers a contrasting metaphor for awakened imagination. Here as the walkers travel slowly up rue Victor Hugo discovering unexpected images of Charlotte's *doudou* that *détourne* this section of the route that seems to lack any personality, we realize that the doudou is leading us along a transformed city street. This non-descript block suddenly becomes magical as the doudou *guides* the tourist-spectator to look into windows and listen to sound installations that reveal obscure historical moments that bring the site to life. We even notice the name of the street.

Clearly, the most obvious democratic performative in *Witness/N14* is participation in art-making that contributes to or intervenes in official discourses. The community collaborators discover a voice, an agency or an embodied sociality as they engage in artworks to tell their version of the character and uniqueness of the N14 along their section of the route, and in so doing, they both articulate and begin to construct a communal identity that did not exist or was invisible. The local residents are co-creators of the art works, but also the subject of the art and its primary audience. They exhibit the art in their homes and shops and on their walls and streets for each other and for a visiting tourist public. As they *perform* the roles that they *live* in everyday life, their perspective shifts, and the distance that the aesthetic performance establishes, enables them to see their personal role in a larger social context as a key element in the social fabric. They tell their stories, but they also write new ones.

Witness/N14 is radical art that encourages and in many cases achieves active citizenship, but it does not set itself up in opposition to institutional or government support. That does not mean that the various participating groups of people rubber stamp official policies; on the contrary, these community formations use the art-making process to begin to articulate aloud what they love about where they live and work and what troubles or angers them and to share their concerns and their propositions for the future in the art works that they choose to show to a wider public that can easily include policy-makers. As Solnit insists, 'the streets are where the people become public and where their power resides' (2001: 176). And, *Witness/N14* has begun to establish connections between local inhabitants and the previously nameless and faceless individuals working for various social services and governmental institutions – groups that had assumed indifference or hostility toward each other. It has introduced a role that art can play in creating that more sustainable future.

I think that *Witness/N14 witnesses* and reveals layers of social, economic, and cultural history (both actual and imagined) and contemporary realities that give the route its unique character to a range of publics all of whom observe and participate in varied levels of intensity. The specifics change as one walks along the road, but each section offers an embodied social space of community and cultural debate. *Witness/N14* makes what is often invisible if one is just passing through, hurrying from one place to another, or if one passes through so often that the place is no longer *seen*, visible and engaging. Perhaps even more significantly, *Witness/N14* encourages the neighborhood participants and tourist-spectators who walk the public *parcours* to witness community collaboration and the empowerment of individuals who live and work along the route as they become involved in the artistic process. I particularly enjoyed chatting with M Lenore, the owner of Librairie La Boîte à Lettres, who said he made his first artwork in the poster he created to advertise the writers who had published books on walking that he had invited to the shop as *his* part of the performance. His tiny shop was filled not only with audience members, but also with passers-by who came to buy a book or just glanced in the shop window and wanted to know what was going on. Later in Parcours 2, I was quite moved as I watched Sarah Harper help an elderly community member from the café to the shipping container showing the film, *Au Port des Quatre Routes,* in which he played a major role so he could see himself on screen. He grinned with pride.

In another manifestation of the project, *Le Glissement des Axes sur la Route avec nos Voisins,* Harper tests the ideas and guiding principles of *Witness/N14* by creating a 'spectacle-performance-conférence' in which the specific sites along the route are documented in soundscapes, photographs, videos and installations, but they come alive through the actual and virtual presence of the local residents with whom she collaborated. '"I invite some of my neighbours to come on stage with me 'to play with me' and tell their stories. For the more timid, I will call them during the performance, and others will be integrated into the text through videos taken over the past several years', explains Harper (2010: 2). Personal anecdotes are braided with social debate on the issues important to the participants: the explosion in the number of cars on the roads, youth violence, unemployment, demolishment of neighbourhoods in the name of urban renewal, the breaks in biodiversity corridors made by the motorways and urban expansion. In *Le Glissement des Axes,* neighbours from different distant parts of the route (and participating in different Parcours) are in dialogue with each other 'on stage', via video conferencing, or by shared recordings.

The success of the community collaborations established in *Witness/ N14* has led to a new commissioned project in which Harper seeks to establish connections across difference and in dangerous and confrontational public spaces with an art-making community response to a serious social conflict. After an incident in 2011 between rival gangs from Asnières and Gennevilliers (towns in *Witness/N14:* Parcours 2), in which a young boy was killed at the metro station Les Courtilles, city officials and police officers asked Harper to add art-making to the work of the social workers, the police and others. In *Lieu Commun,* an ongoing artistic project developing over several years, Harper and multiple generations of the competing communities develop common art-making initiatives that encourage conversation and collaboration across antagonism. Harper and the collaborators in *Lieu Commun* seek to establish a peaceful and legal re-appropriation of public space by local inhabitants of the rival communities together to begin a process of lessening the split between them. The project thus asks how can we share a common space. It seeks answers in the stories and experiences of an equal number of participants from both communities and, significantly, in the transformation of the contested site around the metro station into a shared public space of dialogue and debate. Harper seeks to create art with the local inhabitants that draws on the poetics of youth street culture and to develop meeting places and situations for the exchange of ideas.

For the initial stage, *Espaces Rêvés*, the focus is on the metro station, a site of confrontation for the youth. Harper and photographer Juliette Dieudonné started the work by establishing a series of social encounters between residents from the two towns. Each encounter revolved around a particular theme important to a specific sub-group within the community, for example, mothers of the gang members, teenagers, or grandparents. The encounter was guided by a specialist who explored topics like notions of one's territory, biodiversity in nature and society, and combat, but the discussion was really led by an equal number of participants from Asnières and Gennevilliers. The encounters initiated communal art-making as the inhabitants from one town collected photographs, sketches, interviews and stories from the other and together, they created large collages depicting the two communities and their hopes for the future. These collages have been displayed as a permanent installation on tall glass walls of the metro station, Les Courtilles, since October 2011. *Espaces Rêvés* thus seeks to explore collective ways to bridge difference through art and shared public space.

The walking, witnessing, and conversing throughout the entire project of *Witness/N14* and its varied offshoots create a dynamic site of encounter that revises political and personal links between geographic location, historical traces, and embodied identities in order to make visible what no longer exists or never existed except in the imagination. Augé wrote that the old *routes nationales*, like the N14, 'used to penetrate the intimacy of everyday life' (98). Walking and talking the route questions that nostalgic idea of intimacy, but it also provides a space for spontaneous connection. As Claire Bishop argued:

> Art should not have to surrender itself to exemplary gestures, but it can instead use the medium of participation to articulate a contradictory pull between autonomy and social intervention; moreover, it can reflect on this autonomy both in the structure of the work *and* in the conditions of its reception to subsequent audiences. (2009: 255)

While this approach may be disconcerting or confusing, as Bishop points out, it does offer a challenging and provocative approach to social engagement with community performance like *Witness/N14*.

Postscript: Beyond the Street

The concept of the *street* or public space is shifting and elusive. It lacks a clear and permanent identity and instead reflects a Deleuzian 'becoming'. Art historian Patricia Phillips writes:

> Public space has not disappeared, but it often appears in new guises....There remains a physical and territorial dimension to public space, but there is a growing recognition of its more quixotic, intangible characteristics. Public space has become cellular and molecular, dynamic and granular... immaterial and invisible. (2003: 129)

As many of the performances in this book attest, public space is not just a geographic place, but it is also a discursive site linked to concepts of democracy and civil society, interpretations of what (the) public means, and issues of institutional power, individual agency and inclusion/exclusion.[1] Artists who work in public spaces relish these ambiguities and constantly seek to discover innovative ways not only to use, but also to conceive public space. The social practice in Opéra Pagaï's *Entreprise de Détournement* and *Safari Intime*, Compagnie Kumulus' *Itinéraire Sans Fond(s)* and *Les Rencontres Internationales de Boîtes*, and Friches Théâtre Urbain's *Witness/N14* and *Lieu Commun* create dialogic public spaces through community collaboration, often tied to a geographic place, but not always. Cyberspace, as seen most blatantly in the work of Liu Bolin, Desiree Palmen, Lili Jenks and Fallen Fruit, creates a limitless public space not restricted by actual locations. In some recent work, the human body has become a public space for interventions. But just as actual streets can go unexpected places, street artists constantly try to identify surprising and not-previously-imagined public spaces. I would like to end with two examples that highlight the diversity and unpredictability of the art form, but there are many others that I could have chosen.

Belgian artist, Kurt Demey, stretches the concept of the *street* into the human mind in *L'Homme Cornu* (The Horned Man) where he exposes the mind as a form of public space that challenges clear demarcations between public and private. Here, the text and special world of the performance are created through the thoughts of spectators in the audience, and Demey uses mind-reading techniques to guide, manipulate and reveal these thoughts. In this piece, the public space is ambiguous and intangible, actual and imagined, private and public simultaneously as the most intimate of our personal spaces – our mind – 'becomes' the public space in spite of us. Demey's art participates in what is now called the 'new magic' movement that uses magic and mentalism (mind-reading) as a theatrical language to explore alternative levels of reality and comprehension. Raphael Navarro, one of the initiators of this movement defines 'new magic':

> an art whose language is the diversion of the real within the real. Magic is a way to situate oneself in relationship with the real—space, time, objects...—in a special kind of way. Movies and paintings divert the real into the physical space of the image. Theatre and literature suggest it in a metaphoric space. New magic plays with the real within the real: that is to say, within the same space-time offered by perception. Images no longer correspond with an illusionist act. They make up a proper order to reality. (*New Magic*: 5)

New magic is not about sleight of hand and rabbits pulled from hats, but rather about making an audience question what they think they see and know, about creating doubt and reflection, and about changing what reality might mean. It is not about a series of tricks, but rather about contextualizing the effects and *affects* of the magic into a story or encounter that opens the door to different perceptions and understandings of the logical and the knowable. Navarro continues, 'Since magic is a threshold to the invisible, its goal is to bring into existence what does not exist....As an artistic form, it represents an ability to transform the world....It suggests another approach to reality' (*New Magic*: 5).

Demey's company, Rode Boom, was founded in 2006 to explore new magic and paraphysics and to discover links between the mind and the street. Public space exists in one's mind as much as in the city, claims Demey. The city is a physical space, but it is also a psychological space of people's favourite paths or places they avoid and memories of encounters there. But, for Demey, these individual stories of particular places represent the *mind* of the city – the city is occupied by stories. When we go into the street, we experience our individual stories *and* others' stories that inhabit the public space and influence or affect our responses even when we are unaware of that happening. The interconnected stories thus break down the barrier between the street and the mind. Demey's art strives to reveal those links.

In an early work, *Avec ma tête dans l'arbre* (With my head in a tree) Demey created a form of land art that suggested a physical link between public spaces and the mind. White plaster life-size figures bury their faces in a tree trunk becoming like a strange branch or root. Passers-by often approach the figures and put their ears close to the point where face and tree fuse as if to listen in on a conversation between the two. There is no taped dialogue to hear, and yet, many stand with their ears to the tree for a very long time. The land art here creates a striking visual image, but the affective response it arouses comes from the imaginary world it conjures up. For Demey, magic creates an environment of poetic illusion and surreality that enables his audiences to experience and begin to accept an alternate reality.

L'Homme Cornu begins as the audience enters a garden or courtyard. Two men, each with large curved horns growing from their backs where wings would be if they were angels, sit at a table playing with chestnuts. Around them are five small tables with glass bowls filled with a clear liquid. One man gets up and begins to play haunting music on a bass; the other walks to a tree and scratches his horns against the bark. 'The horns grow under my skin where one waits to see wings grow. That was the first thing I felt. The second... it was lies becoming clearer and sharper. How can we live without lies? What is truth but acceptable lies? Our lies seem secure in our heads, but our bodies betray us', Demey begins. Throughout the piece, Demey alternates a lyrical and cryptic narrative reinforced by the music with participatory exchanges with audience participants – so many that they cannot be planted – that reveal that he can read their minds and manipulate their thoughts. He hands four chestnuts, three brown and one white, to the audience and asks them to pass the chestnuts around until he stops them. He turns away as spectators try to come up with unpredictable ways to move the nuts among them. He soon says stop and asks the four with the chestnuts to join him. He explains that the three with the brown nuts will respond to his questions with lies, but the one with the white chestnut will give truthful answers. It does not take long for him to know who is holding the white. He asks four others to come join him and choose one of the five bowls to stand by. He confides that four are water, but one is a flammable liquid. Demey goes to each person, one by one, giving him or her the option to change bowls, but once the participant settles on a bowl, he or she must have a sip. By the time he reaches the fourth, this last person knows that one of the two bowls is not water. He or she always chooses the water however. Demey then goes to the fifth bowl and lights the liquid. He has manipulated the participants' thoughts so that they choose the correct bowls. It is surprising to speak to the participants after the show who repeat over and over how sure they were that they would be drinking water. Even they were surprised by their certainty.

In another encounter, a spectator thinks he is standing upright whereas he is falling backward to be caught by Demey. One spectator reacts to a feather tickling his nose, but there was nothing. On a video on the Rode Boom website, a young participant expresses his disbelief at the disconnect between what he thought he knew and what he saw. He shakes his head, saying 'strange'. The exchange that I found the most startling, however, was the one that showed an ability to reproduce a line drawing that a participant was imagining. A spectator was asked to draw a simple design on a card. Demey then asks a few questions and shakes his head saying that she is able to block his mind-reading. He asks his musician, Joris Van Vinckenroye, to sit facing her as she mentally erases her design line by line. As she does that, Van Vinckenroye draws the image – a musical note when I saw it, but other images in other shows. Both drawings are shown to the audience, and they match perfectly. As spectator after spectator proves that their thoughts are being read or manipulated, the audience's sense of reality and assumptions about privacy are overturned. Demey interrogates where public space ends and private space begins when people's thoughts can be exposed and manipulated. He demonstrates that our thoughts cannot remain private, that non-verbal communication is much clearer and stronger than we imagine, and that what we think about can be manipulated. Thus, *L'Homme Cornu* also raises questions about free will and whether we can make independent choices or whether we are simply responding to stimuli – that, of course, draws attention to the power of advertising and echoes the ideas of Guy Debord.

L'Homme Cornu is the first piece of a quartet called *Evidence Inconnue* (Unknown Evidence) that challenges the certainty of what we believe or want to believe about our world from a range of perspectives. In *La Ville Qui Respire* (The City that breathes), the audience participates in the stories embedded in the city, not one's own stories associated with a place, but the stories of strangers that permeate the city even if they are not seen or heard. A person inhabits the city, but the city also inhabits the person, says Demey, and in this piece he seeks to expose the hidden life of the city by presenting scenes that the audience knows cannot be true but that are true as they are actually happening on the street. The city becomes the mind-reader. In *Des Objets avec un pouvoir* (Powerful Objects), Demey teaches the spectator how to use objects to read the minds of others and so raises questions about non-verbal communication, but also about the use of such a power. And the final piece, *Vous-même* (Yourself) is an interactive film that confronts the participant with the questions about free will. The worlds of these performances come into existence through the thoughts of the public, and they confront the public with a new reality that contradicts what they thought they knew, yet a reality that has the force of *truth* since audiences are seeing and experiencing it. It puts into practice what Deleuze and Guattari claim is the aim of art: 'to make perceptible the imperceptible forces that populate the world, affect us, and make us become' (1994: 182). Demey uses mind-reading and affective suggestion to enable spectators to begin to see those 'imperceptible forces', but in so doing he also shakes the spectators' sense of reality and makes them doubt their ability to ascertain the difference between truth and untruth or even whether there is a clear separation. Demey's work opens new and controversial ways to think about the links between public space and democratic practices as he addresses issues of control, power and freedom.

Dutch artist, Dries Verhoeven's work asks the spectator to re-assess an understanding of intimacy and intensity between solo performer and solo spectator and to rethink notions of being together in a public space. But he also suggests that public space is located in ordinary daily routines that strangers share with each other and with individuals worldwide. Thus the *public space* has shifted from a tangible geographic location to a conceptual one that resides both in cyberspace and in bodily activities. Verhoeven experiments with a public cyber/body space in *Life Streaming*, performed in London at the London International Festival of Theatre in 2010. For this encounter, Verhoeven created two internet cafés on opposite sides of the world so that strangers separated by great geographic distances and by very different life experiences could talk to each other face-to-face (or computer-to-computer). In London, Verhoeven set up a trailer with twenty computers in separate cubicles all facing the same way on London's South Bank River Walk near the National Theatre.

And on a beach in Sri Lanka, the performers sit at identical computers in another temporary internet café. Each participant in London must remove his or her shoes before entering to sit in front of a computer. As spectators put on their headphones, an image of an individual from the other side of the world appears on the screen. The *performance* is the real-time conversation with this stranger, so there are twenty similar, but also unique, one-to-one performances happening simultaneously. While the anecdotes and questions spoken by the performer-participant at the computer on the beach are scripted to a large extent, there is also space for improvisational responses to information exchanged as the conversation moves from one topic or interlude to the next.

The impetus for the performance installation was Verhoeven's desire to put a face and a voice to the images of victims of the tsunami in 2004. Each of the performers in Sri Lanka, all survivors of the tsunami, has a story of loss and fear that is told at some point during the performance, but the piece is less about documenting disaster experiences and more about establishing an ephemeral relationship of intimacy and trust. The spectators in London are asked several personal questions and can ask questions in return as the two share information through words and images. As soon as the London spectator gives his or her home address, for example, the building appears on the screen through Google Earth. These exchanges lead to a discussion between the spectator-performer in London and the one in Sri Lanka about their respective homes, neighbourhoods and life styles. They share their interests, fears and hopes for the future, and they speak about how close each one lives to the sea. At one point in the conversation, the performer in Sri Lanka asks the London participant if he or she has lost someone close and reveals his or her own loss caused by the tsunami. The conversation nudges the London spectator into some form of compassion, but the Sri Lankan partner gently admonishes with 'I don't want your pity.' The encounter is about sharing trust that must banish feelings of superiority in whatever form they take. Verhoeven's scripting of the structured conversations keeps the dialogue moving but also allows for spontaneity and unplanned questions and confessions. It is structured but not obstructed. At the end of the conversation, the spectator watches his or her new friend walk to the sea. At the same moment that the Sri Lankan steps into the waves, the spectator feels warm water flow into the trailer as its temperature rises to match Sri Lanka. Both of us are ankle-deep in water, and those physical links powerfully shift the interpersonal connection from cyberspace to actual space as we are connected by the sea. It becomes very clear that the piece is not about the information exchanges. The one-to-one conversation is the means to establish an intimate encounter, across distance and difference, that thrusts an individual from London into a shared public space with another individual from Sri Lanka, a shared space that lacks a *geographic* presence and yet has a strong *affective* presence. Through a dialogue that uses words certainly, but relies as heavily on unspoken memories, suggestions and feelings, *Life Streaming* makes visible and tangible, the invisible and intangible through what Deleuze and Guattari call the 'bloc of pure sensations that owe their preservation only to themselves and that provide the event with the compound [of percepts and affects] that celebrates it' (1994: 167–8). Art here is not a reflection or 'resemblance' of reality; it is pure sensations that compel the spectator to rethink encounter and dialogue as affect and becoming rather than meaning. Here the democratic performatives do not reclaim a physical street, but rather reclaim the affective and imagined paths between our experiences, impressions and bodies, across distance and difference. As Eisenstein suggested, 'thinking...with our bodily desires and needs promises a possibility for recognizing human connectedness' (2004: 53), and it offers a new way to imagine democratic practices of liberty, equality and the common good.

All of the interventions discussed in this book seek to 'emancipate' the spectator by intervening in public spaces, actual or metaphoric, in order to change perceptions and understandings of the everyday world. While they rely on tactics of interruption or disruption, *détournement*, and social or political action, the goal is not necessarily (or not solely) oppositional actions of resistance to the state or official institutions. Instead these performance interventions offer a way to reimagine how we live in the world and provide a range of public spaces in which to practice new models. In their work (and many other performances not mentioned), the artists seek to redefine the political and to disassociate politics from government, what Rancière called the police since it has the power to enforce a particular distribution of the sensible. 'Politics, before all else,' he explains, 'is an intervention in the visible and the sayable' (2010: 37), and like politics, art is 'a way of changing existing modes of sensory presentations and forms of enunciation, of varying frames, scales and rhythms; and of building new relationships between reality and appearance, the individual and the collective' (2010: 141). Many contemporary street artists assert that to be political is to insert one's voice into the social experience and to influence what is seen and said. That voice is both the artist's and the emancipated spectator's.

By creating situations in which the audiences can construct and practice their new knowledge in actual public spaces (even when that public space is not a geographic location) and in which they gain a sense of personal and communal agency as they take on the role of citizen-artist and active citizen, the street artists create affective encounters rather than reproductions of reality. These encounters encourage each participant to become an aesthetic and political being that can be *affected by* the immediate surrounding public space and the encounters experienced there as well as less tangible public spaces. But through these encounters, this citizen-artist can also *affect* the larger social world. The belief here is that until the public, from city resident to city official, begins to sense the role art can play in affecting socio-political change and to practice what they have learned, they will enjoy the arts, but miss the opportunity the arts offer to merge artistic creation and cultural action.

Notes

Preface: Into the Street

1. Sue Harris (2004) in her article, '"Dancing in the Streets": The Aurillac Festival of Street Theatre' demonstrates the same thrill although in somewhat more measured tones of academic discourse. These 'astonished reactions' are discussed in more detail in the Introduction as forms of 'shock'.
2. 'Street arts' and 'street theatre' are contested terms. Many artists who work with some form of live performance in public spaces do not come from theatre backgrounds, but rather from music, film, dance, painting, sculpture, architecture, or installation art and reject the labels of 'street theatre' and 'street arts' for their creative work. Charlotte Granger lists several terms: *'arts de la rue, théâtre de rue, théâtre itinérant, arts forains, théâtre in situ, arts urbains, animation, divertissement cultures urbains, arts dans l'espace public, arts publics, spectacles en plain air'* and claims that the range of terms signifies a range of forms and thus thwarts any common definition (Freydefont and Granger, 2008: 27). For many years in France, there was discussion over whether to call the work *théâtre de rue, théâtre de la rue,* or even *théâtre dans la rue*: a distinction hard to translate with the same connotations, but one that prioritizes essential characteristics over location. In this book, I will rely on the terms street arts, street theatre, and performance in public spaces, using them interchangeably.
3. HorsLesMurs was created in 1993 by the Minister of Culture as a resource to document and disseminate information, both scholarly and practical, about street theatre and circus.
4. I have limited my study to performance interventions that have occurred somewhere in Europe even though a few of the artists are based elsewhere. Outdoor performance is a vibrant theatrical form in many areas of the world outside the European context, but often the traditions, performance practices, sources of inspiration, and engagement of the audience are quite different. These street performances are outside the scope of this book. There are many sources on these performances, but a good place to start an exploration of this street theatre is Jan Cohen-Cruz, *Radical Street Performance: An International Anthology* (1998).

Introduction: Aesthetics and Politics of Street Arts Interventions

1. Some of the most important pioneering radical theatre companies that experimented with outdoor performance were Bread and Puppet Theatre, San Francisco Mime Troupe, El Teatro Campesino, and Living Theatre in the United States; Augusto Boal's Theatre of the Oppressed in Brazil; El Comediants in Catalonia; Il Gorilla Quadrumano, Piccolo Teatro di Pontedera, and Dario Fo in Italy; Kollektif Rote Rübe in Germany; Welfare State International, People Show, Natural Theatre Company, I.O.U., and

Notes 185

John Bull Puncture Repair Kit in England; Dogtroep in Holland; Akademia Ruchu in Poland; Squat Theatre in Hungary; and Théâtre de l'Unité, Théâtre à Bretelles, Théâtracide, Urban Sax, and Troupe Z in France.
2. Grant Peterson, in his doctoral thesis, traces the trajectory of the Natural Theatre Company from the 1960s to the present. This pioneering British street arts company created provocative and confrontational walkabout characters who mocked various characteristics of British national identity. Peterson uses the work of the company as a case study to explore a shift from political oppositional art to corporate entertainment.
3. Grant Kester, in *The One and the Many: Contemporary Collaborative Art in a Global Context*, also suggests an alternate model in 'dialogic, collaborative projects' that rely on 'a reciprocal testing of both ethical and aesthetic norms, the outcome of which can only be determined through the subsequent forms of social interaction mobilized by a given work' (2011: 185). I will return to Kester's model later in the book.
4. See Hirschhorn's interview with Okwui Enwezor in *Thomas Hirschhorn: Jumbo Spoons and Big Cake* (Chicago: Art Institute of Chicago, 2000, pp. 27–9). Grant Kester points out that Hirschhorn 'appropriated' the phrase from Jean-Luc Godard who said, 'I don't make political films, I make films politically' (2011: 234, footnote 24).
5. See Claire Bishop, 'Antagonism and Relational Aesthetics' and 'The Social Turn: Collaboration and Its Discontents' where she explores shock and rupture as key aspects of the art experience.
6. In a later book, however, Kester questions the power of shock to initiate insight and increased agency since the disorientation it causes resembles trauma in its psychological impact. He identifies shock as a key tactic of avant-garde art and offers an alternative model in dialogic collaboration (2011: 182–4).
7. Michael Warner in *Publics and Counterpublics* distinguishes between *the* public ('a kind of social totality... the people in general') and *a* public ('a concrete audience, a crowd witnessing itself in visible space, as with a theatrical public. Such a public also has a sense of totality, bounded by the event or by the shared physical space'), pp. 65–6. When I use 'public' to refer to audiences in this book, I am using the term like Warner's '*a* public'.
8. See Laura Cull, *Deleuze and Performance* (2011).
9. Nigel Thrift, in *Non-Representational Theory: Sapces, Politics, Affect*, identifies five schools of thought about affect in the social sciences. Each one places significant emphasis on the body (2008: 223–5).
10. Boal (1985) and Dolan (2005) use the term 'rehearsal' in this way.
11. A loose translation is 'Those with no balconies.'
12. To see a video clip of the many performances, go to: http://www.rueetcirque.fr/index/en/search_simple. Search by the name of the company or the name of the show.

1 Looking Back: A Socio-Historical and Intellectual Context for Contemporary Street Arts in Europe

1. Some sources on entertainments at the fairs are Sybil Rosenfeld, (1960) *The Theatre at the London Fairs in the Eighteenth Century* (Cambridge: Cambridge

University Press); Émile Compardon, (1970) *Les Spectacles de la foire: théâtres, acteurs, sauteurs et danseurs de corde...des Foires Saint-Germain et Saint-Laurent, des Boulevards et du Palais-Royal depuis 1595 jusqu'à 1791: documents inédits recueillis aux Archives Nationales* (Geneve: Slatkine, photographic repr. of 1877 edition); Virginia Scott, (1972) 'The Infancy of English Pantomime 1716–1723', *Educational Theatre Journal* 24.2: 125–34; Meg Armstrong (1992–3) '"A Jumble of Foreignness": The Sublime Musayums of Nineteenth-Century Fairs and Expositions', *Cultural Critique* 23: 199–250. I wrote my doctoral dissertation on the London fairs: *'From Booths, to Theatre, to Court': The Theatrical Significance of the London Fairs, 1660–1724* (University of Michigan, 1984).
2. See footnote 1 in the Introduction.
3. Lieux Publics (http://www.lieuxpublics.fr/index.php) was founded in Marne la Vallée near Paris in 1983 by Michel Crespin (who remained its director until 2001) and Fabien Jannelle as a centre to encourage artistic reflection and creation. It moved to Marseille in 1990. Today, under the direction of Pierre Sauvageot, director of street music company Décor Sonore, Lieux Publics is a major national creation center that hosts companies to develop artistic creations, leads conferences and symposia, and publishes books, journals, and articles on art in public space.
4. See Gaber, *40 Years of Street Arts* (2009a: 71–2).
5. See also Delfour (1997) and Chaudoir (1997) who both acknowledge the importance of the long history of outdoor performance, but argue that the 'street arts' that flourished from the 1970s were fundamentally different. Delfour explores the problematics of urban and cultural action that he feels are unique to this period and art form. Chaudoir looks at the issues of ubanism and locates the historical roots of contemporary street theatre in agit-prop, happenings (and Fluxus), and radical theatre.
6. Many books have been written on the events of 1968 and the circumstances leading up to them, especially in the American and French contexts. Some of the most helpful are Anderson (1999), Berman (1996), Bloom and Breines (1995), Cavallo (1999), Feenberg and Freedman (2001), Gitlin (1987), Gregoire and Perlman (1969), Macedo (1997), Miller (1994), Ross (2002), Seidman (2004), Singer (2000), Starr (1995) and Unger and Unger (1998), but there are many others. Fink, Gassert, and Junker (1998) is one of the few books that has collected essays on the events internationally. Each of the essays has an excellent bibliography that covers sources specific to the geographical location being analysed.
7. See also Kershaw (1999: 89–125).
8. Throughout his book, *The One and the Many: Contemporary Collaborative Art in a Global Context*, Kester assesses the impact of May 1968 on the ideas of the major post-structuralists, in part as a way to locate and validate the paradigm of collaboration that he sets up in contrast to the oppositional paradigm represented in art works and theory that elevate shock, dissensus and affect (or somatic experience) to the level of key tactic to change the way the public thinks.
9. A short clip of one of the early performances is available on the HorsLesMurs website (street theatre and circus archive in Paris). To see a video clip of the performance, go to http://www.rueetcirque.fr/ and search by company name or title of the performance.

10. Floriane Gaber (2009b), in *How It All Started: Street Arts in the Context of the 1970s*, offers an excellent and comprehensive description and analysis of the origins of street theatre emphasizing the work in France, but always with an eye to influences and developments outside France. The first chapter, 'The Cultural Policy', looks in detail at cultural policies in France that led to the development of street theatre. Gaber's other book, *40 Years of Street Arts*, looks at developments of street theatre from the 1970s to the present. These two books provide the most detailed information on street arts in France.
11. The major documents of the Situationists, many of which were originally published in *Internationale Situationiste* between 1959 and 1969, are available online or have been anthologized. See Knabb (1981 and rev. edn, 1995), McDonough (2004) and Dark Star (2001). Key book-length texts are Guy Debord, *The Society of Spectacle* (1995) and *Comments on the Society of Spectacle* (1990) as well as Raoul Vaneigem, *Revolution of Everyday Life* (1994). Other interesting sources on the Situationists are Ford (2005), Jappe (1999), Plant (1992), and Sadler (1998).
12. Juhani Pallasmaa (2005), an architectural theorist, echoes these ideas years later when he blames the inhumanity of modern architecture and the consequent alienation felt by individuals in today's world on the privileging of sight over the other senses (9–10). And he certainly is not alone – David Harvey, Fredric Jameson, and Susan Sontag (to name just a very few in other fields of scholarship) warn of the dangers of understanding our three-dimensional world as a two-dimensional image.
13. See 'The Situationists and the New Forms of Action in Politics and Art' (1963) in Knabb (2006).
14. The production that I saw was performed in Paris in March 2010.
15. As Debord expressed: 'A use of the commodity arises that is sufficient unto itself; what this means for the consumer is an outpouring of religious zeal in honor of the commodity's sovereign freedom' (1994, thesis 67: 43). He warned that certain products in the society of spectacle were gaining cult status as they were produced in order to be collected like '*indulgences* – the glorious tokens of the commodity's immanent presence among the faithful' (1994, thesis 67: 44).
16. See information about the UK Shopocalypse Tour on Reverend Billy's website: http://www.revbilly.com/campaigns
17. See, for example, Suzanne Lacy, *Mapping the Terrain: New Genre Public Art* (1995); Nicolas Bourriaud, *Relational Aesthetics* (2002); Grant Kester, *Conversation Pieces: Community + Communication in Modern Art* (2004) and *The One and the Many* (2011); Erika Fischer-Lichte, *The Transformative Power of Performance: A New Aesthetics* (2008); Claire Bishop, 'The Social Turn: Collaboration and Its Discontents' (2009); and Shannon Jackson, *Social Works: Performing Art, Supporting Publics* (2011).
18. See *Art and Objecthood* (1998).
19. 'The Legacy of Jackson Pollock' in Kaprow (1993).
20. Bishop (2005) looks in more depth at the legacy of Kaprow's ideas and work. Floriane Gaber (2009b: 103–14) looks at the influence of Kaprow, John Cage, Fluxus and Land Art on European street arts.
21. See Chaudoir (1997): 179–85.

22. Jean-Jacques Delfour, Professor of Philosophy who writes extensively on street theatre, claims that street arts can begin:

> to change life, but in the sense of an alternate experience of life and of social reality, ... [Street theatre] does not erase the difference between theatre and social life. It transforms this difference between theatre and not-theatre, between theatre and communal reality, not to abolish it, but to make it function differently. It is precisely in the juxtaposition of theatre and normal social life that street theatre occurs and asserts another way of living. (Delfour, 1997: 147–8; my translation)

23. That braiding of aesthetics and politics is a commonplace in both popular and more scholarly discussions of street theatre. See, for example, Ostrowetsky (1997), Delfour (1997), Chaudoir (1997), Le Floc'h (2006), and Freydefont and Granger (2008). Jan Cohen-Cruz, in the Introduction to *Radical Street Performance*, emphasizes the link between aesthetics and politics and connects the concept of *radical* to *street theatre*:

> Radical street performance draws people who comprise a contested reality into what its creators hope will be a changing script.... Radical street performance strives to transport everyday reality to something more ideal.... Potentially, street performance creates a bridge between imagined and real actions, often facilitated by taking place at the very sites that the performance makers want transformed. (1998: 1)

24. Nicolas Bourriaud was one of the early voices to respond to this criticism by describing a shift in art from a revolutionary utopian agenda to a more practical one as a contemporary change in attitudes toward the possible scope or reach of social change. Artists, he argues, no longer seek to change the world, but rather to alter small pockets of society, perhaps even just temporarily. Provisional solutions replace all-encompassing ones: 'Art was intended to prepare and announce a future world: today it is modelling possible universes....The role of artworks is no longer to form imaginary and utopian realities, but to actually be ways of living and models of action within the existing real, whatever the scale chosen by the artist' (2002: 13).
25. Kester offers an interesting critique of Bishop (2011: 31–3, 59–64). In his book, he offers a detailed analysis of the tension between autonomy and heteronomy in contemporary art.

2 Democratic Performatives and an Aesthetics of Public Space

1. See Haedicke, 'Breaking Down the Walls: Interventionist Performance Strategies in French Street Theatre' (2011) for a more detailed analysis of this production.
2. See Rancière (2004: 12), discussed in the Introduction.
3. The word *trespass* retains connotations of transgression and offence from its original meaning that color its current definition of unlawful entry. See Ethel Seno, ed., *Trespass: A History of Uncommissioned Urban Art* (2010).

4. There are many videos of their work on the street on YouTube, for examples: http://www.youtube.com/watch?v=KTUQBxpMa5Q or http://www.youtube.com/watch?v=O-7kXJV1Cto
5. See also Laclau and Mouffe (2001: 186–8). I will return to Laclau and Mouffe's ideas on dissensus (or what they call antagonism or agonism) as key to radical democracy later in the book, especially in the analysis of the London performance of *The Sultan's Elephant*.
6. Deutsche's notion of public space is closely associated with the work of Jürgen Habermas who identified the public sphere as an arena with open access in which the public could debate and hold the state accountable. Many years after the publication of *The Structural Transformation of the Public Sphere*, Habermas responded to his critics by explaining, 'the concept of the public sphere, *Öffentlichkeit*, is meant as an analytic tool for ordering certain phenomena and placing them in a particular context as part of a categorical frame' (1992: 462). Debates about Habermas's ideas have filled many pages and are outside the scope of this study, but for further work on this debate, see, in particular, Nancy Fraser, 'Rethinking the Public Sphere: A contribution to the Critique of Actually Existing Democracy' (1992), Warner, *Publics and Counterpublics* (2002) and Reinelt, 'Rethinking the Public Sphere for a Global Age' (2011).
7. Many books and articles have been published on public art, particularly since the late 1980s, and it is impossible to list them all. The writers that I have found the most useful in my analysis of street theatre are Rosalyn Deutsche, Tom Finkelpearl, Miwon Kwon, Lucy Lippard, Malcolm Miles, W.J.T. Mitchell, Patricia Phillips and Harriet F. Senie.
8. See, in particular, the well-documented controversies over Richard Serra's *Tilted Arc* and John Ahearn's community sculptures, discussed in Deutsche (1996), Finkelpearl (2001), and Kwon (2004).
9. I will return to these ideas of radical democracy and public art in subsequent chapters.
10. See Patricia C. Phillips, 'Public Art: A Renewable Resource' (2003).
11. See Glass (2001), Freire and Kirby (1982), and McLaren (1999) for informative summaries and analyses of Freire's ideas.
12. Freire originally called this process of developing critical awareness *conscientization*, but he abandoned that term by the 1980s because he felt the simple label led to an oversimplification and distortion of the process. See Freire and Kirby (1982).
13. Director Nicola Danesi de Luca explained to me that 'overweight myth' in the title also means 'overrated myth', apparently clearer in Italian. He provided many other insights into the production.
14. A loose translation of the title is 'The Business of Hijacking Reality'.
15. See Haedicke (2012a and 2012b) for other essays on *L'Entreprise de Détournement*.
16. Information on audience responses was shared with me in an interview with Cyril Jaubert, Artistic Director of Opéra Pagaï, on 12 March 2010.
17. Another way to understand Rancière's efficacy of dissensus is to look at his summary of Schiller's paradox and promise. Schiller, he explains:

> declares that 'Man is only completely human when he plays,' and assures us that this paradox is capable 'of bearing the whole edifice of the art of

the beautiful and the still more difficult art of living'. We could reformulate this thought as follows: there exists a specific sensory experience that holds the promise of both a new world of Art and a new life for individuals and the community, namely *the aesthetic*. (2010: 115)

Rancière declares that 'the entire question of the "politics of aesthetics"... turns on this short conjunction. The aesthetic experience is effective inasmuch as it is the experience of that *and*. It grounds the autonomy of art, to the extent that it connects it to the hope of "changing life"'. (2010: 116)

18. On their flyers for *Darwin and the Dodo*, they include a quotation from Dr Paul D. Taylor of the Natural History Museum in London on the accuracy of their science: 'I must admit to having been skeptical of Darwin and the Dodo before I saw your performance. However, I was won over by the accuracy of the science in your performance and how you were able to convey difficult issues about evolution in an intelligent yet light-hearted way.'
19. A video clip of the performance in Buenos Aires is available on the company website at http://www.ilotopie.com/.
20. Rosalyn Deutsche explores this phenomenon in many of her essays on public art, but especially 'Uneven Development: Public Art in New York City' and 'Agoraphobia' in *Evictions: Art and Spatial Politics* (1996).
21. See the work of Mark C. Taylor, *The Moment of Complexity: Emerging Network Culture* (2001) and John Urry, *Global Complexity* (2003).

3 Performing Democracy on a Grand Scale

1. The French title is *La Visite du Sultan des Indes sur son elephant à voyager dans le temps*. There are many websites with photographs from the performances of *La Visite du Sultan des Indes sur son elephant à voyager dans le temps* in Nantes and Amiens. The Artichoke website (www.artichoke.uk) has photographs, information and a documentary video of the London production, and several video clips have been posted on YouTube. Surprisingly, there is very little scholarly work on this production, but see Patel (2009).
2. The negotiations began in 1999 to bring one of Royal de Luxe's earlier shows, *Les Chasseurs des Giraffes* that was created in the 1990s. As the new production with the Elephant and the Girl developed, negotiations shifted to bringing that show to London. *The Sultan's Elephant* was co-produced by Artichoke and LIFT (London International Festival of Theatre). The budget for *The Sultan's Elephant* was around £1.5 million, based on the figures given to me by Helen Marriage in our February 2007 interview. The largest percent came from Arts Council London and Mayor of London. It was also supported by BBC London, Power Station in Battersea, Grange Hotels, The Wolseley, Association française d'action artistique, London Development Agency, City of Westminster, Transport for London, NESTA, Totally Lond(on), West One Infrastructure Services, WSP, and ARK. The operational partners included Westminster City Council, Greater London Authority, GLA/Trafalgar Square, Royal Parks, Visit London, Metropolitan Police, London Buses, London Underground, Transport for London, London Ambulance Service, London Fire Brigade, and London Traffic Control Centre.

3. Available online at www.thesultanselephant.com and reprinted in Webb (2006).
4. The provocative presence of the Sultan and his Court, especially in London, and the contradictory signals of the faux welcoming ceremonies will be explored later in the chapter.
5. The Girl's face was manipulated by several technicians turning her head, opening and closing her mouth, and moving her eyes and eyelids. One technician stood at a distance facing her to control her eye movements by remote control. This technician, led by another guiding her by holding onto a large belt loop, walked backwards in front of the Girl.
6. This video is available on the Artichoke website: http://www.artichoke.uk.com/events/the_sultans_elephant/
7. This mechanical elephant was larger than an actual elephant, so his pace was slowed down to what an actual elephant would walk if he were that size, about 1.5 kilometres an hour.
8. To enable the huge elephant to walk down the streets of London required that tree branches, traffic lights, street lamps, pedestrian crossings and railings be removed before the weekend events, said Helen Marriage in my interview with her on 5 February 2007. Five miles of some of London's busiest streets were closed to traffic over the weekend.
9. Eighty square metres of leather were used to make the Elephant's ears.
10. The route for the bus tour was designed by London Transport. (Marriage interview).
11. Courcoult is adamantly opposed to advertising his spectacles and so relies primarily on word-of-mouth, but cryptic notices that something would happen in early May appeared in the Underground and by Thursday, street closure notices were posted along the show's route.
12. David Harvey writes that unlike modernist 'large-scale, metropolitan-wide technologically rational and efficient urban *plans*....Postmodernism cultivates, instead, a conception of the urban fabric as necessarily fragmented, a "palimpsest" of past forms superimposed upon each other, and a "collage" of current uses, many of which may be ephemeral' (1990: 66).
13. Other terms for post-political democracy of consensus are cosmopolitan, dialogic and participatory democracy. The Introduction to Helen Gilbert and Jacqueline Lo's *Performance and Cosmopolitics: Cross Cultural Transactions in Australasia* offers an overview of cosmopolitan democracy and performance.
14. Justine Simons, from Mayor Ken Livingstone's office, exclaimed:

> I loved it because it did everything great art should do—it was truly transformative. It moved the city and its people in an extraordinary way. Over one unforgettable weekend, it animated the city, drew people together and captured imaginations. These days we tend to measure success in the form of targets, outputs, tickets sold, number of key rings bought in the gift shop etc, but looking at the value of culture in this way kind of misses the point. Reading through the audience responses after the event couldn't have made this clearer. People talked of their amazement, the magic, the way it made them look at the world in a new way, talk to the person next to them. It reduced adults to tears and got them trekking

around town following the elephant and the girl in a cult-like fashion. And this is no mean feat. Londoners are a cynical, no-nonsense bunch. I often hear filmmakers talk about why they like making movies here, and apart for the iconic backdrops, the fact that Londoners just go about their business, too cool to be star-struck, is often cited as a big plus. Well, I think that all went to pot the weekend the Elephant came to town! (Webb, 2006: 35)

15. And Baroness McIntosh, in a House of Lords debate on the Arts on 11 May 2006, affirmed:

"I spent a large part of last Friday in the elephant's company along with an amazingly disparate crowd of others, and I can honestly say that it was one of the most uplifting, joyous, life-enchanting days I have ever spent. Upwards of a million people turned out to see the elephant and its entourage over a four-day period and many of them have testified to the power of the event. But, although it is wonderful to know that statistic, no amount of statistical analysis will capture the value of the elephant's visit or why it will be remembered, and there will be no way of demonstrating any direct causal relationship between it and economic, social, or educational outputs. So what were all these people responding to? I think that they were recognizing that art, like cuckoos and spring, makes you feel better just by being itself. (Webb, 2006: 36)

16. A cabinet reshuffle on Friday, 5 May 2006 because of the resignation of the Home Office Minister meant that many British and foreign journalists were in the downtown area and happened on the show and ended up following it. As a result, it got quite extensive coverage, even appearing in the *New York Times*, on page 3.
17. On Monday, 8 May 2006, LIFT (London International Festival of Theatre) and Artichoke presented a one-day symposium entitled 'How Many Elephants Does It Take…?' on the event to explore 'how the cultural sector and the city infrastructure can work creatively together to change the way we experience the city' (http://www.thesultanselephant.com/about/otherevents.php, p. 2, accessed 6 April 2006). The symposium featured keynote speakers who were responsible for the logistics of producing *The Sultan's Elephant*, but a major part of the day was spent in break-out sessions where we swapped stories and reactions to the weekend's events.
18. The success of *The Sultan's Elephant* in London to reframe urban futures gave city officials in Liverpool the courage to try a similar event. The over-sized outdoor spectacle of La Machine's *La Princesse* was commissioned by the city of Liverpool as a major event in its year-long celebration as European Capital of Culture in 2008. From 3–7 September, the city enjoyed the antics of a huge spider, created by François Delarozière who was the engineer who designed the mechanical giants in *The Sultan's Elephant*. The background story revealed that the spider lived deep beneath Concourse Tower, marked for demolition, but as the wrecking crews began their noisy work, the frightened creature emerged to walk the city until she made her dramatic escape on Sunday night through the Queensway tunnel under the River Mersey. Although large crowds came

to see the spider walk through the city, she lacked the personified humanity of the Elephant and the Girl. Many people expressed a fear and dislike of real spiders and although La Princesse did not rouse the same level of loathing, no one I spoke to wanted to believe that she had come alive. Her tiny static cartoonish spider head and eyes did not move or enable us to feel as though we had made eye contact, and although her legs had an incredible range of movement, they looked as though they were just waving around her rather than being the parts of her body that she used to move (in spite of the meticulous calculations of Delarozière and many permutations of the hydraulics). Thus rather than a visit from an over-sized creature whose live-ness and difference enabled the spectators to learn something about themselves, the mechanical spider always remained a clever and efficient machine in a carnival parade. In April 2012, Liverpool again hosted giant visitors. Royal de Luxe performed *Sea Odyssey* in honour of the one-hundredth anniversary of the sinking of the Titanic, using the Girl and the Giant from an earlier spectacle.

19. See Mouffe (1992): 117–28.
20. Mouffe writes:

   To be sure, I am not the only one to use that term and they [sic.] are currently a variety of 'agonistic' theorists. However they generally envisage the political as a space of freedom and deliberation, while for me it is a space of conflict and antagonism. This is what differentiates my agonistic perspective from the one defended by William Connolly, Bonnig Honig or James Tully. (2005: 131, footnote 9)

   While the basic concept of the two traditions does not change significantly in her books and articles, the terms do. For example, in 'Democratic Citizenship and the Political Community' (1992), she uses the term civic republicanism, whereas in *The Democratic Paradox* (2000), she calls it the democratic tradition.

21. Rancière explains:

   The collective power shared by the spectators does not stem from the fact that they are members of a collective body or from some specific form of interactivity. It is the power of each of them to translate what she perceives in her own way, to link it to the unique intellectual adventure that makes her similar to all the rest in as much as this adventure is not like any other. This shared power of the equality of intelligence links individuals, makes them exchange their intellectual adventures, in so far as it keeps them separate from one another, equally capable of using the power everyone has to plot her own path. What our performances—be they teaching or playing, speaking, writing, making art or looking at it—verify is not our participation in power embodied in the community. It is the capacity of anonymous people, the capacity that makes everyone equal to everyone else. (Rancière, 2009: 16–17)

22. See Prussin, *Hatumere: Islamic Design in West Africa* (1988), pp. 11–17. I would like to thank my colleague Yvette Hutchison for drawing my attention to this source.

23. When I spoke to Indian colleagues about the Girl, they said her face belied Indian or Middle Eastern origins. Asian colleagues saw Asian features. That ethnic ambiguity contributes to her iconic power.
24. The mechanical elephant appears to be inspired by both Asian and African elephants, and I cannot find any documentation on which elephants were the source. However, the differences between African and Asian elephants (size, tusks, and wrinkled skin) seem to indicate that the body of the mechanical elephant more closely resembled an African elephant, but the elaborate tapestries evoke the *Orient*. As with the face of the Girl, that ambiguity represents a significant aspect of the power of the image. The presence of the black concubine is a modification of the written narrative where one of the concubines longs to be black and so bathes in octopus ink everyday. During the performance, some of the concubines did take bubble baths on the elephant's back.
25. There is an evocative photograph of the Horse Guards, in their official capacity, riding their horses to the Changing of the Guard at Buckingham Palace, but looking as though they are leading the huge Elephant behind them to an official welcome. It can be found in the Gallery of photographs for Saturday, 6 May 2006 at www.thesultanselephant.com
26. The importance of the use of the fifty local volunteers in the spectacle cannot be overestimated in terms of the impact on their sense of 'owning' the show. One volunteer, John Ellingsworth, wrote a long impassioned blog entry soon after the show that detailed his experience as a volunteer following the Girl. It is reprinted in Webb, 2006: 27–33.
27. Webb (2006) in *Four Magical Days in May*, includes several testimonies from city officials: Tim Owen, Head of Special Events for Westminster City Council; Sargeant Trevor Jenner, Special Coordinator, Public Order Branch, Metropolitan Police; John Gardner, Events Planning Manager for London Bus Services, Central London, Network Operations; Sarah Weir, Executive Director of Arts Council London; Justine Simmons in the office of Ken Livingstone, Mayor of London; and Mark Wasilewski, Royal Parks Manager for St. James Park and Green Park. Other testimonies from Baronness McIntosh, Ken Livingstone, Peter Hewitt (Chief Executive of Arts Council London) and many more are available on the Artichoke website and in their other published newsletters.
28. The media contributed as well by honouring the request to remain silent about the event before it began, and so to allow the mystery to build with hints 'leaked' in small announcements by the company. Surprise was key: 'It is important that what we do is free and in public places. Audiences in cinemas or theatre have already crossed a threshold. They know they are there for art, and that is where they expect to find it. I want to reach people as they are and surprise them', explained Jean Luc Courcoult to *The Sunday Times* (30 April 2006). The only violation of that silence occurred just as the show began. The company had been rehearsing for a month at Battersea Power Station, an out-of-the-way derelict industrial site. Their activities were visible only to a block of flats opposite the site. The residents of the flats, let in on the 'secret', agreed to silence, but just before the weekend, a photographer for *The Guardian* got into the building and took an unauthorized photograph of the rehearsal. The story ran on Friday morning of the show.

4 Trespassing in Urban Places

1. This early daguerrotype was on display in 'On the Move' at Estorick Collection of Modern Italian Art in London, 13 January–18 April 2010.
2. Henri Lefebvre in *The Production of Space*, develops a triad of social space (or spatial concepts). One of these is 'representational space': 'space as directly *lived* through its associated images and symbols, and hence the space of "inhabitants" and "users," ... It overlays physical space, making use of its objects' (1991: 39). The sites of street performances become like these representational spaces.
3. Sadie Plant, *The Radical Gesture: The Situationist International in a Postmodern Age* and Simon Sadler, *The Situationist City* explain and develop these Situationist tactics and ideas in great depth.
4. Several photographs and videos of the performances in Berlin, Paris, London, and Philadelphia are on the Compagnie Willi Dorner website, http://www.ciewdorner.at. Willi Dorner developed and expanded the ideas in this piece in *Fitting* (2012).
5. The image is available at http://www.ciewdorner.at/index.php?page=photos&anode=18#album18
6. There are many websites of Liu Bolin's camouflage art: http://liubolin.sino-web.net, http://www.artnet.com/artist/425227158/liu-bolin.html, http://www.toxel.com/inspiration/2009/10/04/camouflage-art-by-liu-bolin/, http://www.webdesignerdepot.com/2010/02/the-hidden-art-of-camouflage-photography/ and http://www.youtube.com/watch?v=mxEstgh6cAM
7. I have not seen Liu Bolin's work in China and there is very little in English on its reception in his homeland, although the Chinese artists with whom I have spoken say he is not well known in China.
8. For images of Palmen's street interventions, go to www.desireepalmen.nl and http://www.designboom.com/weblog/cat/10/view/3189/camouflage-art-by-desiree-palmen.html
9. Several of these animations can be found on YouTube. See, for example, http://www.youtube.com/watch?v=3JlJnjw0cug, http://www.youtube.com/watch?v=n8jfxyUNoqM, http://www.youtube.com/watch?v=VTOMiOKnwow
10. See http://www.youtube.com/watch?v=xJLzJapBXpw
11. Part 1 at http://www.youtube.com/watch?v=2uh2GureA2w; Part 2 at http://www.youtube.com/watch?v=VTOMiOKnwow; and Part 3 at http://www.youtube.com/watch?v=n8jfxyUNoqM
12. This scene is part of *Windar's Theory, Part 2* (one series of interventions in *PAPAERGLUEnScotch*) at http://www.youtube.com/watch?v=4ORXlNK4rYI
13. The name of the company, Jeanne Simone, is the first name of each of Terrier's grandmothers.
14. See Haedicke (2011) for an analysis of this production.
15. For two versions of the performance (one short and another more complete one) on the rue Daguerre in Paris in September 2010, see http://globulefilms.com/index.php?/project/mademoiselle/
16. I have had numerous informal conversations with Laure Terrier since 2008. Her comments on her practice come from these conversations.
17. For additional information and videos, see http://www.operapagai.com/spectacle_safari.php

18. See Beatriz Colomina (1994), *Privacy and Publicity: Modern Architecture as Mass Media*, especially 'Window', pp. 283–335.
19. The panel announcements were sent to me by the company in French. The translations are my own.

5 Subversive Imaginaries: Performing the Other

1. In *The Archive and the Repertoire: Performing Cultural Memory in the Americas*, Taylor analyses *Two Undiscovered Amerindians Visit* through the lens of scenarios of discovery that explain aspects of colonial expansion and the construction of the Other. See Chapter 2: 'Scenarios of Discovery: Reflections on Performance and Ethnography', pp. 53–78.
2. A video clip of the show is available at http://www.kumulus.fr/repertoire/les-squames and in the HorsLesMurs archives at http://www.rueetcirque.fr
3. Recent experiments in neuroscience support the idea that memories can be created by embodied experiences certainly, but also by watching an experience or by participating in an enacted situation. Mark Johnson describes an experiment conducted by several cognitive science researchers on how a monkey observing a manual activity like holding a banana will experience the same neural activation as if the monkey itself were holding the banana. This activation of neural activity through observation was observed in humans as well, and it has also been confirmed when an individual merely imagines an activity. As Johnson explains, 'this mirroring capacity extends to even merely imagining that one is performing an action. My understanding of bodily actions performed by others is based on the activation of my own bodily sense of performing such an action' (2007: 40). This *mirror-neuron system*, or what Damasio calls the 'as-if-body-loop', 'involves an internal brain simulation that consists of a rapid modification of ongoing body maps' (2003: 115). In other words, witnessing an action or participating in an activity within a theatrical frame (as in the democratic performatives) activates the same sensorimotor areas as performing an action in real life. 'It can produce alterations in working memory, attention' (2003: 148). These findings of neuroscience offer significant support for the potential for efficacy of metaphoric memory in street performances. See Damasio (2003), Johnson (2007) and McConachie (2008).
4. See Haedicke (2008) for a more detailed analysis of *Melgut* in the context of French immigration policy.
5. The title combines two French words, *vitupérer* and *errance*, that for Laurent link a biting criticism with a dérive (representing both his physical act of meandering through the public space and his improvisational tactic that finds unexpected links between ideas).
6. For information and photographs, go to http://www.friches.fr/spip.php?article80
7. Earlier choreographies include *Migrant* (1998), *Migrant Mother* (2000), *Migrant Mother Memories* (2001), *Flesh* and *La Silence des Mémoires* (both in 2003).
8. An extract of this performance is available in the HorsLesMurs online archives (www.rueetcirque.fr).
9. A video of *Alhambra Container* is available in the HorsLesMurs online archives (www.rueetcirque.fr).

10. The video clip of *Alhambra Container* on the Osmosis Compagnie website (www.osmosiscie.com) is of this scene.
11. McConachie calls this process 'visuomotor representatations' (2008: 63). According to the recent work of neuroscientists, the embodied witnessing of a refugee's clandestine voyage and the moment of arrival in a new country would cause neural activation in the spectator that is the same as if he or she were doing the action.
12. See the Back-to-Back Theatre website (http://backtobacktheatre.com).
13. The title *Itinéraire Sans Fond(s)* is difficult to translate because of the play on the word fond(s). 'Fond' means 'end' or 'bottom'; 'fonds' means resources. So the literal translation of the title is 'Journey without end or resources' which lacks the poetics of the French. A video clip of the performance is on the Compagnie Kumulus website (www.ciekumulus.fr). Barthélémy Bompard, Joel Cramesnil, Jean-Pierre Tutard et La Compagnie Kumulus published *Rencontres de Boîtes* in 2007 that includes extensive pictures and descriptions of *Itinéraire Sans Fond(s)* and *Les Rencontres Internationales de Boîtes*.
14. This title can be loosely translated as 'International Encounters of Shoeboxes'.
15. This quotation is from an unpublished interview that can be found in the Kumulus box (literally a cardboard box) of documents donated by the company, located at HorsLesMurs. The interview took place during the residency at Bonlieu Scène Nationale at Annecy in 2003.
16. See Mouffe, *The Democratic Paradox* (2000), especially Chapter 4, and *On the Political* (2005).

6 Community Performance: Community Performatives

1. Much of the information about *Witness/N14* comes from unpublished materials: the Artistic Dossiers and Bilans on Parcours 2 and 5. A *Dossier Artistique* is a promotional document that describes the project in detail. It is used by artists creating and promoting their work in France. There are three complete versions of the Artistic Dossier for *Witness/N14* created as the project developed; two in 2007 and one in 2009. In addition, there are Artistic Dossiers for each of the individual parcours, except Parcours 1. The Bilans are extended discussions providing more details. The Artistic Dossiers and Bilans are in French; all the translations are my own. While the Artistic Dossiers and Bilans are very helpful, the majority of my information comes from many conversations with Sarah Harper since the project began in 2005.
2. For information and pictures of *Witness/N14* go to http://www.witnessn14.org/. Harper continues to document her experience in a blog (http://witnessn14.canalblog.com) that has become a key link between the aesthetic project and the public for its duration lasting several years.
3. In July 2008, *Stradda*, the journal on street arts and circus published by HorsLesMurs, focused on social practice in street arts in an issue they titled, 'Adventurous Terrains: Composing for and with the Territory' (July 2008). The introduction to the issue asks whether there is a new trend in street arts

that uses the tactics from the past but for contrasting ends. It states that many artists:

> are leaving behind the old beaten path of artistic distribution in search of new, adventurous terrains. What is their motivation? They wish to immerse themselves in the heart of territories to find material for their creations; to speak not only to an audience but also to inhabitants so as to create with them; to renew the relationship between the period of creation and distribution and to invent new forms that are rooted in real life (Dossier #3: 5).

These artists seek to blur the boundaries between art and non-art, performer and spectator, citizen and artist, and even between art object and cultural policy.

4. In *The Reenchantment of Art* written in 1991, Suzi Gablik called for individuals to reject the cultural paradigm of an isolationist and disengaged aesthetics and instead to envisage anew and to reframe sociality to foreground social responsibility. She asked whether a confrontational aesthetic was 'useful' and instead advocated a new aesthetic paradigm that 'reflects a will to *participate* socially: a central aspect of new paradigm thinking involves a significant shift from *objects* to *relationships*' (1991:7). This 'social turn' in art is well established and documented by the early decades of the twenty-first century, and it has had a considerable impact on contemporary street performance interventions as well.
5. The other *parcours* – *Parcours 3: D'Île en île* (from Argenteuil to Franconville), *Parcours 4: La loi fondamentale des flux* (from Pierrelaye to Pontoise), and *Parcours 6: Quels sont les lignes qui persistent?* (from Magny-en-Vixen to St Claire/Epte) are planned to occur between 2012 and 2015. In addition, Harper is developing *Le Glissement des Axes*, a 'spectacle-conference' with 'our neighbours along the route' to go on tour beginning in autumn 2012.
6. This short video appears on the website (http://www.witnessn14.org/) in the section on *D'Ici-Là!*.
7. See, for example, Claire Bishop's essay "The Social Turn: Collaboration and Its Discontents" (2009). This essay was published in an earlier version in *Artforum* 44 (February 2006): 178–83.
8. See Massey's 'Politics and Space/Time' (1994: 249–72) and *For Space* (2005).
9. In 'Theory of the Dérive,' Debord claims 'chance is a less important factor in this activity than one might think: from a dérive point of view cities have psychogeographical contours, with constant currents, fixed points and vortexes that strongly discourage entry into or exit from certain zones' (Knabb, 2006: 62).

Postscript: Beyond the Street

1. See Kwon (2004) for a description of the notion of discursive site for site-specific art. She develops a genealogy of site-specificity since the late 1960s as she traces the development of three paradigms: phenomenological or experiential, social/institutional and discursive.

Bibliography

10 Ans D'Action Artistiques: 1995–2005 (avec la revue *Cassandra*). Preface de Robert Abirached. (2006) Paris: Cassandre-Horschamp/Éditions de l'Amandier.
Abbitt, Erica Stevens, Johanna Frank, Geraldine Gerry Harris and Roberta Mock. (2011) 'Aging Provocateurs and Spect(er)acular Pub(l)ic Performances'. *Performance Research* 16.2: 50–6.
Acconci, Vito. (1990) 'Public Space in a Private Time'. *Art and the Public Sphere*. Ed. W.J.T. Mitchell. Chicago and London: The University of Chicago Press, pp. 158–76.
Adorno, Theodor. (1977) 'Commitment'. *Aesthetics and Politics*. Trans. Ed. Ronald Taylor. London: NLB, pp. 177–95.
'Adventurous Terrains [Composing for and with the territory]'. (July 2009) *Stradda* Dossier 3: 1–20. English translation of 'Terrains d'aventures [Ecrire pour et avec le territoire]'. *Stradda* 9 (Juillet 2008): 7–27.
Adriani, Götz, Winifired Konnertz and Karin Thomas. (1979) *Joseph Beuys: His Life and Works*. Trans. Patricia Lech. New York: Barron's.
Agamben, Giorgio. (1978) *Infancy and History: On the Destruction of Experience*. Trans. Liz Heron (1993) London and New York: Verso.
Anderson, Terry H. (1995) *The Movement and the Sixties: Protest in America from Greensboro to Wounded Knee*. New York and Oxford: Oxford University Press.
Anderson, Terry H. (1999) *The Sixties*. New York: Addison Wesley Longman, Inc.
Anselme, M. (1991) 'Les Delices de l'Espace Pubic: Remarques à propos du spectacle d'Ilotopie, *Le Palace à Loyer Modéré (P.L.M.)*'. La Castellane, May 1990. Study on *P.L.M.* realized by S. Anselme, S. Bensasson, C. Gontier, A. Ottaviano, A. Pierrot and N. Spinousa. Article in the box on Ilotopie at HorsLesMurs.
Aron, Raymond. (1968) *La Révolution Introuvable*. Paris: Fayard.
Art into Society/Society into Art: Seven German Artists. (1974) London: Institute of Contemporary Arts.
Artangel. (2002) *Off Limits: 40 Artangel Projects*. London: Merrell.
Artichoke News. September 2006.
Artichoke Productions (www.artichoke.uk.com).
Audooren, Fabien, ed. (2008) *ISTF: Internationaal Straattheater Festival vzw (International Street Theatre Festival)*. ISTF vzw.
Audooren, Fabien, ed. (n.d.) *Straattheater: Impressies in Woord en Beld/ Théâtre de Rue: Impressions et Images/ Street Theatre: Impressions and Images*. Ghent, Belgium: Internationaal Straattheaterfestival VZW.
Augé, Marc (1995) *Non-Places: Introduction to an Anthropology of Supermodernity*. Trans. John Howe. London and New York: Verso.
Aurillac 2005: Vingtième Festival International de Théâtre de Rue. Catalogue des Compagnies. (2005) Aurillac: Association Eclat.
Austin, J.L. (1962 and 1975) *How To Do Things With Words*. 2nd edn. Cambridge, MA: Harvard University Press.
Bachelard, Gaston. (1994) *The Poetics of Space*. Trans. Maria Jolas. Boston: Beacon Press.

Back to Back Theatre. http://backtobacktheatre.com
Banes, Sally and Andre Lepecki, eds. (2007) *The Senses in Performance*. New York and London: Routledge.
Barber, Benjamin R. (31 August 2009) 'The Art of Public Space'. *The Nation*: n.p.
Barrett, Lisa Feldman, Paula M. Niedenthal and Piotr Winkielman, eds. (2005) *Emotion and Consciousness*. New York and London: The Guilford Press.
Becker, Carol and Ann Wiens, eds. (1995) *The Artist in Society*. Chicago: Chicago New Arts Association.
Belifore, Eleonora and Oliver Bennett. (2008) *The Social Impact of the Arts: An Intellectual History*. Basingstoke: Palgrave Macmillan.
Beneath the Paving Stones: Situationists and the Beach, May 1968. (2001) Texts Collected by Dark Star. Edinburgh and San Francisco: AK Press.
Benjamin, Walter (1968) *Illuminations*. Trans. Harry Zohn. New York: Schocken Books.
Bennett, Susan. (1990) *Theatre Audiences*. London: Routledge.
Berger, John. (1972) *Ways of Seeing*. London: Penguin Books.
Berleant, Arnold. (1970) *The Aesthetic Field: A Phenomenology of Aesthetic Experience*. Springfield, IL: Charles C. Thomas, Publisher.
Berman, Paul. (1996) *A Tale of Two Utopias: The Political Journey of the Generation of 1968*. New York and London: W.W. Norton & Company.
Bishop, Claire. (Autumn 2004) 'Antagonism and Relational Aesthetics'. *October* 110: 51–79.
Bishop, Claire. (Winter 2005) 'Art of the Encounter: Antagonism and Relational Aesthetics'. *Circa* 114: 32–5.
Bishop, Claire. (2005) *Installation Art*. New York: Routledge.
Bishop, Claire, ed. (2006) *Participation*. Cambridge, MA: MIT Press.
Bishop, Claire. (2009) 'The Social Turn: Collaboration and Its Discontents'. *Rediscovering Aesthetics: Transdisciplinary Voices from Art History, Philosophy, and Art Practice (Cultural Memory in the Present)*. Eds. Francis Halsall. Julia Jansen, and Tony O'Connor. Stanford: Stanford University Press, pp. 238–55.
Bloom, Alexander and Wini Breines, eds. (2003) *'Takin' it to the Streets': A Sixties Reader*. Oxford: Oxford University Press.
Boal, Augusto. (1985) *Theatre of the Oppressed*. Trans. by Charles A. and Maria-Odilia Leal McBride. New York: Theatre Communications Group.
Bompard, Barthélémy, Joel Cramesnil, Jean-Pierre Tutard and La Compagnie Kumulus. (2007) *Rencontres de Boîtes*. Montpellier: Éditions L'Entretemps.
Bordenave, Julie. (October 2007) 'Utopie ou divertissement poétique?' *Stradda* 6: 2–7.
Bordenave, Julie. (January 2009) '2008, une 'Rue Libre!' partagée'. *Stradda* 11: 33–5.
Bordenave, Julie. (April 2010) 'Est-ce que le monde sait qu'il me parle?' *Stradda* 16: 24.
Borreca, Art. (1993) 'Political Dramaturgy: A Dramaturg's (Re)View'. *The Drama Review: TDR* 37.2: 56–79.
Bourges, Hervé. (1968) *The French Student Revolt: The Leaders Speak*. Trans. B.R. Brewster. New York: Hill and Wang.
Bourriaud, Nicolas. (2002) *Relational Aesthetics*. Trans. Simon Pleasance and Fronza Woods. Dijon-Quetigny: Les Presses de réel.

Bradford, Gigi, Michael Gary, and Glenn Wallach, eds. (2000) *The Politics of Culture: Policy Perspectives for Individuals, Institutions, and Communities*. New York: The New Press.
Bradley, Will and Charles Esche, eds. (2007) *Art and Social Change: A Critical Reader*. London: Tate Publishing with Afterall.
Brian, Crystal. (2005) 'Devising Community'. *Theatre Topics* 15.1: 1–13.
Brown, Bernard E. (1974) *Protest in Paris: Anatomy of a Revolt*. New Jersey: General Learning Press.
Buckley, Anne. (October 2009) 'Fallen Fruit: Another Year in LA and LACE'. *Art in America*: 176.
Bruno, Giuliana. (2002) *Atlas of Emotion: Journeys in Art, Architecture, and Film*. New York: Verso.
Burton, Richard. (1989) 'The Arguments for Public Art'. *Art for Public Spaces: Critical Essays*. Ed. Malcolm Miles. Winchester: Winchester School of Art Press, pp. 1–15.
Calhoun, Craig, ed. (1992) *Habermas and the Public Sphere*. Cambridge, MA and London: The MIT Press.
Canivet, Pascale, ed. (1997) *Theatre Ambulant: Nouvelles formes, nouveaux lieux*. Orléans: Éditions HYX.
Carlson, Allen. (1993) 'Aesthetics and Engagement'. *British Journal of Aesthetics* 33.3: 220–7.
Carter, Erica, James Donald, and Judith Squires, eds. (1993) *Space and Place: Theories of Identity and Location*. London: Lawrence & Wishart.
Cavallo, Dominick. (1999) *A Fiction of the Past: The Sixties in American History*. Basingstoke: Palgrave.
'Chalon-dans-la-rue. Festival Transnational des artistes de la rue'. (21–24 July 2005) Brochure.
Chambers, Samuel A. (April 2004) 'Giving up (on) Rights? The Future of Rights and the Project of Radical Democracy'. *American Journal of Political Science* 48.2: 185–200.
Chaudoir, Philippe. (2000) *Discours et figures de l'espace public à travers les 'arts de la rue': La ville en scènes*. Paris: l'Harmattan.
Chaudoir, Philippe. (1999) 'Distance/Décalage Intervention Artistique et Regard Sociologique: Une Impossible Alliance?' *Pour une Sociologie de la forme*. Ed. Sylvia Ostrowetsky. Paris: L'Harmattan, pp. 341–63.
Chaudoir, Philippe. (1999) 'L'Interpellation dans les Arts de la Rue'. *Les Langages de la Rue*. Paris: L'Harmattan, pp. 167–92.
Christie, Julie, Richard Gough and Daniel Watt, eds. (2006) *A Performance Cosmology*. London: Routledge.
Clidière, Sylvie. (Juillet/Août 2003) 'L'Exode des comédiens'. *Cassandre*. n.p.
Clidière, Sylvie. (2008) 'Exterior Dance'. *Ballettanz. Das Jahrbuch*. pp. 12–25.
Clidière, Sylvie and Alix de Morant. (2009) *Extérieure Danse: Essai sur la dance dans l'espace public*. Montpellier: Éditions L'Entretemps. (Includes DVD).
Clough, Patricia Ticineto, ed. (2007) *The Affective Turn: Theorizing the Social*. Durham and London: Duke University Press.
Cohen-Cruz, Jan. (2010) *Engaging Performance: Theatre as Call and Response*. London and New York: Routledge.
Cohen-Cruz, Jan, ed. (1998) *Radical Street Performance: An International Anthology*. London and New York: Routledge.

Colebrook, Claire. (2002) *Gilles Deleuze*. London and New York: Routledge.
Coles, Alex, ed. (2000) *Site-Specificity: The Ethnographic Turn*. Volume 4. London: Black Dog Publishing Ltd.
Colomina, Beatriz. (1994) *Privacy and Publicity: Modern Architecture as Mass Media*. Cambridge, MA: MIT Press.
Compagnie Kumulus. Folder. HorsLesMurs. Paris, France.
Compagnie Kumulus. *Itinéraire Sans Fond(s)*, a preliminary preparation dossier (PPD), Box A00380. HorsLesMurs. Paris, France.
Compagnie Kumulus. *Itinéraire Sans Fond(s)* dossier from the residence at Bonlieu Scène Nationale at Annecy (DA), Box A00380. HorsLesMurs. Paris, France.
Compagnie Kumlus. *Itinéraire Sans Fond(s)*, Notes post-créatrices (PC), Box A00380. HorsLesMurs. Paris, France.
Compagnie Kumulus. www.kumulus.fr
Compagnie Willi Dorner. http://www.ciewdorner.at/
Community Arts Network, http://www.communityarts.net
Conquergood, Dwight. (June 1991) 'Rethinking Ethnography'. *Communication Monographs* 58: 179–94.
Coverley, Merlin. (2006) *Psychogeography*. Harpenden, Herts: Pocket Essentials.
Cresswell, Tim. (1996) *In Place/Out of Place: Geography, Ideology, and Transgression*. Minneapolis: University of Minnesota Press.
Cresswell, Tim. (2004) *Place: A Short Introduction*. Oxford: Blackwell Publishing.
Crossley, Nick and John Michale Roberts, eds. (2004) *After Habermas: New Perspectives on the Public Sphere*. Oxford: Blackwell Publishing.
Cull, Laura. (2011) 'Performing Presence, Affirming Difference: Deleuze and the Minor theatres of Georges Lavaudant and Carmelo Bene'. Eds. Clare Finburgh and Carl Lavery. Basingstoke: Palgrave Macmillan, pp. 99–110.
Cull, Laura. (2012) 'Performance as Philosophy: Responding to the Problem of "Application"'. *Theatre Research International* 37.1: 207.
Cull, Laura, ed. (2009) *Deleuze and Performance*. Edinburgh: Edinburgh University Press.
'Culture et Société, Arts dans l'Espace Publique: Quelles Articulations? Les Arts de la rue et les arts du cirque dans la politique de la ville'. (2010) Compte-rendu de la Rencontre Professionelle du 15 décembre 2009. Organisée par HorsLesMurs.
Damasio, Antonio. (1994/2006) *Descartes' Error*. London: Vintage Books.
Damasio, Antonio. (2003) *Looking for Spinoza: Joy, Sorrow and the Feeling Brain*. London: Vintage Books.
Dapporto, Elena and Dominique Sagot-Duvauroux. (2000) *Les Arts de la Rue: portrait économique d'un secteur en pleine effervescence*, Paris: La Documentation française.
David, Gwénola. (Mai 2002) 'Public Chéri: Un Autre Rapport?' *Scènes Urbaines* 1: 26.
Davis, Tracy C. and Thomas Postlewait, eds. (2003) *Theatricality*. Cambridge and New York: Cambridge University Press.
de Certeau, Michel. (1988) *The Practice of Everyday Life*. Trans. Steven Rendall. Berkeley, CA: University of California Press.
de Certeau, Michel. (1998) *The Capture of Speech and Other Political Writings*. Ed. Luce Giard. Trans. Tom Conley. Minneapolis and London: University of Minnesota Press.

De La Boulaye, Pauline. (Avril 2010) 'L'art confondant du camouflage'. *Stradda* 16: 37–40.
de Lage, Christophe Renaud. (2000) *Intérieur Rue: 10 Ans de théâtre de rue (1989–1999)*. Montreuil-Sous-Bois: Éditions Théâtrales.
De Marinis, Marco. (1987) 'Dramaturgy of the Spectator'. *The Drama Review: TDR* 31.2, pp. 100–14.
De Morant, Alix. (November 2009) 'Dancing the Space: New Terrain for Choreographers'. *Stradda*. Special Edition in English: 13–20.
Dean, Tacita and Jeremy Millar. (2005) *Place*. Thames and Hudson: Art Works Series.
Debord, Guy. (1990) *Comments on the Society of Spectacle*. Trans. Malcolm Imrie. London and New York: Verso.
Debord, Guy. (1994, repr. 2004) *The Society of Spectacle*. Trans. Donald Nicholson-Smith. New York: Zone Books.
Delarozière, François. (2003) *Le Grand Repertoire: Machines de Spectacle*. Arles: Actes Sud.
Deleuze, Gilles. (1964) *Proust and Signs*. Trans. R. Howard. New York: Columbia University Press.
Deleuze, Gilles. (1995) *Negotiations: 1972–90*. Trans. Martin Joughin. New York: Columbia University Press.
Deleuze, Gilles. (1997) 'One Less Manifesto'. Trans. E. Dal Molin and T. Murray. *Mimesis, Masochism, and Mime*. Ed. T. Murray. Ann Arbor: University of Michigan Press, pp. 239–58.
Deleuze, Gilles and Félix Guattari. (1988) *A Thousand Plateaus: Capitalism and Schizophrenia*. Trans. Brian Massumi. London: The Athlone Press.
Deleuze, Gilles and Félix Guattari. (1994) *What Is Philosophy?* Trans. Hugh Tomlinson and Graham Burchill. London and New York: Verso.
Delfour, Jean-Jacques. (1997) 'Rue et théâtre de rue: habitation de l'espace urbain et spectacle théâtral'. *Espaces et Sociétés 90/91: Les Langages de la Rue*. Paris: L'Harmattan, pp. 145–66.
Delfour, Jean-Jacques. (2009a) '*Le Cri* de Kumulus, *Élu* du Théâtre Group et *En Campagne* de Générik Vapeur: de spectacles politiques?' *Philosophie du visible*—Blog LeMonde.fr. http://jjdelfour.blog.lemonde.fr
Delfour, Jean-Jacques. (2009b) 'Zoo humaine et ethnographie imaginaire: *Safari Intime* d"Opéra Pagaï'. *Philosophie du visible*—Blog LeMonde.fr. http://jjdelfour blog.lemonde.tr
Demey, Kurt. Rode Boom. http://www.artefake.com/RODE-BOOM-compagnie. html
Desperate Men. http://www.desperatemen.com/
Deutsche, Rosalyn. (1992) 'Art and Public Space: Questions of Democracy'. *Social Text* 33: 34–53.
Deutsche, Rosalyn. (1996) *Evictions: Art and Spatial Politics*. Cambridge, MA and London: The MIT Press.
Deutsche, Rosalyn, Hans Haacke, and Miwon Kwon. (Summer 2004) 'Der Bevölkerung: A Conversation' *Grey Room* 16: 60–81.
Dewey, John. (1934) *Art as Experience*. New York: Penguin.
Dissanayake, Ellen. (2000) *Art and Intimacy: How the Arts Began*. Seattle and London: University of Washington Press.
Docherty, Thomas. (2006) *Aesthetic Democracy*. Stanford: Stanford University Press.

Dodds, George. (2008) 'Performance Anxiety'. *Journal of Architectural Education* 61.4: 3.
Doherty, Claire. (2004) 'The New Situationists'. *Contemporary Art: From Studio to Situation*. Ed. Claire Doherty. London: Black Dog Publishing, Ltd., pp. 7–13.
Doherty, Claire, ed. (2009) *Situation*. London: Whitechapel Gallery and Cambridge, MA: MIT Press.
Dolan, Jill. (2005) *Utopia in Performance: Finding Hope at the Theater*. Ann Arbor: University of Michigan Press.
Donald, James. (1999) *Imagining the Modern City*. Minneapolis, MN: University of Minneapolis Press.
Donald, Merlin. (Spring 1993) 'Human Cognitive Evolution: What We Were, What We Are Becoming'. *Social Research* 60.1: 143–70.
Dossier #3: 'Adventurous Terrains: Composing for and with the Territory' (July 2009) Online publication translating articles from *Stradda #9: Terrains d'Aventures [Ecrire pour et avec le territoire]* (2008) into English. www.stradda.fr.
Dreyfus, Emmanuelle. (Janvier 2010) 'La Compagnie des riverains'. *Stradda* 15: 42–5.
Edelman, Murray. (1995) *From Art to Politics: How Artistic Creations Shape Political Conceptions*. Chicago and London: University of Chicago Press.
Eisenstein, Zillah. (2004) *Against Empire: Feminisms, Racism, and the West*. London and New York: Zed Books.
ERICarts, Parlement européen (November 2006) 'Mobilité des artistes et sécurité sociale'. http://www.europarl.europa.eu/activities/expert/eStudies.do?language=EN
ERICarts 'The status of artists in the European Union'.http://www.europarl.europa.eu/activities/expert/eStudies.do?language=EN
Espaces st Sociétés 90/91: Les Langages de la rue. (1997) Paris: L'Harmattan.
Estournet, Jean-Pierre and Bernard Begadi. (1992) *Scènes de Rue*. Paris: Éditions Mermon.
Eversmann, Peter. (2004) 'The Experience of the Theatrical Event'. *Theatrical Events: Borders Dynamics Frames*. Eds. Vicky Ann Cremona, Peter Eversmann, Hans van Maanen, Willmar Sauter and John Tulloch. Amsterdam and New York: Rodopi.
Fallen Fruit, http://www.fallenfruit.org/
Feenberg, Andrew and Jim Freedman. (2001) *When Poetry Ruled the Streets: The French May Events of 1968*. Albany, NY: State University of New York Press.
Felshin, Nina, ed. (1995) *But is it Art? The Spirit of Art as Activism*. Seattle: Bay Press.
Feuer, Wendy. (1989) 'Public Art from a Public Sector Perspective'. *Art in the Public Interest*. Ed. Arlene Raven. Ann Arbor and London: U.M.I. Research Press, pp. 139–53.
Fink, Carole, Philipp Gassert and Detlef Junker, eds. (1998) *1968: The World Transformed*. Washington, DC: German Historical Institute and Cambridge: Cambridge University Press.
Finkelpearl, Tom. (2001) *Dialogues in Public Art*. Cambridge, MA: MIT Press.
Fischer-Lichte, Erika. (2008) *The Transformative Power of Performance: A New Aesthetics*. Trans. Saskya Iris Jain. London and New York: Routledge.
Fleming, Ronald Lee. (2007) *The Art of Placemaking: Interpreting Community Through Public Art and Urban Design*. London and New York: Merrell.

Floch, Yohann, coordinator. (2006) *Public Policies in Favour of Street Arts and Circus Arts in Europe – Preliminary Study*, CRCMD-Université de Bourgogne, Paris, HorsLesMurs.
Floch, Yohann. (Juillet 2007) 'L'Artiste a-t-il sa place dans l'espace public européen?' *Stradda* 5: 54–5.
Floch, Yohann (2007) *Street Artists in Europe*, Brussels: European Parliament's Committee on Culture and Education. http://www.europarl.europa.eu/activities/expert/eStudies.do?language=EN or www.fitzcarraldo.it/pdf/street_arts.pdf
Ford, Simon. (2005) *The Situationist International: A User's Guide*. London: Black Dog Publishing Ltd.
Foster, Hal, ed. (1987) *Discussions in Contemporary Culture*. Number 1. Seattle: Bay Press.
Foster, Susan Leigh. (1995) 'An Introduction to Moving Bodies'. *Choreographing History*. Ed. Susan Leigh Foster. Bloomington and Indianapolis: Indiana University Press, pp. 3–21.
Foster, Susan Leigh. (2003) 'Choreographies of Protest'. *Theatre Journal* 55: 395–412.
Foucault, Michel. (1986) 'Of Other Spaces'. Trans. J. Miskowiec. *Diacritics* 16.1: 22–7.
Fraser, Nancy. (1992) 'Rethinking the Public Sphere: A Contribution to the Critique of Actually Existing Democracy'. *Habermas and the Public Sphere*. Ed Craig Calhoun. Cambridge, MA and London, UK: The MIT Press, pp. 109–42.
Fraser, Nick. 'Philosophy in the Streets'. BBC Radio 4. 30 April 2008. http://www.bbc.co.uk/radio4/1968/
Freire, Paulo. (1989) *Pedagogy of the Oppressed*. Trans. Myra Bergman Ramos. New York: Continuum.
Freire, Paulo. (1994) *Pedagogy of Hope: Reliving Pedagogy of the Oppressed*. Trans. Robert R. Barr. New York: Continuum.
Freire, Paulo. (1998) *Pedagogy of Freedom: Ethics, Democracy, and Civic Courage*. Trans. Patrick Clarke. Lanham, Boulder, New York, Oxford: Rowman & Littlefield Publishers, Inc.
Freire, Paulo and Peader Kirby. (1982) 'Interview with Paulo Freire'. *The Crane Bag* 6.2: 45–8.
Freydefont, Marcel and Charlotte Granger, eds. (2008) *Théâtre de rue, un théâtre de l'échange*. Louvain-la-Neuve, Belgium: Études Théâtrales.
Friches Théâtre Urbain. Folder. HorsLesMurs. Paris, France.
Friches Théâtre Urbain. www.friches.fr/
Fried, Michael. (1998) *Art and Objecthood*. Chicago and London: The University of Chicago Press.
Fuchs, Elinor and Una Chaudhuri, eds. (2002) *Land/Scape/Theater*. Ann Arbor: University of Michigan Press.
Fuller, Peter. (1980) *Seeing Berger: A Reevaluation*. Whitstable, Kent: Writers and Readers.
Gaber, Floriane. (2009a) *40 Years of Street Arts*. Trans. Kate Merrill. Paris: Éditions ici & là.
Gaber, Floriane. (2009b) *How It All Started: Street Arts in the Context of the 1970s*. Trans. Kate Merrill. Paris: Éditions ici & là.
Gaber, Floriane, Project Co-ordinator. (n.d.) *The Street Arts Publics in Europe*. Ghent, Belgium: Study commissioned by EUNETSTAR.

Gablik, Sue. (1991) *The Reenchantment of Art*. New York and London: Thames and Hudson.
Gallagher, Shaun. (2005) *How the Body Shapes the Mind*. Oxford: Clarendon Press.
Gallagher, Winifred. (1993) *The Power of Place: How Our Surroundings Shape Our Thoughts, Emotions, and Actions*. New York: HarperCollins Publishers, Inc.
Générik Vapeur. Folder. HorsLesMurs. Paris, France.
Gerard, Naly. (Octobre 2007) 'Stimuler sa propre de politique'. *Stradda* 6: 34.
Gilbert, Helen and Jacqueline Lo. (2007) *Performance and Cosmopolitics: Cross-Cultural Transactions in Australia*. Basingstoke: Palgrave Macmillan.
Gilcher-Holtey, Ingrid. (1998) 'May 1968 in France: The Rise and Fall of a New Social Movement'. *1968: The World Transformed*. Eds. Carole Fink, Philipp Gassert, and Detlef Junker. Washington, DC: German Historical Institute and Cambridge: Cambridge University Press, pp. 253–76.
Gitlin, Todd. (1989, rev. 1993) *The Sixties: Years of Hope, Days of Rage*. New York: Bantam Books.
Glass, Ronald David. (2001) 'Freire's Philosophy of Praxis and the Foundations of Liberation Education'. *Educational Researcher* 30.2: 15–25.
Glenberg, Arthur M. (1997) 'What Memory Is For' and 'Open Peer Commentary'. *Behavioral and Brain Sciences* 20: 1–55.
Gonon, Anne. (2006) 'Experiencing "Imaginary Realism": How French Street Theatre Companies Offer Theatrical Experiences to their Audience'. *Culture and Communication, Proceedings of the XIX Congress International Association of Empirical Aesthetics*. 524–45.
Gonon, Anne. (2011) *In Vivo: Les Figures du spectateur des arts de la rue*. Montpellier: Éditions L'Entretemps.
Gonon, Anne. (2007) 'Les Spect'Acteurs'. *Stradda* 6: 17–19.
Gonon, Anne, ed. (2006) *La Relation au Public dans les Arts de la Rue*. Vic la Gariole: L'Entretemps Editions.
Goodman, Lizbeth with Jane de Gay, eds. (2000) *The Routledge Reader in Politics and Performance*. London and New York: Routledge.
Goodwin, Jeff and James M. Jasper. (2004) *Rethinking Social Movements: Structure, Meaning, and Emotion*. Lanham, Boulder, New York, Toronto, and Oxford: Rowman & Littlefield Publishers, Inc.
Goodwin, Jeff, James M. Jasper and Francesca Polletta. (2001) *Passionate Politics: Emotions and Social Movements*. Chicago: University of Chicago Press.
Gourdon, Jean-Loup. (2001) *La Rue: Essai sur l'économie de la forme urbaine*. Gémenos: Éditions de l'Aube.
Granger, Charlotte. (2008) 'En Guise d'épilogue'. Marcel Freydefont and Charlotte Granger, eds. *Théâtre de rue, un théâtre de l'échange*. Louvain-la-Neuve, Belgium: Études Théâtrales, pp. 261–2.
Gregoire, R. and F. Perlman. (1969) *Worker–Student Action Committees, France, May '68*. Detroit, MI: Black and Red.
Gregory, Derek. (1994) *Geographical Imaginations*. Cambridge, MA and Oxford, UK: Blackwell.
Greenberg, Clement. (1940) 'Towards a Newer Laocoon'. In *Clement Greenberg: The Collected Essays and Criticism*, Volume 1. Ed John O'Brien. (1986) Chicago and London: University of Chicago Press, pp. 23–38.
Guénoun, Denis. *Aurillac aux Limites: Théâtre de Rue*. (2005) Arles: Actes Sud.

Guattari, Félix. (2006) 'Chaosmosis: An Ethico-Aesthetic Paradigm, 1992'. *Participation*. Ed. Claire Bishop. London: Whitechapel, pp. 79–82.
Habermas, Jürgen. (1992) 'Concluding Remarks'. *Habermas and the Public Sphere* Ed. Craig Calhoun. Cambridge, MA and London, UK: The MIT Press, pp. 462–79.
Habermas, Jürgen. (1995) *The Structural Transformation of the Public Sphere: An Inquiry into a Category of Bourgeois Society*. Cambridge, MA: The MIT Press.
Haedicke, Susan C. (September 2002) 'Politics of Participation: *Un Voyage Pas Comme Les Autres Sur Les Chemins De L'Exil'*. *Theatre Topics* 12.2: 99–118.
Haedicke, Susan C. (2006) 'Discomfort at the Intersections of the Imaginary and Everyday Worlds in Friches Théâtre Urbain's *Macbeth* for the Street'. *Text and Performance Quarterly* 26.3: 253–73.
Haedicke, Susan C. (2008) 'The Outsider Outside: Performing Immigration in French Street Theatre'. *Performance and Violence: Local Roots and Global Routes of Conflict*. Eds. Patrick Anderson and Jisha Menon. Basingstoke: Palgrave/Macmillan, pp. 31–53.
Haedicke, Susan C. (2011) 'Breaking Down the Walls: Interventionist Performance Strategies in French Street Theatre'. *Theatre and Performance in Contemporary France*. Eds. Clare Finburgh and Carl Lavery. Basingstoke: Palgrave/Macmillan, pp. 162–73.
Headicke, Susan C. (2012a) 'Beyond Site-Specificity: Environmental Heterocosms on the Street'. *Performing Site-Specific Theatre*. Eds. Anna Birch and Joanne Tompkins. Forthcoming with Palgrave/Macmillan.
Headicke, Susan C. (2012b) 'Opéra Pagaï's *Entreprise de Détournement*: Collage of Geographic, Imaginary and Discursive Spaces'. *Theatre and the Politics of Space*. Eds. Erika Fischer-Lichte and Benjamin Wihstutz. Forthcoming with Routledge in "Routledge Advances in Theatre and Performance" series.
Hall, Felicity. (2002) *Strategy and Report on Street Arts*, London: Arts Council of England.
Hall, Tim and Chereen Smith. (2005) 'Public Art in the City: Meanings, Values, Attitudes, and Roles'. *Interventions: Advances in Art and Urban Futures Volume 4*. Eds. Malcolm Miles and Tim Hall. Bristol, England and Portland, OR: Intellect, pp. 175–9.
Hall, Stuart. (1988) 'Popular-Democratic vs. Authoritarian Populism: Two Ways of Taking Democracy Seriously'. *The Hard Road to Renewal: Thatcherism and the Crisis of the Left*. London: Verso, pp. 123–49.
Hamon-Siréjols, Christine and Anne Surgers, eds. (2003) *Théâtre: espace sonore, espace visuel. Theater: Sound Space, Visual Space*. Lyon: Presses Universitaires de Lyon.
Hanna, Dorita and Omar Khan. (2008) 'Performance/Architecture'. *Journal of Architectural Education* 61.4: 4–5.
Hardt, Michael. (2007) 'Foreword: What Are Affects Good For?' *The Affective Turn: Theorizing the Social*. Patricia Ticineto Clough. Durham and London: Duke University Press, pp. ix–xiii.
Harper, Glenn, ed. (1998) *Interventions and Provocations: Conversations on Art, Culture, and Resistance*. Albany: State University of New York Press.
Harper, Sarah. (2007a) *Dossier Artistique: Witness/N14*.
Harper, Sarah. (2007b) *Dossier Artistique: Witness/N14*.
Harper, Sarah. (2009a) *Dossier Artistique: Witness/N14: 5 Parcours de randonnées artistiques en Ile de France De Levallois à St Clair/Epte*.

Harper, Sarah. (2009b) *Witness/N14: Parcours 02, Au-delà du périph*. Bilans.
Harper, Sarah. (2010) *Witness/N14: Parcours 05, Un pas de côté*. Bilans.
Harper, Sarah. (2011) *Le Glissement des axes sur la route avec mes voisins*. Promotional Brochure.
Harris, Sue. (2004) '"Dancing in the Streets": The Aurillac Festival of Street Theatre'. *Contemporary Theatre Review* 14.2: 57–71.
Harrison-Pepper, Sally. (1990) *Drawing a Circle in the Square*. Jackson and London: University Press of Mississippi.
Harvey, David. (1990) *The Condition of Postmodernity: An Inquiry into the Origins of Cultural Change*. Cambridge, MA and Oxford, UK: Blackwell.
Harvey, David. (2000) *Spaces of Hope*. Berkeley and Los Angeles: University of California Press.
Harvie, Jen. (2009) *Theatre and the City*. Basingstoke: Palgrave Macmillan.
Harvie, Jen. (2011) 'Democracy and Neoliberalism in Art's Social Turn and Roger Hiorns's Seizure'. *Performance Research* 16.2: 113–23.
Hayden, Dolores. (1992) 'An American Sense of Place (with an afterword)'. Eds. Harriet Senie and Sally Webster. *Critical Issues in Public Art: Content, Context, and Controversy*. Washington and London: Smithsonian Institution Press, pp. 261–9.
Hayden, Dolores. (1995) *The Power of Place: Urban Landscapes as Urban History*. Cambridge: MIT Press.
Heilmann, Éric, Françoise Léger, Jean-Louis Sagot-Duvaroux and Bruno Schnebelin. (2008) *Les Utopies à l'Epreuve de l'Art: Ilotopie*. Montpellier: L'Entretemps Éditions.
Hewitt, Andy and Mel Jordan (Freee). (2005) *Futurology: Issues, Contexts and Conditions for Contemporary Art Practice Today*. UK: The New Art Gallery Walsall.
Hill, Leslie and Helen Paris. (2006) *Performance and Place*. Basingstoke and New York: Palgrave Macmillan.
Hoffman, Jens and Joan Jonas. (2005) *Perform*. Thames and Hudson: Art Works Series.
Hiss, Tony. (1990) *The Experience of Place*. New York: Random House, Inc.
hooks, bell. (2009) *Belonging: A Culture of Place*. New York and London: Routledge.
Hopkins, D.J., Shelley Orr, and Kim Solga. (2009) *Performance and the City*. Basingstoke: Palgrave Macmillan.
Howes, David, ed. (2005) *Empire of the Senses: The Sensual Cultural Reader*. Oxford and New York: Berg.
Hussey, Andrew (2008) 'The Paris Intifada: The Long War in the Banlieue'. *Granta* 101: 41–59.
In Situ: Voyages d'Artiste Européens/European Artists on the Road. (2006) Éditions l'Entretemps.
Ilotopie. Folder. HorsLesMurs. Paris, France.
Ilotopie, www.ilotopie.com
Independent Street Arts Network (ISAN), www.streetartsnetwork.org.uk.
Jackson, Shannon. (2011) *Social Works: Performing Art, Supporting Publics*. New York and London: Routledge.
Jackson, Shannon. (2011) 'Working Publics'. *Performance Research* 16.2: 8–13.
Jakovljivic, Branislav. (Autumn 2005) 'The Space Specific Theatre: "Skewed Visions" *The City Itself*'. *The Drama Review* 49.3: 96–106.

Jameson, Fredric. (1977) 'Reflections in Conclusion'. *Aesthetics and Politics*. Trans. Ed. Ronald Taylor. London: NLB, pp. 196–213.
Jappe, Anselm. (1999) *Guy Debord*. Trans. Donald Nicholson-Smith. Berkeley, Los Angeles, and London: University of California Press.
Jasper, James M. (1997) *The Art of Moral Protest: Culture, Biography, and Creativity in Social Movements*. Chicago and London: University of Chicago Press.
Jasper, James M. (1998) 'The Emotions of Protest: Affective and Reactive Emotions in and Around Social Movements'. *Sociological Forum* 13.3: 397–424.
Jasper, James M. and Jane D. Poulsen. (1995) 'Recruiting Strangers and Friends: Moral Shocks and Social Networks in Animal Rights and Anti-Nuclear Protests'. *Social Problems* 42.4: 493–512.
Jeanne Simone. Folder. HorsLesMurs. Paris, France.
Jeanne Simone (2007–2008) *Le Goudron n'est pas meuble*. Unpublished Artistic Dossier (English translation by the company), personal correspondence with company.
Jeanne Simone. (2010) *Mademoiselle*. Unpublished Artistic Dossier (English translation by the company).
Jeanne Simone. (12 October 2007) www.dailymotion.com/video/x36yqq_compagnie-jeanne-simone_fun
Jeanne Simone. (26 November 2008) *Le Goudron n'est pas meuble*. www.dailymotion.pl/video/x7j67z_le-goudron-nest-pas-meublecie-jeann_creation
Jeanne Simone. (September 2011) *Mademoiselle*. http://globulefilms.com/index.php?/project/mademoiselle/
Johnson, Mark. (1990) *The Body in the Mind: The Bodily Basis of Meaning, Imagination, and Reason*. repr. Chicago: University of Chicago Press.
Johnson, Mark. (2007) *The Meaning of the Body: Aesthetics of Human Understanding*. Chicago and London: The University of Chicago Press.
Johnstone, Stephen, ed. (2008) *The Everyday*. London: Whitechapel and Cambridge, MA: MIT Press.
Jones, Seitu. (1992) 'Public Art That Inspires: Public Art That Informs'. Eds. Harriet Senie and Sally Webster. *Critical Issues in Public Art: Content, Context, and Controversy*. Washington and London: Smithsonian Institution Press, pp. 280–6.
Kahn, Fred. (October 2007) 'Françoise Léger, La Vie en Ilotopie'. *Stradda* 6: 15.
Kaprow, Allan. (1993) *Essays on the Blurring of Art and Life*. Ed. Jeff Kelley. Berkeley: University of California Press.
Karp, Ivan and Steven D. Lavine, eds. (1991) *Exhibiting Cultures: The Poetics and Politics of Museum Display*. Washington, D.C. and London: Smithsonian Institution Press.
Kaye, Nick. (2000) *Site-Specific Art: Performance, Place, and Documentation*. New York and London: Routledge.
Kelley, Jeff. (1995) 'The Body Politics of Suzanne Lacy'. *But is it Art? The Spirit of Art as Activism*. Ed. Nina Felshin. Seattle: Bay Press, pp. 221–49.
Kennedy, Dennis. (2009) *The Spectator and the Spectacle: Audiences in Modernity and Postmodernity*. Cambridge: Cambridge University Press.
Kershaw, Baz. (1992) *The Politics of Performance: Radical Theatre as Cultural Intervention*. London: Routledge.
Kershaw, Baz. (1999) *The Radical in Performance: Between Brecht and Baudrillard*. London: Routledge.

Kershaw, Baz. (December 2003) "Curiosity or Contempt: On Spectacle, the Human, and Activism." *Theatre Journal* 55.4: 591–612.
Kester, Grant H. (2004) *Conversation Pieces: Community + Communication in Modern Art*. Los Angeles: University of California Press.
Kester, Grant H. (2005) 'Conversation Pieces: The Role of Dialogue in Socially-Engaged Art'. *Theory in Contemporary Art: From 1985 to the Present*. Eds. Zoya Kucor and Simon Leung. Oxford: Blackwell, pp. 76–88.
Kester, Grant H. (2011) *The One and the Many: Contemporary Collaborative Art in a Global Context*. Durham and London: Duke University Press.
Khan, Omar and Dorita Hannah. (2008) 'Performance/Architecture: An Interview with Bernard Tschumi'. *Journal of Architectural Education* 61. 4: 52–8.
Kieran, Matthew. (2005) *Revealing Art: Why Art Matters*. London and New York: Routledge.
Klanten, Robert. (2010) *Urban Interventions: Personal Projects in Public Spaces*. Berlin: Die Gestalten Verlag.
Klanten, Robert, Matthias Hübner, Alain Bieber, Pedro Alonzo and Gregor Jansen,eds. (2011) *Art & Agenda: Political Art and Activism*. Berlin: Gestalten.
Knabb, Ken, ed. (2006) *Situationist International Anthology*. Revised and Expanded Edition. Berkeley, CA: Bureau of Public Secrets.
Knight, Cher Krause. (2008) *Public Art: Theory, Practice and Populism*. Oxford: Blackwell Publishing.
Král, Petr. (2007) *Enquête sur des lieux*. Normandie: Flammarion.
Krasner, David. (2006) 'Empathy and Theater'. *Staging Philosophy: Intersections of Theater, Performance, and Philosophy*. Eds. David Krasner and David Z. Saltz. Ann Arbor: University of Michigan Press, pp. 255–77.
Krasner, David and David Z. Saltz, eds. (2006) *Staging Philosophy: Intersections of Theater, Performance, and Philosophy*. Ann Arbor: University of Michigan Press.
Ktha Compagnie. www.ktha.org/
Kumar, Krishna. (1998) 'Freire's Legacy'. *Economic and Political Weekly* 33.46: 2912–15.
Kurlansky, Mark. (2004) *1968: The Year That Rocked the World*. New York: Random House.
Kwon, Miwon. (2004) *One Place After Another: Site-Specific Art and Locational Identity*. Cambridge: MIT Press.
Lacombe, Robert. (2004) *Le spectacle vivant en Europe: modèle d'organisation et politiques de soutien*, Paris: La Documentation française.
Lachaud, Jean-Marc, ed. (1999) *Art, culture et politique*. Paris: Presses Universitaires de France.
Lachaud, Jean-Marc, ed. (2006) *Art et Politique*. Paris: L'Harmattan.
Laclau, Ernesto and Chantal Mouffe. (1985, 2nd edn 2001) *Hegemony and Socialist Strategy: Towards a Radical Democratic Politics*. London and New York: Verso.
Lacy, Suzanne. (1989) 'Fractured Space'. *Art in the Public Interest*. Ed. Arlene Raven. Ann Arbor and London: U.M.I. Research Press, pp. 287–301.
Lacy, Suzanne, ed. (1995) *Mapping the Terrain: New Genre Public Art*. Seattle, WA: Bay Press.
Lakoff, George and Mark Johnson. (1980, with new Afterword, 2003) *Metaphors We Live By*. Chicago and London: University of Chicago Press.
Lakoff, George and Mark Johnson. (1999) *Philosophy in the Flesh: The Embodied Mind and its Challenge to Western Thought*. New York: Basic Books.

Lane, Jill. (2002) 'Reverend Billy: Preaching, Protest, and Postindustrial Flânerie'. *TDR* 46.1: 60–84.
Larsen, Lars Bang. (2006) 'Social Aesthetics, 1999'. *Participation*. Ed. Claire Bishop. London: Whitechapel, pp. 172–83.
Latour, Bruno. (2005) *Making Things Public: Atmospheres of Democracy*. Cambridge, MA: MIT Press.
Lebel, Jean-Jacques. (1998) 'Notes on Political Street Theatre, Paris: 1968, 1969'. *TDR: The Drama Review* 13.4 (1969) and reprinted in *Radical Street Performance: An International Anthology*. Ed. Jan Cohen-Cruz. London and New York: Routledge, pp. 179–84.
Ledrut, Raymond. (1986) 'Speech and the Silence of the City'. *The City and the Sign: An Introduction to Urban Semiotics*. Eds. M. Gottdeiner and Alexandros Ph. Lagopoulos. New York: Columbia University Press.
Le Floc'h, Maud, ed. (2009) 'Quelle Place pour les artistes?' *Stradda* 12: 12–27.
Le Floc'h, Maud, ed. (2006) *Un Élu, Un Artiste: Missions Repérage(s)*. Vic la Gardiole: Éditions l'Entretemps.
Le Goliath 2002: guide-annuaire des arts de la rue et des arts de la piste. (2002) Paris: HorsLesMurs.
Le Goliath: Guide Annuaire 2005–2006 des Arts de la Rue et des Arts de la Piste. (2005) Paris: HorsLesMurs.
Le Goliath 2008–2010: L'Annuaire des Professionnels. (2008) Fontenay-sous-Bois: HorsLesMurs.
'Le Temps des Arts de la Rue'. (2005) Présentation du programme en faveur des arts de la rue, initié en 2005 par le ministère de la culture et de la communication (Direction de la musique, de la danse, du théâtre et des spectacles). Pamphlet. HorsLesMurs.
Lefebvre, Henri. (1969) *The Explosion: Marxism and the French Revolution*. Trans. Alfred Ehrenfeld. New York: Monthly Review Press.
Lefebvre, Henri. (1991) *The Production of Space*. Trans. Donald Nicholson-Smith. Oxford: Blackwell Publishing.
Lefebvre, Henri. (1996) *Writings on Cities*. Trans. and edited by Eleonore Kaufman and Elizabeth Labas. Oxford: Blackwell.
Lefebvre, Henri. (2004) *Rhythmanalysis: Space, Time and Everyday Life*. Trans. Stuart Elden and Gerald Moore. London and New York, Continuum.
Lefebvre, Henri. (2007) *Everyday Life in the Modern World*. Trans. Sacha Rabinovitch. With a new introduction to the Transaction Edition by Philip Wander. New Brunswick, USA and London, UK: Transaction Publishers.
Lefort, Claude. (1988) *Democracy and Political Theory*. Trans. David Macey. Cambridge: Polity Press.
Levine, Caroline. (2007) *Provoking Democracy: Why We Need the Arts*. Oxford: Blackwell Publishing.
Liggett, Helen. (2003) *Urban Encounters*. Minneapolis and London: University of Minnesota Press.
Light, Andrew and Jonathan M. Smith, eds. (2005) *The Aesthetics of Everyday Life*. New York: Columbia University Press.
Lippard, Lucy R. (1989) 'Moving Targets/Moving Out'. *Art in the Public Interest*. Ed. Arlene Raven. Ann Arbor and London: U.M.I. Research Press, pp. 209–28.
Lippard, Lucy R. (1997) *The Lure of the Local: Senses of Place in a Multicentered Society*. New York and London: New Press.

Lippard, Lucy R. (1999) *On the Beaten Track: Tourism, Art, and Place*. New York: The New Press.
Looseley, David L. (1995) *The Politics of Fun: Cultural Policy and Debate in Contemporary France*. Oxford and Washington, D.C.: Berg Publishers.
Loxley, James. (2007) *Performativity*. London and New York: Routledge.
Lyotard, Jean-Francois. (1984) *The Postmodern Condition: A Report on Knowledge*. Trans. Goeff Bennington and Brian Massumi. Minneapolis: University of Minnesota Press.
Macedo, Stephen. (1997) *Reassessing the Sixties: Debating the Political and Cultural Legacy*. New York: W.W. Norton & Co., Inc.
Machon, Josephine. (2009) *(Syn)aesthetics: Redefining Visceral Performance*. Basingstoke: Palgrave Macmillan.
Madral, Philippe. (1969) *Le Théâtre hors les murs*. Paris: Éditions Le Seuil.
Marcuse, Herbert. (1970) *Five Lectures*. Harmondsworth: Penguin
Marcuse, Herbert. (1978) *The Aesthetic Dimension: Toward a Critique of Marxist Aesthetics*. Boston: Beacon Press.
Margolies, Eleanor, ed. (2009) *Theatre Materials*. London: Centre for Excellence in Training for Theatre. The Central School of Speech and Drama.
Martin, Bradford D. (2004) *The Theater is in the Street: Politics and Public Performance in Sixties America*. Amherst and Boston: University of Massachusetts Press.
Mason, Bim. (1992) *Street Theatre and Other Outdoor Performance*. London and New York: Routledge.
Mason, Jeffrey D. (1996) 'Street Fairs: Social Space, Social Performance'. *Theatre Journal* 48.3: 301–19.
Massey, Doreen. (1994) *Space, Place, and Gender*. Minneapolis: University of Minnesota Press.
Massey, Doreen. (2005) *For Space*. Los Angeles, London, New Delhi, Singapore, Washington, DC: Sage.
Massey, Doreen, John Allen, and Philip Sarre, eds. (2005) *Human Geography Today*. Malden, MA: Polity Press.
Massumi, Brian. (2002a) *Parables for the Virtual: Movement, Affect, Sensation*. Durham and London: Duke University Press.
Massumi, Brian. (2002b) *A Shock to Thought: Expression after Deleuze and Guattari*. London and New York: Routledge.
Mauret, Nathalie. (April 2007) 'Les Arts de la rue: sonti-ils devenus politiquement correct?' *Stradda* 4: 46–9.
McClellan, Andrew. (2003) 'Introduction'. *Art and Its Publics: Museum Studies at the Millennium*. Malden, MA: Blackwell Publishing, pp. xiii–viii.
McConachie, Bruce. (2008) *Engaging Audiences: A Cognitive Approach to Spectating in the Theatre*. Basingstoke: Palgrave Macmillan.
McConachie, Bruce and F. Elizabeth Hart, eds. (2006) *Performance and Cognition: Theatre Studies and the Cognitive Turn*. London and New York: Routledge.
McDonough, Tom, ed. (2004) *Guy Debord and the Situationalist International: Text and Documents*. Cambridge, Ma and London: The MIT Press.
McGrath, John. (2002) 'Theatre and Democracy'. *New Theatre Quarterly* 18: 133–9.
McLaren, Peter. (Spring 1996) 'Paulo Freire and the Academy: A Challenge from the U.S. Left'. *Cultural Critique* 33: 151–84.

McLaren, Peter. (1999) 'A Pedagogy of Possibility: Reflecting on Paulo Freire's Politics of Education: In Memory of Paulo Freire'. *Educational Researcher* 28.2: 49–54 + 56.
McManus, Helen. (October 2008) 'Enduring Agonism: Between Individuality and Plurality'. *Polity* 40.4: 509–25.
Menger, Pierre-Michel. (2005) *Les Intermittants du spectacle: Sociologie d'une exception*. Paris: Éditions de l'École des Hautes Études en Science Sociales.
Meyer, James. (2000) 'The Functional Site: or, The Transformation of Site-Specificity'. *Space Site, Intervention: Situating Installation Art*. Ed. Erika Suderburg. Minneapolis: University of Minnesota Press.
Micklem, D. (July 2006) *Street Arts Healthcheck*, Arts Council England, www.artscouncil.org.uk/documents/publications/phpYfKdxY.rtf
Miles, Malcolm. (1997) *Art, Space and the City*. London and New York: Routledge.
Miles, Malcolm. (2004) 'Critical Practice: Art, Intervention and Power'. http://www.malcolm.org.uk/CriticalPractice.html (Accessed 9 February 2010).
Miles, Malcolm. (2010) 'A Really-Possible Public Sphere?' Lecture given at Utopian Studies Conference, Marie Curie University, Lublin, Poland, http://www.malcolmmiles.org.uk/PossiblePublicSphere.html (Accessed 7 May 2011).
Miles, Malcolm. (2008/2009) 'Society as a Work of Art'. Paper based on radio talk given in London July 2008 and presentations at Royal Holloway College, University of London and Brunel University, http://www.malcolmmiles.org.uk/SocietyAsAWorkOfArt.html (Accessed 7 May 2011).
Miles, Malcolm. (2004) *Urban Avant-Gardes: Art, Architecture, and Change*. London and New York: Routledge.
Miles, Malcolm. (2008) *Urban Utopias: The Built and Social Architectures of Alternative Settlements*. London and New York: Routledge.
Miles, Malcolm. (2007) 'Whose City? Whose Culture?' http://www.malcolmmiles.org.uk/WhoseCityWhoseCulture.html. (Accessed 9 February 2010).
Miles, Malcolm, ed. (1989) *Art for Public Spaces: Critical Essays*. Winchester: Winchester School of Art Press.
Miles, Malcolm and Tim Hall. (2005) *Interventions: Advances in Art and Urban Futures*. Volume 4. Bristol: Intellect Books.
Miles, Malcolm and Tim Hall. (2003) *Urban Futures: Critical Commentaries on Shaping the City*. London and New York: Routledge.
Miles, Malcolm and Tim Hall, with Iain Borden, eds. (2004) *The City Cultures Reader*. 2nd edn. London and New York: Routledge.
Milin, Gildas, ed. (2002) *L'Assemblée Théâtrale*. Paris: Les Éditions de l'Amandier.
Miller, James. (1994) *Democracy in the Streets: From Port Huron to the Siege of Chicago, with a New Preface by the Author*. Cambridge, MA: Harvard University Press.
Mitchell, W.J.T., ed. (1990a) *Art and the Public Sphere*. Chicago and London: The University of Chicago Press.
Mitchell, W.J.T. (1990b) 'The Violence of Public Art: *Do the Right Thing*'. *Art and the Public Sphere*. Ed. W.J.T. Mitchell. Chicago and London: The University of Chicago Press, pp. 29–48.
Mouffe, Chantal. (1993, repr. 2005) *The Return of the Political*. London and New York: Verso.
Mouffe, Chantal. (2000) *The Democratic Paradox*. London and New York: Verso.

Mouffe, Chantal. (2005) *On the Political*. London and New York: Routledge.
Mouffe, Chantal, ed. (1992) *Dimensions of Radical Democracy: Pluralism, Citizenship, Community*. London and New York: Verso.
Mouffe, Chantal, Rosalyn Deutsche, Branden W. Joseph and Thomas Keenan. (Winter 2001) 'Every Form of Art Has a Political Dimension'. *Grey Room* 2: 98–125.
National Street Arts Audience. (Summer 2003) Independent Street Arts Network (ISAN), www.streetartsnetwork.org.uk
New Magic: The Emergence of a Contemporary Art. (2010). Dossier 7 extracted from *Stradda #16* and translated into English. Coordinated by Julie Bordenave.
Nguyen, Patrick and Stuart Mackenzie. (2010) *Beyond the Street: The 100 Leading Figures in Urban Art*. Berlin: Die Gestalten Verlag.
Niedenthal, Paula M., Lawrence W. Barsalou, François Ric and Silvia Krauth-Gruber. (2005) 'Embodiment in the Acquisition and Use of Emotion Knowledge'. *Emotion and Consciousness*. Eds. Lisa Feldman Barrett, Paula M. Niedenthal and Piotr Winkielman. New York and London: The Guilford Press, pp. 21–50.
Noble, Richard, ed. (2009) *Utopias*. London: Whitechapel and Cambridge, MA: MIT Press.
Nora, Pierre. (Spring 1989) 'Between Memory and History: Les Lieux de Mémoire'. *Representations* 26: 7–25.
Oddey, Alison. (2007) *Re-Framing the Theatrical: Interdisciplinary Landscapes for Performance*. London: Palgrave Macmillan.
Oddey, Alison and Christine White, eds. (2009) *Modes of Spectating*. Bristol, UK and Chicago, USA: Intellect.
Opéra Pagaï. *L'Appartement Cultivable*. http://www.dailymotion.com/video/x1mghs_l-appartement-cultivable-par-opera_creation
Opéra Pagaï. *Le Safari Intime*. http://www.dailymotion.com/video/xcal9b_safari-intime-par-opera-pagai_creation
Opéra Pagaï. *L'Île de Carhaix-Bretagne*. http://www.dailymotion.com/video/xc86fl_l-ile-de-carhaix-bretagne_creation
Opéra Pagaï. Folder. HorsLesMurs. Paris, France.
Opéra Pagaï. *Mobile-Home Container*. http://www.dailymotion.com/video/x1hh0y_mobil-container-home-par-opera-paga_creation
Opéra Pagaï. www.operapagai.com/
Osmosis Compagnie. Folder. HorsLesMurs. Paris, France.
Osmosis Compagnie. http://www.osmosiscie.com/
Ostrowetsky, Sylvia. (1999) 'Port-Royal de Luxe'. *Pour une Sociologie de la forme*. Ed. Sylvia Ostrowetsky. Paris: L'Harmattan.
Ostrowetsky, Sylvia. (1997) 'La Rue et la thébaïde'. *Espaces st Sociétés 90/91: Les Langages de la rue*. (1997) Paris: L'Harmattan, pp. 139–44.
Pallasmaa, Juhani. (2005) *The Eyes of the Skin: Architecture and the Senses*. Chichester, UK: John Wiley & Sons, Ltd.
Parker, Andrew and Eve Kosofsky Sedgwick, eds. (1995) *Performativity and Performance*. New York and London: Routledge.
Parker-Starbuck, Jennifer. (2011) 'The Spectatorial Body in Multimedia Performance'. *Performing Arts Journal* 33.3: 60–71.
Patel, Roma. (2009) 'Touched by Human Hands: City and Performance'. *Modes of Spectating*. Eds. Alison Oddey and Christine White. Bristol, UK and Chicago, USA: Intellect, pp. 177–93.

Pearson, Lynn F. (1999) *Public Art Since 1950*. Princes Risborough: A Shires Book.
Pearson, Mike. (1998) 'My balls/your chin', *Performance Research* 3.2: 35–41.
Pearson, Mike. (2010) *Site-Specific Performance*. Basingstoke: Palgrave Macmillan.
Pearson, Mike and Michael Shanks (2001) *Theatre/Archeology* London and New York: Routledge.
Pellegrin, Julie. (January 2008) 'Recolonizing Public Space: Direct Action and Delinquency'. *Art Press* 2: 69–77.
Peterson, Grant Tyler. (2012) *'Partly Political' Street Performance? British Alternative Theatre History and the Natural Theatre Company*. Diss. Royal Holloway, University of London.
Phillips, Patricia C. (2003) 'Creating Democracy: A Dialogue with Krzysztof Wodiczko'. *Art Journal* 62.4: 33–47.
Phillips, Patricia C. (1992) 'Temporality and Public Art'. *Critical Issues in Public Art: Content, Context, and Controversy*. Eds. Harriet Senie and Sally Webster. Washington and London: Smithsonian Institution Press, pp. 295–304.
Phillips, Patricia C. (1995) 'Maintenance Activity: Creating a Climate for Change'. *But Is It Art? The Spirit of Art as Activism*. Ed. Nina Felshin. Seattle: Bay Press, pp. 165–93.
Phillips, Patricia C. (2003) 'Public Art: A Renewable Resource'. *Urban Futures: Critical Commentaries on Shaping the City*. Eds. Malcolm Miles and Tim Hall. London and New York: Routledge, pp. 122–34.
Plant, Sadie. (1992) *The Most Radical Gesture: The Situationist International in a Postmodern Age*. London and New York: Routledge.
Prinz, Jesse J. (2005) 'Emotions, Embodiment, and Awareness'. *Emotion and Consciousness*. Eds. Lisa Feldman Barrett, Paula M. Niedenthal and Piotr Winkielman. New York and London: The Guilford Press, pp. 363–83.
Rancière, Jacques. (2009) *The Emancipated Spectator*. Trans. Gregory Elliott. London, Verso.
Rancière, Jacques. (2010) *Dissensus: On Politics and Aesthetics*. Trans. Steven Corcoran. London and New York: Continuum.
Rancière, Jacques. (2004) *The Politics of Aesthetics*. Trans. Gabriel Rockhill. London and New York: Continuum.
Rancière, Jacques. (2006a) 'Aesthetics and Politics: Rethinking the Link'. Lecture given at the University of California, Berkeley, 6 May 2006. Transcript posted on 16 Beaver Group website, http://www.16beavergroup.org/
Rancière, Jacques. (2006b) 'Problems and Transformations in Critical Art, 2004'. *Participation*. Ed. Claire Bishop. London: Whitechapel, pp. 83–93.
Raven, Arlene, ed. (1989) *Art in the Public Interest*. Ann Arbor and London: U.M.I. Research Press.
Read, Alan. (1993/1995) *Theatre and Everyday Life: An Ethics of Performance*. London: Routledge.
Read, Alan. (2008) *Theatre, Intimacy and Engagement*. Basingstoke, UK: Palgrave Macmillan.
Reinelt, Janelle. (1998) 'Notes for a Radical Democratic Theater: Productive Crisis and the Challenge of Indeterminacy'. *Staging Resistance: Essays on Political Theater*. Eds. Jeanne Colleran and Jenny S. Spencer. Ann Arbor: University of Michigan.
Reinelt, Janelle. (2001) 'Performing Europe: Identity Formation for a "New" Europe'. *Theatre Journal* 53.3: 365–87.

Reinelt, Janelle. (2002a?) 'Approaching the Sixties: Between Nostalgia and Critique'. *Theatre Survey* 43.1: 37–6.
Reinelt, Janelle. (2002b?) 'The Politics of Discourse: Performativity meets Theatricality'. *SubStance* 31.2 &3: 201–15.
Reinelt, Janelle. (2011) 'Rethinking the Public Sphere for a Global Age'. *Performance Research* 16.2: 2, 16–27.
Reinelt, Janelle, ed. (1996) *Crucibles of Crisis: Performing Social Change*. Ann Arbor: University of Michigan Press.
Reverend Billy and the Church of Life After Shopping. http://www.revbilly.com/
Roach, Joseph. (1996) *Cities of the Dead: Circum-Atlantic Performance*. New York: Columbia University Press.
Roach, Joe. (2007) *It*. Ann Arbor: University of Michigan Press.
Roche, Jennifer. (2006) '"Socially Engaged Art, Critics and Discontents: An Interview with Claire Bishop'. Community Arts Network: Reading Room http://www.communityarts.net/readingroom/archivefiles/2006/07/socially_engage.php
Rode Boom Compagnie, http://www.rodeboom.be/
Rose, C. 'Audience Participation'. *Essential Audiences, issue 69*, Arts Council England, New Audiences Program, http://www.newaudiences.org.uk/resource.php?id=306
Ross, Kristin. (2002) *May '68 and Its Afterlives*. Chicago: University of Chicago Press.
Royal de Luxe. http://www.royal-de-luxe.com/
Royal de Luxe. Folder. HorsLesMurs. Paris, France.
Royal de Luxe: 1993–2001. (2001) Arles: Actes Sud.
Royal de Luxe. *Le Géant Tombé du Ciel* and *Le Dernier Voyage*. (1995). DVD. HorsLesMurs. Paris, France.
Ruan, François-Xavier, ed. (Juillet 2009) 'Au-Delà des murs: Le Son'. *Stradda* 13: 39–49.
Sadler, Simon. (1999) *The Situationist City*. Cambridge, MA and London: The MIT Press.
Said, Edward W. (1979) *Orientalism*. New York: Vintage Books.
Salmi, Ali. (2012) 'The Artistic Research Work on the Body and the Image in the Creations of Compagnie Osmosis'. Presentation at ArtVU: ArtVisualUrban, organized by the Pôle National Cirque et Arts de la Rue d'Amiens, in partnership with the University of Picardy and HorsLesMurs. Amiens, France.
Salom-Gomis, Sébastien. (Avril 2007) 'Un Éléphant sur une île'. *Stradda* 4: 2–3.
Saltz, David Z. (2006) 'Infiction and Outfiction: The Role of Fiction in theatrical Performance'. *Staging Philosophy: Intersections of Theater, Performance, and Philosophy*. Eds. David Krasner and David Z. Saltz. Ann Arbor: University of Michigan Press, pp. 203–20.
Salverson, Julie. (2001) 'Change on whose Terms? Testimony and an Erotics of Injury'. *Theatre* 31.3: 119–25.
Sanderson, Christopher Carter. (2003) *Gorilla Theatre: A Practical Guide to Performing New Outdoor Theatre Anytime, Anywhere* New York and London: Routledge.
Scant, Renata. (2004) *20 ans de Festival de Théâtre Européen: De l'Atlantique à l'Oural*. Grenoble: Presses Universitaires de Grenoble.

Scarry, Elaine. (1985) *The Body in Pain: The Making and Unmaking of the World*. New York: Oxford University Press.
Scarry, Elaine. (2000) 'The Difficulty of Imagining Other Persons'. *The Handbook of Interethnic Coexistence*. Ed. Eugene Weiner. New York: Continuum, pp. 40–62.
Schmidt, Mary and Randy Martin, eds. (2006) *Artistic Citizenship*. New York and London: Routledge.
Sedgewick, Eve Kosofsky. (2003) *Touching Feeling: Affect, Pedagogy, Performativity*. Durham and London: Duke University Press.
Seidman, Michael. (2004) *The Imaginary Revolution: Parisian Students and Workers in 1968*. New York and Oxford: Berghahn Books.
Senie, Harriet and Sally Webster. (1992) *Critical Issues in Public Art: Content, Context, and Controversy*. Washington and London: Smithsonian Institution Press.
Senie, Harriet F. (2003) 'Reframing Public Art: Audience Use, Interpretation, and Appreciation'. *Art and Its Publics: Museum Studies at the Millennium*. Ed. Andrew McClellan. Malden, MA: Blackwell Publishing, pp. 185–200.
Sennett, Richard. (1971) *The Uses of Disorder*. London: Allen Lane The Penguin Press.
Sennett, Richard. (1994) *Flesh and Stone: The Body and the City in Western Civilization*. London and Boston: Faber and Faber.
Seno, Ethel, ed. (2010) *Trespass: A History of Uncommissioned Urban Art*. Köln: Taschen.
Servan-Schreiber, J.-J. (1968) *The Spirit of May*. Trans. Ronald Steel. New York: McGraw-Hill Book Company.
Sheets-Johnstone, Maxine. (2009) *The Corporeal Turn: An Interdisciplinary Reader*. Exeter, UK and Charlottesville, VA: Imprint Academic.
Sherlock, Maureen. (1998) 'Postscript – No Loitering: Art as Social Practice'. *Interventions and Provocations: Conversations on Art, Culture, and Resistance*. Ed. Glenn Harper. Albany, NY: State University of New York Press, pp. 219–25.
Sholette, Gregory. (2010) *Dark Matter: Art and Politics in the Age of Enterprise Culture*. London: Pluto Press.
Siminot, Michel. (1999) 'L'Art de la rue. Scène urbaine – Scène commune?' *Rue de la Folie* 3.1: Dossier Spécial 01. pp. 1–15.
Singer, Daniel. (2002) *Prelude to Revolution: France in May 1968*. 2nd edn. Cambridge, Massachusetts: South End Press.
Smith, Anna Marie. (1998) *Laclau and Mouffe: The Radical Democratic Imaginary*. London and New York: Routledge.
Soja, Edward W. (1989) *Postmodern Geographies: The Reassertion of Space in Critical Social Theory*. London and New York: Verso.
Solnit, Rebecca. (2001) *Wanderlust: A History of the Art of Walking*. London: Penguin Books.
Spielmann, F. (January 2000) *Les questions de formation, qualification, transmission dans le domaine des arts de la rue*, DMDTS-French Ministry of Culture and Communication.
Starr, Peter. (1995) *Logics of Failed Revolt: French Theory After May '68*. Stanford, CA: Stanford University Press.
Stiles, Kristine and Peter Selz, eds. (1996) *Theories and Documents of Contemporary Art: A Sourcebook of Artists' Writings*. Berkeley, Los Angeles, and London: University of California Press.

Suderburg, Erika. (2000) *Space, Site, Intervention: Situating Installation Art*, Minneapolis: University of Minnesota Press.
Sugiera, Malgorzata. (2002) 'Theatricality and Cognitive Science: The Audience's Perception and Reception'. *SubStance* 31. 2 & 3: 225–35.
Taussig, Michael. (1993) *Mimesis and Alterity – a Particular History of the Senses*. New York and London: Routledge.
Taylor, Diana, (1994) 'Opening Remarks'. Eds. Diana Taylor and Juan Villejas. *Negotiating Performance*. Durham, NC and London: Duke University Press, pp. 1–16.
Taylor, Diana. (2003) *The Archive and the Repertoire: Performing Cultural Memory in the Americas*. Durham and London: Duke University Press.
Taylor, Mark C. (2001) *The Moment of Complexity: Emerging Network Culture*. Chicago and London: University of Chicago Press.
Thiébaut, Jeff. (Janvier 2010) 'Dialogue à une voix (et nombreux commentateurs)'. *Stradda* 15: 4–5.
Thompson, James. (2009, 2011) *Performance Affects: Applied Theatre and the End of Effect*. Basingstoke: Palgrave Macmillan.
Thompson, Nato and Gregory Sholette, eds. (2004) *The Interventionists: Users' Manual for the Creative Disruption of Everyday Life*. North Adams, MA: MASS MoCA Publications and Cambridge, MA and London, UK: The MIT Press.
Thrift, Nigel. (2008) *Non-Representational Theory: Space/Politics/ Affect*. London and New Yourk: Routledge.
Tony Clifton Circus. http://www.tonycliftoncircus.com/
Tuan, Yi-Fu. (1977) *Space and Place: The Perspective of Experience*. Minneapolis: University of Minnesota.
Tucker, Anne. (April 2005) *UK Street Arts and Mainland Europe: Opportunities and barriers to exploiting work form England in the rest of Europe*, London: Arts Council England.
Turner, Cathy. (2010) 'Mis-Guidance and Spatial Planning: Dramaturgies of Public Space'. *Contemporary Theatre Review* 20.2: 149–61.
Tusa, John. '1968: The Year of Revolutions'. BBC Radio 4. Programmes #1–4. 18 March, 29 April, 19 August, and 26 August 2008. http://www.bbc.co.uk/radio4/1968/yearofrevolutions.shtml
Unger, Irwin and Debi Unger. (1998) *The Times were a Changin': the Sixties Reader*. New York: Three Rivers Press.
Urry, John. (2003) *Global Complexity*. Cambridge, England: Polity Press.
Vaneigem, Raoul. (1994) *Revolution of Everyday Life*. Trans. Donald Nicholson-Smith. London: Rebel Press; Seattle: Left Bank Books.
Varela, Francisco J. (1992) *The Embodied Mind: Cognitive Science and Human Experience*. Cambridge: MIT Press.
'La Ville Éphémère'. (Octobre 2006) *Stradda*: 2: 31–40.
Verhoeven, Dries. www.driesverhoeven.com
Vitilio, Paul. (2000) *A Landscape of Events*. Trans. Julie Rose. Cambridge, MA and London: The MIT Press.
Voisin, Thierry. (July 2006) 'Paroles d'habitants, paroles de commerçants'. *Stradda* 1: 36.
Voisin, Thierry and Jean Pierre Estournet, eds. (2009) *Viva Cité: 20 ans, Sotteville-lès-Rouen*. Bonsecours: Éditions point de vues.
Warner, Michael. (2002) *Publics and Counterpublics*. New York: Zone Books.

Webb, Nicky, ed. (2006) *Four Magical Days in May: How an Elephant Captured the Heart of a City*. London: Artichoke Trust.
Whybrow, Nicolas. (2011) *Art and the City*. London and New York: I.B. Tauris.
Wilson, Frank. (Juillet 2006) 'Londres en Piste'. *Stradda* 1: 8–11.
Wielant, Catherine. (2002) *Le Nomade: Guide des arts de la rue, arts du cirque, et arts forains*. Bruxelles: Olé Olé.
Wolin, Sheldon. (1992) 'What Revolutionary Action Means Today'. *Dimensions of Radical Democracy: Pluralism, Citizenship, Community*. Ed. Chantal Mouffe. London and New York: Verso, pp. 240–53.
Wolin, Sheldon. (1997) 'The Destructive Sixties and Postmodern Conservatism'. *Reassessing the Sixties: Debating the Political and Cultural Legacy*. Ed. Stephen Macedo. New York and London: W.W. Norton & Company.
Zukin, S. (1995) *Cultures of Cities*, Malden, MA: Blackwell Publishers Inc. and Oxford: Blackwell Publishers Ltd.

Index

Entries of figures are indicated in italics.

1960s, 2, 20, 22–4, 30, 33, 41, 185n2, 198n1
1968, 8, 20, 22–31, 41, 83, 186n6, 186n8

about-ness, 7
Abramovic, Marina: *Lips of Thomas*, 12
activism, 8, 28, 29, 30, 32, 39, 105, 152, 171
   citizen, 14, 24
   political, 63
   social, 46, 69, 164
   socio-political, 20, 23
aesthetic rupture, 6, 63, 68
aesthetics, 3–6, 8, 18, 20, 21, 24, 35, 69, 159, 168, 171, 188n23, 190n17, 198n4
   of public space, 8, 20, 44, 45, 188
   relational, 185n5, 187n17
affect, 3, 8–13, 19, 33, 46, 53, 60, 89, 103, 177, 182, 183
affective response, 11–13, 19, 45, 53, 68–70, 93–5, 97, 103, 127, 132, 137, 140, 147, 178
agency, 9, 41, 44, 47, 52, 59, 153, 159, 172, 183, 185n6
   individual, 9, 32, 33, 39, 50, 53, 58, 176
   loss of, 32, 35, 39
   personal, 28, 34, 38, 69, 88
   See also individual freedom
agonism, 79, 80, 89, 95, 126, 159, 193n20
agonistic pluralism, 79, 125
Ahearn, John, 189n8
Akademia Ruchu, 184n1
Alhambra Container, 137–40, *138*
   See also Osmosis Compagnie
anti-establishment, 2, 20, 22, 32
Apocalypse, Parts 1, 2 and 3, 105, 108

   See also Lili Jenks
Artichoke, 71, 88, 190n1, 194n27
   The Sultan's Elephant, 73, 76, 190n2, 192n17
Arts Council London, 76, 85–86, 194n27
audience-constructed stories, 80, 81–3
audiences, 1, 11, 13, 14, 19, 22, 35–6, 37, 41, 45, 47, 55, 56, 57, 64, 77, 86, 88, 93, 96, 98, 100, 105, 115, 120–1, 122, 129, 133, 140, 141, 143, 145, 146, 171, 173, 175, 177, 180, 182, 184n4, 185n7, 197n3
   accidental, 31, 43
   actions, 14–15
   attention of, 75
   barriers between actor and, 29
   casting of, 38
   communication, 75
   compelling of, 54, 160
   complicit, 159
   and democracy, 44, 46
   engagement, 30, 68, 158
   enthusiasm, 74
   experience, 20
   intentional, 110–12, 116
   knowledge, 66
   mass, 83
   media, 88
   participatory, 147, 153, 159, 178, 179
   physical distance between actor and, 23
   pre-existing, 52
   primary, 172
   proper, 36
   reactions, 136
   reception, 161
   responses, 12, 65, 189n16, 191n14
   seducing of, 72
   small, 137

Index

spectatorship, 113
The Sultan's Elephant, 83
theatrical, 8, 194n28
twenty-first-century, 84
unsuspecting, 46, 61, 112, 127, 134
walking, 116
wandering, 35
well-informed, 128
Au Port des Quatre Routes, 168, 174
Aurillac Festival (France), xi, 23, 137, 184n1
Austin, J. L.: *How To Do Things With Words*, 14

Baby, where are the fine things you promised me?, 17–18, *18*
See Bain, Stephen
Back to Back Theatre: *Small Metal Objects*, 140–2, *142*
Bain, Stephen: *Baby, Where are the Fine Things You Promised Me?*, 17–18, *18*
Battersea Arts Centre, 39, 40
Battersea Power Station, 190n2, 194n28
Baudelaire, Charles, 95
becoming, 9, 10–11, 13, 19, 160, 172, 176, 182
sensory, 11, 18
Beedell, Jon, 65, 66
Berlin Wall, 29, 30, 195n4
Berman, Paul, 25, 186n6
Billington, Michael, 77
Bishop, Claire, 42, 74, 175, 185n5, 187n20, 188n25
Bivouac, 20–30, Plate 2
Boal, Augusto, 47, 185n10
Bodies in Urban Spaces, 97–102, Plates 6–7
Bourriaud, Nicolas, 188n24
Bread and Puppet Theatre, 23, 184n1
Bruno, Giuliana: *Atlas of Emotion*, 99
Buckingham Palace, 86, 194n25
Burns, David, 57

camouflage, 102, 103–4, 195n6
Capital of Culture, 192n18
Chalon-dans-la-rue, xi, 119, 136
Chaudoir, Philippe, 186n5

choreography, 39, 120, 139
Christo, 'Iron Curtain', 30
Church of Life After Shopping, 38, 39
Circostrada Network, 23
citizen, 5,14, 24, 25, 31, 33, 48, 52, 70, 77, 78, 80, 88–89, 95, 104, 122, 125, 132, 153, 159, 162, 172, 198n3
-artist, 183
citizenship, 20, 23, 41, 46–8, 52, 54, 58, 69, 70, 89, 93, 122, 132, 159, 172, 173, 193n20
Cohen-Cruz, Jan, 153; *Radical Street Performance: An International Anthology*, 184n4, 188n23
Colebrook, Claire, 10
collaboration, 2, 14, 42, 76, 88, 110, 143, 152–5, 158–61, 173–6, 185n6, 186n8
collage, 1, 7, 38, 78, 96, 105, 175, 191n12
chaotic, 85
politics, 84
thematic, 109
Colomina, Beatriz, 98, 117
community, 3, 5, 9, 20, 40, 42, 44, 47, 52, 57, 58, 59–60, 67–8, 74–7, 80, 81, 83, 88, 117–18, 121, 142–7, 149–75, 176, 189n8, 190n17, 193n21
art-making, 142–8, 153
communitas, 74
performance, 20, 149–75
Compagnie Kumulus:
Itinéraire Sans Fond(s), 142–8, 176, 197n13
Les Rencontres Internationales de Boîtes, 142–8, *144*, *147*, 176, 197n13
Les Squames, 45, 127–32, *130*, 142, Plate 10
Compagnie Willi Dorner, 95
Bodies in Urban Spaces, 94, 97–102, *100*, *101*, 195n4, Plates 6–7
Compagny Teatro Gestual de Chile intervention, 51
Su-Seso Taladro, 48–50, *48*, 52
concepts, 9–10, 50, 69
contamination, 79

corporeal turn, 9
counter-narratives, 20, 74, 78–90, 94
Courcoult, Jean Luc, 71, 83, 191n11, 194n28
Crespin, Michel, 23, 186n3
critical theory, 9, 28
Crouch, Julian, 72
Cull, Laura, 185n8
cultural tourism, 2, 42, 86

Daguerre, Louis: *View of Boulevard du Temple*, 91
Damasio, Antonio, 9, 196n3
Dario Fo, 184n1
Darwin and the Dodo, 65–6, *67*
See also Desperate Men
Debord, Guy, 28, 37, 96, 115, 179, 187n15
  Comments on the Society of Spectacle, 187n11
  'Introduction to a Critique of Urban Geography', 95
  situations, 32–4, 44, 75
  The Society of Spectacle, 32, 38, 187n11
  'Theory of the *Dérive*,' 198n9
  'Theses on Cultural Revolution', 34
de Certeau, Michel, 26–7, 28, 31
Décor Sonore, 186n3
de Lage, Christophe Renaud, 31
Delarozière, François, 83, 192n18
Deleuze, Gilles, 3, 9–12, 28, 103, 172, 176, 180, 182
  'One Less Manifesto', 9
Delfour, Jean-Jacques,186n5, 188n22
de Luca, Nicola Danesi, 54–5, 189n13
Demey, Kurt:
  Avec ma Tête dans l'arbre (With My Head in a Tree), 178
  Des Objets avec un pouvoir (Powerful Objects), 180
  Evidence Inconnue (Unknown Evidence), 179
  La Ville Qui Respire (The City that Breathes), 179–80
  L'Homme Cornu (The Horned Man), 177–80

democracy, 4, 21, 24, 33, 44–7, 48, 51, 69, 70, 88, 94, 124, 131, 176, 185n6
  activities, 41, 42, 43, 46, 52, 69, 77, 103
  civil rights, 47
  communities, 5
  consensual, 42, 51, 58
  cosmopolitan, 77, 78, 80
  democratization of culture, 30–1
  initiatives, 23, 25
  liberal, 2
  paradoxes, 79
  participatory, 20, 74–8
  politics, 4, 79, 125
  post-political, 76,191n13
  power, 51
  practices, 2, 4, 14, 19, 29, 47, 52, 54, 58, 64, 69, 78, 80, 89, 93, 153, 171, 180, 182
  public spaces, 52, 57, 77, 94, 98, 126, 148
  radical, 52, 69, 78–80, 122, 125, 126, 159, 172, 189n5
  radical practices, 78
  revolutions, 51
  societies, 24, 29, 131
  traditions, 193n21
democratic performatives, 14, 20, 44–70, 126, 171, 172, 182, 196n3
  developing critical awareness of social constructions, 53–8
  participating in art-making as a social practice, 59–64
  radical, 20
  reclaiming public spaces, 47–52
dérive, 32, 95–7, 115, 151, 153, 164, 196n5, 198n9
Desperate Men
  Darwin and the Dodo, 65–66, *67*
  The Rubbish Heads, 65
détournement, 32, 84, 95, 96, 158, 182
Deutsche, Rosalyn, 42, 51–2, 123, 125–6, 189nn6–8, 190n20
Dieudonné, Juliette, 151, 162, 171, 175
Disaparicion, La, 105
  See also Jenks, Lili

disorientation, 1, 7, 96, 162, 185n6
dissensus, 5, 19, 46, 52, 60, 63–4,
    69, 74, 78, 89, 90, 105, 186n8,
    189n5, 189n17
    and radical democracy, 78–80
    see also Rancière, Jacques
distribution of the sensible, 5, 182
Dogtroep, 184n1
Doherty, Claire, 155
Dolan, Jill: *Utopia in Performance:
    Finding Hope at the Theater*, 12,
    75, 78, 185n10
dramaturgy, 6, 13, 39
durational performatives, 60–1, 71, 84

efficacy, 11, 63–4
    of dissensus, 189n17
    potential for, 3, 9, 15, 19, 20, 21,
        44, 45, 77, 196n3
El Comediants, 184n1
El Teatro Campesino, 184n1
emancipated spectator, 45–6, 80, 83,
    153, 161, 182
emancipation, 45, 79–80, 81
encounter, 7, 8, 10, 13, 14, 19, 59, 64,
    75, 80, 82–83, 93, 95, 98, 110–15,
    126–7, 129, 131, 133, 136, 141,
    146–7, 150–1, 170, 172, 175,
    177–9, 180–2, 183
engagement:
    active, 20, 38, 153
    artistic, 41–2, 63, 115, 140
    critical, 94, 140, 175
    emotional, 93
    political, 2–3, 32, 42, 158
    physical, 59
    social, 175, 184n4
ephemeral public art, 34, 41, 77,
    91–7, 105, 108, 181, 191n12
    sculptures, 98
Est-ce que le monde sait qu'il me parle?,
    35–8, 41
European Parliament: Committee on
    Culture and Education, 23
    Street Artists in Europe, 23
event-ness, 7, 19, 21
exile, 136–40, 142–7
exoticism, 83–86, 127–31
experiential rapport, 1

Fallen Fruit, 57–8, 176
Fer, Nocolas de, 149
festivals (street theatre), x, xi–xii,
    Plate 1
Fink, Carole, 24, 25, 186n6
Finkelpearl, Tom, 189nn7–8
Fira Tàrrega, xi
Fischer-Lichte, Erika, 12, 19
Floch, Yohann, 23
Foucault, Michel, 28, 79
Freire, Paulo, 53–4, 58, 59, 80, 153,
    162–4, 189nn11–12
Friches Théâtre Urbain, 132, 164
Witness/N14, 21, 45, 149–75, 176,
    197nn1–2, Plate 13
Fulgi, Iacopo, 54
Fusco, Coco: *Two Undiscovered
    Amerindians Visit*, 128, 196n1

Gaber, Floriane, 30, 131
    40 Years of Street Arts, 187n10
    *How It All Started: Street Arts in the
        Context of the 1970s*, 187n10,
        187n20
Gardner, Lyn, 75, 88
Gare Montparnasse, 127–8
Gassert, Philipp, 24, 186n6
Gémier, Firmin, 30
Générik Vapeur: *Bivouac*, 29–30, *Plate
    2*
Gens de Couleur, Les, 67–8, *Plate 4*
Gilcher-Holtey, Ingrid, 26
Godard, Jean-Luc, 185n4
Gomez-Peña, Guillermo: *Two
    Undiscovered Amerindians Visit*,
    128, 196n1
Goudron n'est pas meuble, Le, 46
    See also Jeanne Simone
Granger, Charlotte, 184n2
Greenberg, Clement: 'Towards a
    Newer Laocoön', 41
Guattari, Félix, 9–10, 28, 103, 180,
    182
    What is Philosophy?, 11

Habermas, Jürgen: *The Structural
    Transformation of the Public Sphere*,
    189n6
Hardt, Michael, 9, 53–4

Harper, Sarah, 149–52, 154, 155,
    158–9, 160, 162, 168, 169, 170,
    171, 173–5, 197nn1–2
    Espaces Rêvés, 175
    Dossier Artistique, 151, 197n1
    *Le Glissement des Axes sur la Route
      avec nos Voisins*, 174, 198n5
    Witness/N14, 21, 45, 149–75, 176,
      197nn1–2, Plate 13
Harvey, David, 34, 187n12, 191n12
Hirschhorn, Thomas, 6, 185n4
Homme Cornu, L', 177–80
    See also Demey, Kurt
Horse Guards, 71, 73, 82, 84, 86, 88,
    194n25
HorsLesMurs, 19, 23, 184n3, 186n9,
    196n2, 196nn8–9, 197n15, 197n3

identity, 39, 51, 52, 54, 60, 61, 74, 77,
    79, 86, 123, 125–6, 149, 176
    community, 171, 172
Île aux Topies, L', 68
Il Gorilla Quadrumano, 184n1
Ilotopie, 29, 68
    Les Gens de Couleur (Coloured
      People), 67–8, 140, Plate 4
Improbable, 72
individual freedom, 32, 33, 39
    See also agency
insider, 20, 68, 125, 133, 148
intervention, 1, 3, 4, 6, 8, 9, 13–21,
    26, 27, 31, 35–41, 42, 43, 44, 45,
    47, 48, 50, 52, 53–4, 60–1, 63,
    64–70, 92, 94, 95, 96, 102, 103,
    105–6, 107–9, 111, 112, 113, 115,
    116, 123, 124, 126, 127, 128,
    133–4, 140, 143, 147, 148, 154,
    160, 176, 182, 184n4, 198n4
    critical, 163
    cultural, 29, 152
    ephemeral, 91
    impromptu, 105
    large-scale, 74, 86
    provocative, 131–2
    social, 175
    socio-political, 159
    uncomfortable, 49
I.O.U., 184n
It, 81

Itinéraire Sans Fond(s), 142–8, 176,
    197n13
    See also Compagnie Kumulus

Jackson, Shannon, 3
Jacobson, Howard, 74
Jameson, Fredric, 187n12
Jasper, James M., 69
Jaubert, Cyril, 16, 60, 189n16
Jeanne Simone:
    Le Goudron n'est pas meuble, 46, 110
    Le Parfum des Pneus, 110
    Mademoiselle, 45, 94, 97, 110–16,
      Plate 8
Jenks, Lili, 95, 176
    Apocalypse, Parts 1, 2 and 3, 105,
      108
    La Disaparicion, 105
    La Mecanista, 106
    Merry Crisis, 108
    PAPERGLUE-n-SCOTCH, 94, 105–10
    Perdre le Nord, 105, 107
John Bull Puncture Repair Kit, 184n1
Johnson, Mark, 196n3
    The Meaning of the Body, 60
Jowell, Tessa, 76
    *The Jules Verne: Free Illustrated
      Supplement*, 71
Junker, Detlef, 24, 186n6

Kaprow, Allan, 41, 151, 187n20
Kester, Grant, 7, 19, 28, 44, 153,
    185n4, 185n6, 188n25
    *The One and the Many: Contemporary
      Collaborative Art in a Global
      Context*, 185nn3–4, 186n8
Kollektif Rote Rübe, 184n1
Ktha Compagnie: *Est-ce que le monde
    sait qu'il me parle? (Does the
    World Know It Speaks to mM?)*,
    35–8, 41
Kwon, Miwon, 123, 189nn7–8, 198n1

Laclau, Ernesto, 92, 125, 126, 189n5
    *Hegemony and Socialist Strategy:
      Towards a Radical Democratic
      Politics*, 69, 78
Lacy, Suzanne, 158, 187n17
La Machine: *La Princesse*, 192n18

Lammy, David, 76
Lang, David, 85
Laurent, Pascal:
　Melgut, 132–6, 196n4, *Plate 11*
　VitupErrance, 132–6, *135*, 196n5
Le Goliath, xi
Lefebvre, Henri, 27–8, 41, 44, 75, 93
　Everyday Life in the Modern World, 34
　The Production of Space, 195n2
Lefort, Claude, 28, 126
　'The Question of Democracy', 51
Léger, Françoise, 68
Lieu Commun, 174, 176
　See also Harper, Sarah
Lieux Publics, 23, 186n3
Life Streaming, 180–2
Liu Bolin, 94, 95, 102–3, 105, 176, 195nn6–7
　CCTV, 103
　Hiding in the City, 103
living statues, 94, 102–5
　See also, Bolin, Liu; Palmen, Desiree
Living Theatre, 23, 29, 184n1
London International Festival of Theatre, 180, 190n2, 192n17

Mademoiselle, 110–16, *Plate 8*
　See also Jeanne Simone
Madral, Philippe: *Le Théâtre hors les murs*, 30
Marriage, Helen, 71, 88, 190n2, 191n8
Massey, Doreen, 91–2, 127, 149–50, 160, 171
Massumi, Brian, 11–12
McConachie, Bruce, 197n11
McIntosh, Baroness, 192n15, 194n27
Mecanista, La, 106
　See also Lili Jenks
Melgut, 132–33, *Plate 11*
　See also Laurent, Pascal
Merry Crisis, 108
　See also Lili Jenks
metaphoric memory, 132, 136, 140, 147, 196n3
Miles, Malcolm, 93, 189n7
militant performances, 22, 30
MiramirO (festival), 106
mirror-neuron systems, 196n3

Mobil-Home Container, 60–4, *62*
　See also Opéra Pagaï
moments, 14, 19, 30, 32–5
Morte di Babbo Natale: Eutanasia di un mito sovrappeso, La, 54–7, *Plate 3*
Mouffe, Chantal, 69, 76–9, 117, 122, 125, 126, 131, 148, 189n5, 193nn20–1

narratives, 6, 8, 20, 46, 54, 74, 109, 110, 113, 143, 159, 178
　complicated, 81
　consensus and participatory democracy, 74–8, 89, 90
　counter-, 20, 74, 78–80, 83, 89, 94
　dislocated, 121
　of dissensus, 90
　dominant, 59
　of empire, 84, 89
　European colonial expansion, 83
　master, 12, 58
　meandering, 135
　mini-, 118
　nomadic, 123
　official, 60
　post-political, 83
　urban, 94
　written, 194n24
Natural Theatre Company, 185n2
Navarro, Raphael, 177
non-art, 1, 3, 7–8, 13–14, 23, 35, 41, 42, 47, 95, 109, 115, 121, 198n3
norms, 2, 29, 44, 49, 50, 64, 69, 185n3

Opéra Pagaï, 17, 61–2, 95
　L'Entreprise de Détournement, 604, 176
　Les Sans Balcons, 15–17, *15*, 18, 115
　Mobil-Home Container, 60–4, *62*
　Safari Intime, 45, 94, 97, 116–24, *119*, *122*, 176, *Plate 9*
opposition, 1–3, 14, 19, 23, 26–8, 33, 42–43, 173, 182, 185n2, 186n8
Oposito, 29
orientalsim, 84–5, 194n24
Osmosis Compagnie:
　Alhambra Container, 136–40, *138*, 196n9, 197n10
　Transit, 136–40, *Plate 12*

Ostrowetsky, Sylvia, 23, 188n23
Otherness, 2, 11, 20, 36, 37, 45, 64, 67, 99, 105, 124, 125–48, 196n1
outdoor entertainment, 1, 23
outsider, 20, 68, 124, 125–7, 131–6, 140–1, 143, 147, 148, 166, 169, 171

palimpsest, 1, 7, 191n12
   See also collage
Pallasmaa, Juhani, 98, 187n12
Palmen, Desiree, 94, 95, 97, 102, 104–5, 176, 195n8
   Old City Suit, 104
PAPERGLUE-n-SCOTCH, 94, 105–10
   See also Jenks, Lili
Parcours (Witness/N14), 153–5
   1: *D'Ici Là!*, 154, 155, 162, 197n1
   2: *Au-delà du périph*, 154, 155, 162, 163, 164–76, 197n1
   3: *D'Île en île*, 198n5
   4: *La loi fondamentale des flux*, 198n5
   5: *Un pas de côté*, 154, 155, 162, 163, 164–76, 197n1
   6: *Quels sont les lignes qui persistent?*, 198n5
   See also Friches Théâtre Urbain
parody, 40, 80, 82, 83, 84, 85–90, 155
partage du sensible
   See distribution of the sensible
participation, 1, 4, 5, 8–9, 13–14, 29, 33–4, 41, 45–7, 58–9, 74, 78, 93–4, 105, 123, 147, 172, 175, 193n21
participatory practices, x, 1, 9
Pellegrin, Julie, 98, 110, 115
People Show, 184n1
percepts, 3, 10–11, 103, 182
Perdre le Nord, 105, 107
   See also Jenks, Lili
performatives
   See Austin, J. L.; democratic performatives; durational performative; urban dance; utopian performatives; walking performatives
performative turn, 9, 41
Peterson, Grant, 185n2

Phillips, Patricia, 92–3, 94, 95, 176, 189n7
Piccolo Teatro di Pontedera, 184n1
Plant, Sadie, 29, 33, 187n11
   The Radical Gesture: The Situationist International in a Postmodern Age, 195n3
pluralism, agonistic
   See agonistic pluralism
politics, 3–8, 18, 21, 24, 25, 32, 34, 35, 43, 84, 92, 105, 125, 182, 188n23, 189n17
private space, 16, 58, 105, 116–18, 179
procession, 29–30, 48, 80, 86–9
proximity: utopias of, 60
public art, 42, 53, 123, 189n7, 190n20
   definition, 52
   ephemeral, 77, 91–7, 98
   new genre, 158
   sculptures, 99
public space, 2–3
   accessible, 89, 95, 126
   actual, 19, 103, 183
   aesthetics, 6, 8, 20, 44–70
   democratic, 52, 57, 59–64, 77, 78, 94, 98, 126, 148, 171, 172
   celebratory use of, 76
   familiar, 91, 132
   loss of, 88, 151, 176
   metaphoric, 159
   open, 41, 90
   privatized, 105, 106, 118
   re-appropriated, 23, 28, 174
   reclaiming, 47–52
   shared, 182
   See also trespass

Quintin, Erwan, 151, 171

radical democracy, 20, 52, 69, 78, 88, 89, 122, 125, 126, 159, 172, 189n5, 189n9
   dissensus, 78–81
radical theatre, 2, 22, 65, 184n1, 186n5
Rancière, Jacques, 3–8, 28, 45–6, 46, 59
   aesthetic rupture, 3, 68, 94

artistic regimes, 3–4
collage, 78, 84
efficacy of dissensus, 63–4, 189n17
emancipation, 79–80, 81, 83, 153
police, 182
rapport, 1, 31, 72, 81
Rastl, Lisa, 97, 98
rehearsal, 2, 14, 23, 47, 118, 121, 185n10, 194n28
space, 78, 89
Rencontres Internationales de Boîtes, Les, 142–8, *144*, *147*, 176, 197n13
See also Compagnie Kumulus
resistance, 2, 4, 19, 29, 46, 52, 60, 69, 79, 80, 87, 89, 97, 151, 182
Reverend Billy, 38–41
Roach, Joseph, 81, 89
Rode Boom, 177, 179
Royal de Luxe, 29, 83, 90
  Les Chasseurs des Giraffes, 190n2
  Sea Odyssey, 192n18
  The Sultan's Elephant, 20, 44, 71–90, 189n5, 190–3nn1–18, 194nn23–8, Plate 5
  Rubbish Heads, The, 65
See also Desperate Men
rupture, 3, 6–8, 19, 26–8, 34, 45, 63, 68, 78, 80, 84, 94, 185n5

Sadler, Simon: *The Situationist City*, 35, 195n2
Safari Intime, 45, 94, 97, 116–24, *119*, *122*, 176, Plate 9
See also Opéra Pagaï
Said, Edward, 84
Salmi, Ali, 136, 137
See also Osmosis Compagnie
San Francisco Mime Troupe, 184n1
Sans Balcons, Les, 15–17, *15*, 18, 115
See also Opéra Pagaï
Schnebelin, Bruno, 68
Sedgwick, Eve Kosofsky: *Touching Feeling*, 12
Serra, Richard: *Tilted Arc*, 189n8
shock, 7, 8, 10, 27, 38, 53, 54, 78, 80, 88, 91, 95, 103, 126, 131, 184n1, 185nn5–6, 186n8
Simonot, Michel, 23
Singer, Daniel, 25, 186n6

site-specific performances, 30, 60, 72, 83–5, 123, 152, 198n1
Situationists, 32–35, 37, 38, 39, 41, 95, 96, 151, 187n11, 195n3
new, 155
situations, 1, 7, 32–5, 44, 69, 88, 140, 175, 182, 196n3
affect, 9, 13
bewildering, 53
constructed, 34, 35, 41, 95, 96
credible, 63
current, 4
Debord, 75
imaginative, 64
meaningful, 8
new, 155
normal, 45
understanding of, 96
Small Metal Objects, 140–2, *142*
See Back to Back Theatre
Smith, Ritchie, 65
social construction, 2, 47, 53–8
social turn, 41, 42, 198n4
society of spectacle, 32, 33, 35, 38, 96, 187n15
Solnit, Rebecca: *Wanderlust: A History of Walking*, 47–8, 52, 88, 172, 173
Sontag, Susan, 187n12
Sotteville-lès-Rouen, xi, 118
spatio-temporal events, 7, 92, 150
spectagonist, 161–2
spectator, emancipated, 45, 80, 83, 153, 161, 182
Spinoza, Baruch, 9
Squames, Les, 45, 127–32, *130*, 142, Plate 10
See also Compagnie Kumulus
Squat Theatre, 184n1
Stockton International Riverside Festival, xi
storytelling, 8
Street Arts Working Group: 'Dossier Spécial 01', 23
Su-Seso Taladro, 48–50, *48*, 52
See also Compagny Teatro Gestual de Chile
Sultan's Elephant, The, 20, 44, 71–90, 189n5, 190nn1–2, 191nn3–14, 192nn15–18, 194nn23–28, Plate 5

symbolic sites, 27, 31

Talen, Bill (Reverend Billy), 38–41
Taylor, Diana, 128, 139, 196n1
Terrier, Laure, 110–13, 115, 195n13, 195n16
  See also Jeanne Simone
Théâtracide, 23, 184n1
Théâtre a Bretelles, 184n1
Théâtre de l'Unité, 29, 184n1
Théâtre National Populaire (National Popular Theatre/TNP), 30
Theatre of the Oppressed (Augusto Boal) 184n1
Thrift, Nigel: *Non-Representational Theory: Space, Politics, Affect,* 12–13, 46, 185n9
Tony Clifton Circus: *La Morte di Babbo Natale: Eutanasia di un mito sovrappeso* (The Death of Santa Claus, Euthanasia of an Overweight Myth), 54–5, 57, Plate 3
tourism, cultural
  See cultural tourism
Transe Express, 29
transformation, 6, 9–11, 13, 19, 26, 29, 31–4, 51, 75–7, 93, 96, 109, 115, 163, 174
Transit, 136–7, Plate 12
  See also Osmosis Compagnie
trespass, 20, 47, 97, 105, 106, 109, 123, 188n3
Troupe Z, 184n1
Terschelling Oerol, xii

urban dance, 110
Urban Sax, 184n1
utopia, 31, 80, 87

utopian exhilaration, 25
utopian performatives, 12, 20, 23, 34, 35, 41, 68, 75–6, 78, 188n24
utopias of proximity: 60

van Denderen, Ad: *Go No Go,* 136
Vaneigem, Raoul, 96
  Revolution of Everyday Life, 187n11
Van Vinckenroye, Joris, 179
Verhoeven, Dries: *Life Streaming,* 180–1, 182
Verne, Jules, 71, 81, 83
Viegener, Matias, 57
Vilar, Jean, 30
visceral response, 8–9, 13, 136
VitupErrance, 132–36, *135,* 196n5
  See also Laurent, Pascal

walkabouts, 64–5, 66, 67, 185n2
walking performatives, 32, 44, 46, 48, 72, 73, 87, 89, 95, 96, 108, 109, 113, 116, 119, 134, 145, 150–2, 153, 158–62, 171–2, 173, 175, 191nn7–8, 192n18
  See also Parcours
Walmart, 38, 40
Warner, Michael: *Publics and Counterpublics,* 185n7
we/they, 125–27
Webb, Nicky, 71, 88
Weir, Sarah, 76, 80, 194n27
Welfare State International, 72, 184n1
Witness/N14, 149–75, Plate 13
  See also Harper, Sarah
Wodiczko, Krzysztof, 172
Wolin, Sheldon, 24, 29
Wolman, Gil, 96

Young, Austin, 57

GPSR Compliance

The European Union's (EU) General Product Safety Regulation (GPSR) is a set of rules that requires consumer products to be safe and our obligations to ensure this.

If you have any concerns about our products, you can contact us on

ProductSafety@springernature.com

In case Publisher is established outside the EU, the EU authorized representative is:

Springer Nature Customer Service Center GmbH
Europaplatz 3
69115 Heidelberg, Germany

www.ingramcontent.com/pod-product-compliance
Ingram Content Group UK Ltd.
Pitfield, Milton Keynes, MK11 3LW, UK
UKHW041303180426
11947UKWH00009B/653